Second Wave Positive Psychology

Positive psychology is currently equated with theory and research on the positive aspects of life. The reality could not be further from the truth. Positive psychology investigates and researches some of the most difficult and painful experiences. *Second Wave Positive Psychology: Embracing the Dark Side of Life* is an innovative and groundbreaking textbook that explores a variety of topics we consider to be part of the 'dark side' of life while emphasising their role in our positive functioning and transformation as human beings. This more nuanced approach to the notions of 'positive' and 'negative' can be described as the 'second wave' of positive psychology.

Positive psychology is one of the fastest-growing and least understood branches of psychology. Exploring topics at the heart of positive psychology, such as meaning, resilience, human development, mortality, change, suffering and spirituality, this book engages with so-called negative matters from a positive psychology angle, showing how the path of personal development can involve experiences which, while challenging, can lead to growth, insight, healing and transformation.

Containing useful resources, case studies, practical exercises and chapter summaries, *Second Wave Positive Psychology* is an essential guide for undergraduate and postgraduate students studying positive psychology, as well as clinicians wanting to know more about the subject. It will also be relevant to the layperson who is interested in positive psychology.

Itai Ivtzan is a positive psychologist, a senior lecturer and the program leader of Masters in Applied Positive Psychology (MAPP) at the University of East London (UEL). His research areas are mindfulness meditation, spirituality, and meaning in life. In addition to many journal papers and book chapters, he is the author of several books and the leading editor of *Mindfulness in Positive Psychology: The Science of Meditation and Wellbeing*.

Tim Lomas is a lecturer at the UEL, where he is the associate programme leader for the MSc in Applied Positive Psychology and Coaching Psychology as well as having published numerous peer-reviewed papers and books.

Kate Hefferon is a chartered psychologist, senior lecturer and the head of the Posttraumatic Growth Research Unit at the UEL. Her interests lie within the areas of posttraumatic growth (PTG), physical activity, health and wellbeing. She is the author of numerous peer-reviewed papers and book chapters as well as lead author on popular positive psychology textbooks.

Piers Worth is a chartered psychologist, accredited psychotherapist and head of Academic Department – Psychology for Bucks New University. Piers wrote and leads the Bucks MSc Applied Positive Psychology programme.

'*Second Wave Positive Psychology: Embracing the Dark Side of Life* is not only about seeing the reality of positive psychology more clearly, it's about seeing who we are as human beings more clearly. Positive psychology studies and embraces all the vicissitudes of life. And here is the book that outlines this for us. What is most incredible and impactful about this book? Is it that it represents the thought leadership and scholarship of four distinguished positive psychology luminaries? Is it that it is the first positive psychology book to deeply integrate the positive and negative of human experience across a wide array of topics? Is it that it's a clear and interesting read, easily peaking the reader's curiosity page after page? Is it that those who crack the book open will immediately make it required reading for their students? Or, is it that despite being a scholarly, scientific work the book is also eminently practical in its guidance for readers to reflect and explore that which is personal and meaningful? My answer is clear: All of the above.'

  —Ryan M. Niemiec, PsyD, author of *Mindfulness and Character Strengths: A Practical Guide to Flourishing*, and Psychologist and Education Director, VIA Institute on Character

'This timely book is a must read for anybody seriously interested in positive psychology. Rightly or wrongly, positive psychology has been often perceived as focusing only on the positive aspects of human life. However, as it reaches maturity, the discipline is increasingly moving in the direction of embracing human life as a whole from a positive, constructive perspective. For example, can we have something like 'Positive Death'? These are issues that this courageous book is grappling with. Written by scholars who have an excellent knowledge and experience of positive psychology, this book may well become a landmark in the evolution of the field.'

  —Nash Popovic, PhD, author of *Personal Consultancy: A model for integrating counselling and coaching*

'In a climate where the span of positive psychology science so often is reduced to simplistic instructions just to smile, count your blessings, and look on the bright side of life, it is inspiring and exciting to see such a high-quality book guiding us through the most compelling and complex reaches of the field. This book engagingly demonstrates that positive psychology finds its true strength when it unifies happiness and positivity with the kinds of suffering, doubt, and adversity that are part and parcel with human life. It is written with a strong eye toward education, which is completely fitting because *Second Wave Positive Psychology* is written by scientists who are experts at teaching people how to apply research and theory to improve everyday life. Each chapter is an authoritative review of an important topic within positive psychology, from emotions and development to mortality and spirituality. It is a great recipe, blending quality science, insightful reflections and exercises, and new perspectives on the universal human pursuits not just of a brighter smile, but of a richer, more authentic, and more meaningful life.'

  —Michael Steger, PhD, Head of the Laboratory for the Study of Meaning and Quality of Life

'The long awaited book on second wave positive psychology is finally here – clear evidence that positive psychology has entered a new stage of development. Gone are the smiley face and the existential critique. At long last, positive psychology has openly embraced the dark side of life not only as an inevitable aspect of the human condition, but also an essential part in optimal functioning and transformation. The authors have skilfully provided a new narrative, buttressed by empirical evidence that engagement with the challenge and distress in life can contribute to our healing, growth and flourishing. I highly recommend this book to both the positive psychology community and all my friends in the humanistic-existential community."

  —Paul T. P. Wong, PhD, editor of *The Human Quest for Meaning*

Second Wave Positive Psychology

Embracing the Dark Side of Life

Itai Ivtzan, Tim Lomas,
Kate Hefferon and Piers Worth

Routledge
Taylor & Francis Group

LONDON AND NEW YORK

First published 2016
by Routledge
2 Park Square, Milton Park, Abingdon, Oxon, OX14 4RN

and by Routledge
711 Third Avenue, New York, NY 10017

Routledge is an imprint of the Taylor & Francis Group, an informa business

British Library Cataloguing in Publication Data
A catalogue record for this book is available from the British Library

Library of Congress Cataloging-in-Publication Data
A catalog record for this title has been requested.

ISBN: 978-1-138-81865-1 (hbk)
ISBN: 978-1-138-81866-8 (pbk)
ISBN: 978-1-315-74001-0 (ebk)

Typeset in Frutiger and Joanna
by Apex CoVantage, LLC

Contents

Introduction

Thank you for joining us for this adventure of *Second Wave Positive Psychology: Embracing the Dark Side of Life*. What is the first image that comes to our mind when positive psychology (PP) is mentioned? For most of us, it is the smiley emoticon. This symbol of happiness, optimism and joy reflects the way PP is commonly conceived and portrayed, both within the PP discipline and in society at large. In fact, PP is often equated with theory and research on the positive aspects of life. As such, whatever is labelled as 'negative' is frequently rejected and considered to be outside the sphere of PP. But this could not be further from the truth. PP actually investigates and researches some of the most difficult and painful human experiences. The present book explores a variety of topics that could be considered as part of the 'dark side' of life and emphasises the role they play in the positive aspects of our functioning and transformations as human beings. While doing this, cutting-edge theories, research, and practices are also introduced.

The 'dark side' refers to challenging experiences, thoughts, emotions and behaviours which trigger discomfort in us. Such discomfort is frequently avoided as it carries an engagement with fear, pain, distress or confusion. However, engaging with the challenge and discomfort has great potential for growth, healing, insight and transformation. In other words, the 'dark side' contains the seed for a potential positive outcome, even when the path towards this outcome is testing.

This book is a product of our collaborative work on the MSc in Applied Positive Psychology (MAPP) – delivered at the University of East London (UEL) and at Bucks New University. Dr Ivtzan, Dr Hefferon and Dr Lomas run the UEL programme, whereas Dr Worth runs the Bucks programme. The UEL programme is the largest PP postgraduate programme in Europe, with 100 new students every year. Bucks New University opened its programme a couple of years ago and now boasts more than 40 new students. This book is a product of our MAPP work, where we interact with brilliant students who, we believe, are the future of PP. Over the years, we have seen many students feeling uncomfortable about the idea of sharing difficulty and pain in the framework of a PP course. Some of them even felt they were not able to join the weekends of teaching while they were experiencing difficulty in their lives as they felt they were being disingenuous or betraying the need for positivity. We all felt this issue should be cleared up, and this triggered the writing of this book. We wanted students and other people who are interested in this field to feel they were allowed to include the aspects of life we might call 'negative' in their PP experience. Moreover, we wished to make it clear that these aspects of life were frequently *necessary* for the experience of growth and flourishing to be complete. To achieve this, we describe in this book the current state of affairs in the field of PP, with a view to dispel the myth of its 'positivity'. People believe that PP deals only with the positive because they confuse experiences with outcomes. Indeed, the outcomes of PP theory and research are always positive in some way, and yet the paths, the journeys, what we experience on the way to these outcomes may be painful and challenging. PP must recognise and acknowledge this journey, and this is what this book aims to do. This misconception that first emerged within the field of PP has extended to other branches of psychology (clinical, educational, developmental, etc.) and to the general public. The erroneous impression is that discussing the negative is out of bounds in PP. We hope this book allows all concerned to re-conceptualise their view of PP and, hopefully, invite a larger audience to participate in the important ongoing discussions in the field.

PP is one of the fastest-growing and least understood branches of psychology. By exploring various topics that are at the heart of PP, such as meaning, resilience, human development, mortality, change, suffering and spirituality, this book engages with so-called negative matters from the PP angle. Furthermore, this book clearly illustrates how these 'negative' experiences can have positive outcomes if we approach them in a certain way. A trauma, for example, may lead to anxiety and depression as well as, in coexistence, to growth and flourishing. Various topics and aspects of life exemplify the likelihood of such outcomes.

What is the 'second wave of PP' that we are referring to? In its early years, the PP movement differentiated itself from 'psychology as usual' by strongly emphasising the 'positive' (thoughts, emotions, traits, etc.). Whereas psychology as usual was character-ised as focusing mainly on 'negative' mental states and experiences, PP would redress the balance by concentrating on 'positive' qualities and outcomes. Moreover, within this characterisation, there was the implicit message that ostensibly negative states and expe-riences were undesirable, and thus people should aim to avoid or eschew these, whereas 'positive' qualities and outcomes were necessarily beneficial and should be promoted and sought. However, over recent years, scholars within PP have begun to take a far more nuanced approach to the notions of 'positive' and 'negative'. It has been recognised that seemingly positive qualities can be detrimental to wellbeing under certain circumstances. For example, as Seligman (1990) recognised, one must be careful not to be a 'slave to the tyrannies of optimism', but must be 'able to use pessimism's keen sense of reality when we need it' (p. 292). Conversely, as this book summarises, the path of personal development can involve experiences which, while ostensibly challenging, can lead to growth and transformation. Back in 2004, Held (2004) suggested that this more nuanced approach to the notions of 'positive' and 'negative' might be described as the 'second wave' of PP. Thinking along similar lines, Wong (2011) labelled these new developments in the field as PP '2.0'.

We feel that this book reflects and represents these recent currents in the field, cap-turing a key dimension of this emergent second wave, namely an engagement with the 'darker side' of life. In giving this book its title, we must emphasise a number of important points. Firstly, we are certainly not claiming that this book is *creating* this second wave; as we show throughout these pages, research that we are identifying as embodying or reflecting this second wave has been ongoing for years through the combined efforts of scholars worldwide. Secondly, we are not even taking credit for identifying or naming this emergent movement; this due goes to Held (2004), who first used the phrase, and also to Wong (2011), who more actively identified and explained the new movement. Finally, we are not implying that the content of this book exhausts or covers all the strands of this new wave; we are simply highlighting what we see as some important elements in this new wave of research and theory; readers may construe or appraise these developments in their own ways. Nevertheless, we do want to use the name 'second wave' to explicitly name and celebrate these recent developments in the field and to show some of the key ways in which the field is evolving as it matures and progresses as a discipline.

The book will take you through a journey that focuses on aspects of life often regarded as negative and yet ones that could be conducive to our psychological wellbeing. Although we collectively thought of and believe in this book and its components, we independently undertook the creation and writing of two chapters about which we felt the most passionate. Hence, each chapter is clearly linked to its associated writer. The first chapter of the book discusses the 'Dialectics of Emotions' (Dr Tim Lomas) and investigates the way the labels 'positive' and 'negative' are being used in the context of PP and how using these terms is not as straightforward as it might appear at first. The following chapter offers an overview of 'Positive Development – Our Journey of Growth' (Dr Piers Worth), investigating the challenges of different stages in life and the way they can lead to positive change. Based on these different stages of development, the chapter 'The Dark Side of Meaning in Life' (Dr Itai Ivtzan) elaborates on the difficulties and joys that are part of what we experience as meaning and purpose in life. Next is 'Adversity, Resilience and Transformational Growth' (Dr Kate Hefferon), which reviews our capacity to bounce back, stand strong and, in some cases, thrive after trauma and adversity. One of the most challenging human realisations, our mortality, is then discussed ('Mortality and Positive Psychology' by Dr Kate Hefferon), including ways in which our own mortality awareness can create an enhanced existence in the here and now. The chapter on 'Well-Being: Suffering, Compassion and Interconnectedness' (Dr Tim Lomas) explores the way opening ourselves to suffering can generate compassion, which in turn can lead to positive changes in one's sense of self. The chapter 'Spirituality – Transcending the Self' (Dr Itai Ivtzan) relates to the spiritual journey, focusing on self-awareness while recognising the pain and difficulty involved in taking this path. The book's final chapter deals with 'The Hero's Journey' (Dr Piers Worth), inviting us to face our personal challenges and the changes we undergo to fulfil our potential in full.

In addition to theoretical discussions and research, the book also offers practical exercises to give the readers a chance to implement in person the ideas proposed. We believe that reading or talking about an idea is just the beginning of the way to truly understanding it. To be able to grasp the meaning of a certain topic, practical engagement with it is required. That is why each chapter offers you the opportunity to experiment with exercises that would deepen your personal experience of the topic. In addition, the chapters include a number of aids to enhance your reading experience. Learning objectives and outcomes are specified at the beginning of each chapter; throughout the chapter, discussion points are linked explicitly to the learning outcomes; illustrations are brought from previous research and case studies; psychological questionnaires and scales are offered; each chapter ends with a set of questions and a summary; and finally, a detailed reference list is offered for each chapter.

We would like to invite you to engage with and accept aspects of life that are traditionally considered problematic, challenging or negative and are therefore frequently rejected. Such a change in attitude would allow you to increase PP variables such as compassion, joy, meaning, resilience and gratitude and improve at the same time your understanding of the value of the challenging aspects of life. Reformulating your relationship with the 'dark side' of life will allow you to broaden your horizons while also expanding the boundaries of PP. We hope that this book succeeds in transforming the way you perceive difficult experiences and encourages you to include and accept them in full and thus appreciate the complete and genuine meaning of PP.

BIBLIOGRAPHY

Held, B.S. (2004). The negative side of positive psychology. *Journal of Humanistic Psychology, 44*(1), 9–46.

Seligman, M.E.P. (1990). *Learned optimism*. New York: Pocket Books.

Wong, P.T.P. (2011). Positive psychology 2.0: Towards a balanced interactive model of the good life. *Canadian Psychology/Psychologie canadienne, 52*(2), 69–81.

1

The dialectics of emotion

'The darkest hour of the night comes just before the dawn'.

Thomas Fuller

Learning objectives—at the end of the chapter you will be able to do the following:

- Interpret the relationships between 'psychology as usual', 'positive psychology' (PP), and 'second wave' PP
- Understand the dialectics of thesis–antithesis–synthesis
- See the reciprocal codependency of dichotomous terms
- Critique the pursuit of optimism, self-esteem, freedom, forgiveness and happiness
- Find potential value in pessimism, humility, constraint, anger and sadness
- Appreciate the ambivalent nature of the good life via principles of Buddhist aesthetics
- Understand the significance and value of engaging with the 'dark side' of life

List of topics:

- Dialectics
- Second-wave PP
- Contextuality
- Optimism – pessimism
- Self-esteem – humility

- Freedom–restraint
- Righteous anger
- Happiness – sadness
- Love
- Taoist and Buddhist aesthetics

INTRODUCTION

The origin story of psychology (PP) is by now a well worn tale: disenchanted by the way 'psychology as usual' seemed preoccupied with dysfunction, Martin Seligman used his ascension to the American Psychological Association (APA) presidency to inaugurate the new field of PP. Rather than deal in the currency of human failings, the promise of this new movement was to create a forum where scholars could explore the 'brighter sides of human nature' (Linley & Joseph, 2004, p. 4), from pleasure to fulfilment. Its emergence provided the definite sense of a movement within psychology towards ostensibly 'positive' phenomena (even if this territory had already been explored by fields like humanistic psychology; Resnick et al., 2001). Thus, in counterpart to fields like clinical psychology, that endeavour to alleviate the 'negative' states of mind of mental illness, PP might enquire into 'positive' mental states that constitute mental health. In this way, psychology as a whole could be brought into balance. However, in spite of its success, or even *because* of it, PP has drawn flak from critics who have queried its fundamental concepts and have even questioned whether it ought to exist at all (McNulty & Fincham, 2011). What are we to make of these developments?

To understand this apparent movement towards, and then away from, the 'positive' within psychology, I would like to introduce a term that is central to this chapter: 'dialectic'. This refers to the dynamic 'tension of opposition between two interacting forces or elements' (Merriam-Webster, 2014). This tension describes the mysterious way in which binary opposites – positive and negative, light and dark, up and down – while being diametrically opposed, are yet intimately connected and dependent upon the other for their very existence. Indeed, this notion is the very premise of this book as a whole: just as the dark is inextricably connected to the light, so are seemingly 'negative' experiences bound in complex ways to positive ones, with flourishing arising from their mysterious interaction. However, the term 'dialectic' does not simply refer to a static relationship between opposites but to the way in which many phenomena change and evolve through a process of dynamic movement between these opposites, as elucidated by the German idealist philosopher Hegel (1969/1812). An example of this might be the development of ideas. Say that an argument is advanced, perhaps that human beings are fundamentally good. In Hegelian terms, this proposition would be the thesis. People might identify flaws in this, and respond with the counter-argument that people are inherently bad; this retort would be the antithesis. However, this counter-argument may then itself be found to be flawed. This does not mean, though, that people would collectively revert to the original thesis. Rather, what might emerge is a subtle *synthesis* that incorporates aspects of both arguments – for example, suggesting that people have the potential for good and evil – creating a higher unity that transcends and yet preserves the truth of both extremes (Mills, 2000).

We can use this model to understand the emergence of PP: if 'psychology as usual', focusing on the negative, is the thesis, then PP, embracing the positive, represents its bold antithesis. However, as indicated, this may not be the end of the dynamic. In its infancy, in its role as antithesis, the PP movement differentiated itself by strongly emphasising the positive: positive thoughts, emotions and so on. The message was that ostensibly 'negative' phenomena were undesirable, whereas 'positive' qualities and outcomes were necessarily beneficial[1]. Let's refer to this initial embrace of the positive as 'first wave' PP. However, since boldly claiming the academic spotlight in these early years, PP has begun to be assailed by murmurs of dissent, its initial lively optimism punctured by astute critiques from inside and outside the field. In these critiques, we can discern the process of flaws being found in the antithesis. However, as we have seen, this is not the end of the story. Acknowledgment of flaws does not mean we must revert to the original thesis (psychology as usual). Rather, we can hopefully arrive at a new mature synthesis that takes an altogether more nuanced approach to the notions of positive and negative – we might call this the 'second wave' of PP (Held, 2004) or 'positive psychology 2.0' (Wong, 2011). And, one characteristic of this emergent second wave is an embrace of the 'dark side' of life (i.e., seemingly negative experiences and mental states); while the first wave of PP felt uncomfortable with this 'dark side', rejected it in favour of the 'brighter sides' of life, this second wave views it in some strange way as being potentially inherent to flourishing. As elucidated in the introduction, although this 'dark side' can cause us distress and discomfort (which is why we tend to avoid it), engaging with these challenges can bring great potential for growth, healing, insight and transformation; thus, the 'dark side' contains the seed for a potential positive outcome, even when the path towards this outcome is testing.

PRACTICE ESSAY QUESTIONS

- Evaluate the notion that in certain circumstances, ostensibly positive emotions can be detrimental to wellbeing, whereas apparently negative emotions can promote flourishing.
- Conceptually, one can no more hope to eradicate the negative (thereby only having the positive) than one could manage to get rid of down (thereby only having up): Discuss.

In this chapter we shall explore the critiques levelled at first wave PP and examine the emergence of the second wave synthesis. As we shall see, second wave PP means appreciating how emotions[2] themselves exist dialectically. Just as, in a macro-sense, psychology as a field is evolving through its own positive-negative dialectic, in a micro-sense we can see this dialectic playing itself out in our own emotional experiences. Perhaps we feel unhappy; this is our thesis. Consequently, we endeavour to find happiness; this is our antithetic response. However, as Wong (2011) so astutely identified, there are potential downsides to 'seeking the positive' – positive qualities can sometimes be detrimental to wellbeing, whereas negative processes may at times promote our flourishing. Thus, in time, a synthesis may emerge in which we discern that the good life cannot be found by just eschewing negative emotions, or pursuing positive ones, but involves appreciating the nuances of the whole spectrum of our emotional experience.

We will trace these ideas out over three parts here. Part 1 explores the notion that 'positive can be negative': apparently positive qualities can hinder our flourishing under certain circumstances. Conversely, part 2 enquires whether 'negative can be positive': engaging with the 'dark side' of life (i.e., processes we usually regard as negative) might actually be conducive to wellbeing. These sections represent the process of finding flaws in the antithesis position (i.e., our desire to avoid the negative and seek the positive). Finally, Part 3 seeks to establish a synthesis, looking at how some of the most precious experiences in life – like love – inherently involve both positive and negative components; here we shall also explore ways in which we might appreciate this subtle synthesis, based on the aesthetics of Eastern philosophies. However, before we dive into these sections, let me emphasise that in constructing these paradoxical titles – positive can be negative and vice versa – I am not trying to depict an Alice in Wonderland version of mental life, in which black is white, up is down. Rather, I am suggesting that phenomena which appear to be negative may, from a different perspective, not be so harmful after all. Our initial appraisal of the valence of a particular state of mind or affairs may be incomplete or inaccurate, and considered in other lights, contrasting judgments may be reached. As part of that, experiences that one might at first interpret as being part of the darker side of life may actually turn out to herald potentially beneficial outcomes or be unexpected sources of value, meaning or beauty. Let's illustrate this with an old Buddhist parable, titled 'Maybe':

There was an old farmer who had toiled away on his crops for many years. One day his horse ran away. Upon hearing the news, his neighbours came to visit. 'Such bad luck', they said sympathetically. 'Maybe', the farmer replied. The next morning, the horse returned, bringing with it three other wild horses. 'How wonderful', the neighbours exclaimed. 'Maybe', replied the old man. The following day, his son tried to ride one of the untamed horses, was thrown and broke his leg. The neighbours again came to offer their sympathy on his misfortune. 'Maybe', answered the farmer. The day after, military officials came to the village to draft young men into the army. Seeing that the son's leg was broken, they passed him by. The neighbours congratulated the farmer on how well things had turned out in the end. 'Maybe', said the farmer . . . [Can this labyrinthine process ever end?]

Here, the initial negative appraisal becomes relativized when placed in a broader context (i.e., the passage of time and subsequent events). Let us refer to this notion of situating an appraisal in a broader context as 'contextualisation' (Garrett & Schmidt, 2012). This story is an example of 'temporal contextualisation' – the meaning of a current event being altered by perspectives at other points in time. This type of contextualisation is reflected in the notion of posttraumatic growth (PTG) (Tedeschi & Calhoun, 2004), in which some people who have experienced traumatic events report that these events have led to subsequent shifts in aspects of life that are ultimately viewed as being positive (e.g., closer relationships with loved ones). There is also 'spatial contextualisation' – considering the event from a different perspective in the current moment. For example, what if a person makes a self-determined act which he or she feels is integral to his or her flourishing (say, going travelling alone), but this act causes pain to others (the family they are leaving behind). Is this act good or bad? Well, it depends on the context – from whose perspective we are looking at it. As such, one of the messages of this book is that phenomena that may appear at first to be dark (i.e., negative) in nature may in fact become an unanticipated source of light. Conversely, qualities or situations that at first may seem desirable might have their downsides.

Moreover, the range of potential contexts, temporal and spatial, is theoretically infinite and inexhaustible: another can always be found. Thus meaning is always 'deferred', as Lacan (2006) put it. That said, this does not imply moral relativism (i.e., no way of assigning value to phenomena) – ultimately, we can judge situations and behaviours by the extent to which they contribute to the overall wellbeing of as many people as possible (even if making such utilitarian judgements is difficult in practice). Moreover, recognition of contextuality does not render us incapacitated in terms of trying to appraise phenomena; we just do our best with the knowledge we have while retaining the humility that comes from knowing that we are neither omniscient nor faultless in our judgements. So, having introduced some key ideas, we can begin by exploring potential problems with the 'positive'.

POSITIVE CAN BE NEGATIVE

We turn first to the idea that apparently salutary emotions may actually be damaging to our wellbeing in certain circumstances. We'll begin with some individualistic examples, such as optimism, self-esteem and freedom, then explore a few prosocial ones, including forgiveness and altruism. (Needless to say, this is far from a comprehensive critique of the vast scope of qualities of interest to PP but rather a brief foray into a small selection.) Following that, we'll turn to the more unsettling notion that happiness *itself* might be contentious. At this point, you might be thinking, surely these qualities cannot be undesirable? Well, this chapter is not about being contrarian and disavowing these; rather, we can just gently point out that in particular contexts and from certain perspectives, these outcomes might be detrimental to individuals themselves and/or to those around them. And, it is when we begin to appreciate these nuances – to cease simplistically categorising particular qualities as positive or negative – that we have begun to embrace the second wave of PP.

Let's start with optimism. Over the centuries, the dangers of excessive or unrealistic optimism have been critiqued and even lampooned, perhaps most famously by Voltaire (1759), who used the fictional Dr Pangloss to mock Leibniz's assertion that we live in the 'best of all possible worlds'. Even in PP, optimism was recognised from the start as potentially problematic. As Seligman acknowledged in 1990, one must be careful not to be a 'slave to the tyrannies of optimism', but must be 'able to use pessimism's keen sense of reality when we need it' (p. 292). This insight has since been borne out in empirical work, which reveals a diversity of problems associated with undue optimism, many relating to under-appreciation of risk and subsequent maladaptive risk-taking (e.g., smoking; Weinstein et al., 2005). Such actions consequently implicate optimism as a mortality risk: a seven-decade longitudinal study suggested that children who were 'cheerful' (optimism plus a sense of humour) had shorter lives than their conscientious peers (Friedman et al., 1993). Contrariwise though, other studies have found that optimism predicts longevity (Giltay et al., 2004). So, is optimism undesirable? As with everything, context is key; unfortunately, however, context has thus far been under-appreciated in PP. As such, the task going forward is to elucidate the contextual factors that make optimism (and other qualities analysed here) beneficial or otherwise; for now, we might heed Peterson's (2000, p. 51) advice that 'people should be optimistic when the future can be changed by positive thinking but not otherwise'.

There are shades of optimism in our second quality, self-esteem (almost like an optimism of the self). But, surely one would not wish a person to be afflicted with low levels of this barometer of self-worth? Well, no: generally, wellbeing is better served by high rather than low self-esteem. For example, a prospective study found that adolescents with low self-esteem subsequently had relatively greater criminality, worse economic prospects, and poorer mental and physical health in adulthood (Trzesniewski et al., 2006). However, this does not render high self-esteem unproblematic. As with optimism, high self-esteem is associated with perceived invulnerability and subsequent health-risk behaviours (Gerrard et al., 2000). Inflated assessments about one's capabilities also lead people to making commitments that exceed their capacities – particularly if their egos are threatened – leading potentially to failure; if one's self-esteem is contingent on achieving these goals, dependent upon extrinsic validation, such experiences of failure can be damaging (Crocker & Park, 2004), particularly if one has been ennobled by one's culture to regard success as a birthright (a claim often levelled against Western societies). Going further, there are still darker sides to high self-esteem: in combination with noxious qualities like narcissism, the resulting brew is linked to higher levels of aggression, particularly when inflated self-appraisals are threatened (Baumeister et al., 1996). As with optimism, self-esteem is not an unqualified good; as ever, the devil is in the contextual detail.

Turning to freedom – or 'self-determination' in the clinical language of academia – how can this possibly be unwanted? Most thinkers regard freedom as integral to well-being (Ryan & Deci, 2000). Rightly so, given the torments that can arise if freedom is denied, revealed most painfully in unforgivable crimes such as slavery. However, can one have *too much* freedom? The troubling consequences of a life without restrictions have been elucidated by existentialist thinkers. Dostoevsky (1990/1880, p. 589) argued that freedom from religious proscriptions would lead to the erosion of morality ('everything is permitted'). Going further, Kierkegaard (1957/1834) argued that this sense of unlimited possibilities, 'the dizziness of freedom', was profoundly debilitating, leading to ontological dread: even though we are thrown into situations not of our own making (we do not choose the context in which we are born), and though our knowledge is imperfect, we must nevertheless continually make choices that irretrievably determine the course of our lives and assume responsibility for the consequences. It was for this reason that Sartre (1952) said people are 'condemned to be free' (p. 399). These insights have been captured in psychology with the work of Schwartz (2000), who suggests that 'excessive' freedom can be experienced 'as a kind of tyranny' (p. 79). He uses this notion to critique the ideology of 'rational-choice' economic theory – which holds that people are best served by having a diverse array of options – that underpins our consumer–capitalist society. He cites Iyengar and Lepper's (1999) work showing that a greater diversity of consumer choice is associated with *lower* levels of subsequent satisfaction with the chosen item, arguably due to greater scope for regret over the unselected options. While such troubles may be a luxury afforded by contemporary affluence, it still reinforces the existentialists' perceptive linking of freedom and anxiety.

What about prosocial qualities, such as forgiveness and altruism; are these not 'non-zero-sum' goods (win-win), beneficial to both giver and recipient? Usually, yes. Starting with forgiveness, this is generally beneficial to wellbeing; for instance, forgiveness-based therapies have been used successfully in cases such as treating posttraumatic stress disorder (PTSD) in the aftermath of spousal abuse (Reed & Enright, 2006). However, in certain contexts, forgiveness can be harmful – notably, if it means that a person tolerates or acquiesces to a destructive situation that he or she might otherwise be emboldened to resist or change. Here we are indebted to McNulty and Fincham's (2011) seminal work on the need for a 'contextual' approach to PP, who make their point through a summary of studies on abusive relationships. Longitudinal surveys of couples suggest that people who make benevolent 'external' attributions for their partner's abuse (explaining it away as a consequence of situational factors, such as work stress) and/or are more forgiving of such transgressions are at greater risk of ongoing abuse. Needless to say, these studies are not about 'victim-blaming', but trying to help victims to hold aggressors accountable; the real issue of course is the injurious behaviour of their tormentors. Nevertheless, such studies do make the point that the merits of prosocial qualities do depend on context.

Away from the highly charged arena of abusive relationships, it seems difficult to imagine how acts of beneficence such as altruism and kindness could be problematic. In most circumstances, such behaviours do serve the wellbeing of both the protagonist and the recipient (Post, 2005). However, it is possible for these to conflict with *other* prosocial goods in ways that ultimately undermine wellbeing. In one experimental setup, Batson et al. (1995) found that altruism could potentially undercut the moral principle of justice. Participants were encouraged to feel empathy for a (fictional) terminally ill child ostensibly on a waiting list for pain-relieving drugs, while control participants received no such encouragement. The former were more likely to allow the child to skip ahead of other (equally deserving) children on the list, even though they knew this was wrong (they acknowledged that their choice violated principles of justice and could erode social cohesion). This is a good example of the broader concept of the *ethical dilemma*, in which competing goods – *both* of which are valued – are in opposition, such that the fulfilment of one necessarily impedes the other. A salient example of this today, bedevilled as we are by the fear of terrorism and the rapid development of technology, is the competing goods of self-determination, safety, and privacy (Harris, 2011). Each is recognised as being valuable to flourishing, yet in extremis, each impedes the others and must be curbed. That the balancing of these goods is continually being tested, in the courts of law and public opinion, shows how near-impossible this balancing act is.

Above all these particular qualities, we can now turn to perhaps the ultimate concern of PP: happiness itself. Given that the pursuit of this ephemeral goal has been valorised by the finest thinkers throughout the centuries, from Aristotle's (2000/350 BCE) *Nichomachean Ethics* to Thomas Jefferson's American constitution, what problem might there be with this most valued of ends? Although this is a vast, complex terrain, we can touch upon three issues relating to defining, seeking and accepting happiness. First, in terms of defining happiness, PP is developing a nuanced understanding of the different forms of happiness, from the pleasure of hedonic, 'subjective' wellbeing (Diener et al., 1999) to the fulfilment of eudaimonic 'psychological' wellbeing (Ryff, 1989). These distinctions are not new, with analysis of such subtleties being common currency in classical Greek philosophy, for example, where Aristotle describes eudaimonic happiness as 'an activity of the soul that expresses virtue' in contrast to mere hedonic pleasure which he condemns as a 'life suitable to beasts' (McMahon, 2006). As such, qualitative distinctions have long been present in discourses around happiness, with some forms of it being seen as deeper, more fulfilling or in some inchoate way as simply better than others. This point was pithily

captured by John Stuart Mill (1863, p. 9), who said it was 'better to be Socrates dissatis-
fied than a fool satisfied'. On this reading, pursuing hedonic happiness would arguably be
disadvantageous if it hindered one from seeking qualitatively richer states of wellbeing.

However, this last point can itself be critiqued from the perspective of our second
issue here, seeking happiness, as some argue that the very act of pursing this elusive goal
renders it ever more distant. To quote Mill (1960/1873, p. 100) again, 'those only are
happy who have their minds fixed on some object other than their own happiness'. Or,
as (possibly) expressed by Thoreau, 'Happiness is like a butterfly: the more you chase it,
the more it will elude you, but if you turn your attention to other things, it comes and
sits quietly on your shoulder'. This same insight can be found in Buddhism, where the
desire for happiness is seen as the root of unhappiness: the very act of resisting the present and wishing for a happier state of mind is what creates the dissatisfaction one hopes
to alleviate. Or, expressed in the modern terminology of self-regulation theory, Carver
and Scheier (1990) suggest that dysphoria stems from a discrepancy between expectations and reality; yearning for happiness actually widens this discrepancy, thus increasing
dissatisfaction (a theory borne out in empirical studies; Mauss et al., 2011). This yearning may be exacerbated through cultural pressures that turn happiness into something
approaching a social norm; ironically, critical theorists accuse PP of perpetuating this
very process, creating a 'tyranny of positive thinking' (Held, 2002). For example, Barbara Ehrenreich (2009) has written powerfully about her experience of being diagnosed
with cancer and of feeling a certain cultural pressure to disavow her feelings of anger
and despair. The charge is that happiness becomes expected, obligatory even, which may
engender a climate of implicit blame and stigmatisation towards those who fail to achieve
this goal, with unhappiness seen almost as a moral failure (Ahmed, 2007).

REFLECTION

Have you ever felt pressure to be happy? When you are feeling low, is this
feeling compounded by the thought that you shouldn't feel that way?
Does PP contribute to a culture in which there is an expectation to be
happy? If so, how might we reconfigure PP so that it doesn't add to this
oppressive cultural weight?

The third issue concerns, almost perversely, the unforeseen pitfalls of actually believing
oneself to be happy. We may be fortunate enough to enjoy positive states of mind, whether
through our genetic inheritance (Lykken & Tellegen, 1996), our sociocultural position
(Prilleltensky, 2008) or our own efforts through practices like meditation (Kabat-Zinn,
2003). The danger with these small mercies, however, is that these may lull us into believing that life is as good as it could be. We risk becoming tranquilised, acquiescent to a
social context that conspires to undermine collective wellbeing through iniquities such

as societal inequality. In this way, we may be beguiled by happiness into the myopia that Marxist theorists call 'false consciousness', that is, a state of mind that prevents us from acting in our own interests (Jost, 1995). This is what Marx (1975/1844, p. 244) had in mind when he called religion the 'opium of the people'. This is often taken as a criticism of religion, but his real target was society and the desperate conditions in which many people are forced to live. Marx saw dignity in religion, calling it 'the sigh of the oppressed creature, the heart of a heartless world'. His issue, however, was that the comforts provided by religion meant people were pacified into inaction; Marx (1975/1844) thus urged people to relinquish these comforts to realise their full potential as human beings: 'The abolition of religion as the illusory happiness of the people is required for their real happiness', empowering people to overcome social conditions that *need* illusions. It may be that our apparent happiness dissuades us from taking action to really forge a better world. Perhaps we *need* to feel discomfort – to let ourselves become aware of the darker side of life – to propel us into creating the best life we can for ourselves, a question which leads us into the next section . . .

NEGATIVE CAN BE POSITIVE

Thus far we have shone a critical light upon topics conventionally embraced within PP, showing that qualities generally regarded as positive may be problematic in some ways. In terms of the dialectical movement within psychology, if 'psychology as usual' is the thesis, and first wave PP the antitheses, then this critique represents the process of finding flaws in the antithesis, which is the prelude to the synthesis (second wave PP). However, before we discuss this synthesis in the third part of the chapter, we have not finished troubling the antithesis: we can do this by not only destabilising the concept of positive but by finding redeeming features in qualities often regarded as negative, in embracing what appears to be the dark side of life. This is a somewhat unorthodox route to take, certainly within PP; however, the terrain is expansive, mysterious, and certainly worth investigating. There are many potential areas we can explore; indeed, this book as a whole is devoted to this enquiry. So, rather than pre-empt the surprises offered by subsequent chapters, we will content ourselves here with analysing the obverse qualities of those already critiqued, thus lending symmetry to the chapter. So, having considered the pitfalls of optimism, self-esteem, freedom, forgiveness and happiness, we can briefly extol the potential virtues of their antonyms (of near versions thereof) – pessimism, humility, restrictiveness, anger and sadness. Again, the aim is not to argue that black is white and turn these negatives into unalloyed goods but to show that we may find unanticipated value in these unexpected places.

We began by noting the pitfalls of optimism, at least to the extent that it is 'excessive'. Naturally, we can invert this questioning and consider the value of its counterpart, pessimism. So, without engaging in unnecessary repetition – we don't need to revisit the link with risk-taking – we can explore what other qualities it may offer. We might, for example, appreciate the connection between pessimism and proactive coping, or as Norem (2001) puts it, the 'positive power of negative thinking'. Norem is not advocating a trait-like downward cast of mind that sees a cloud in every silver lining. Rather, this is strategic, anticipatory fault finding and problem solving, heeding the advice of Benjamin Franklin – 'He that lives upon hope will die fasting' – and prudently scanning the horizon for storms to thus be better prepared should inclement weather strike. A neat example of this is provided by the astronaut Chris Hadfield (2013) in his account of the training programme at NASA, in which his trainers devised countless simulations of bad-news scenarios to enable him to practice dealing with every conceivable mishap. He articulates of the value of cultivating a pessimistic mindset, crucially though, only with regard to circumstances that he personally has the power to affect. This is the key difference between the strategic pessimism exhibited in proactive coping, and 'pure' pessimism, which simply assumes the worst. Whereas the latter may lead to apathy and even despair, the former can be empowering: one feels emboldened through cultivating the ability to deal with life's challenges. As Hadfield put it, ongoing repetition of such contingency planning enables one to forge 'the strongest possible armor to defend against fear: hard-won competence' (p. 54).

In Hadfield's (2013) cautious and un-hubristic philosophy, we can discern the second of our inverse virtues: humility. Although not strictly an antonym of high self-esteem (whose true opposites are perhaps insecurity or self-pity, neither of which one could realistically advocate), it is often treated as such (Rowatt, Ottenbreit, Nesselroade Jr, & Cunningham, 2002). Etymologically the term derives from the Latin humilis (i.e., lowly, humble or literally 'on the ground'), and it is frequently taken as meaning having a low opinion of oneself, as revealed by the contemptuous derivate 'humiliation' (being reduced to lowliness). However, Rowatt et al. argue that it in fact involves a 'genuine modesty' that is of great value, characterised by 'respectfulness, willingness to admit imperfections, and a lack of self-focus or self-serving biases' (p. 198). Perhaps Tangey (2005, p. 411) best captured the quiet virtue of humility by describing it as a 'forgetting of the self'. Notwithstanding the critique of altruism, many virtuous prosocial acts stem from such self-abnegation (Worthington, 2007). However, the impact of humility on the protagonist themselves may be even more profound. Buddhism holds that an overweening sense of self, and a lack of due humility, is the root of much suffering, generating noxious states like greed (wanting to reward the self) and hatred (for that which threatens the self). As the Buddha said, 'One dwells in suffering if one is without reverence and deference' (Lamotte, 1981). Consequently, the grace of 'self-forgetting' is that it can be a salve for these self-created poisons. Going further, humility can be a doorway to transcendent experiences of great significance. Highlighting the value of humility in the context of medical training, DasGupta (2008, p. 981) argues that it can render one receptive to the gifts the present moment may offer, giving us the opportunity to become spiritually transfigured as we open up to possibilities in the world and encounter new dimensions of ourselves.

This absorbing idea that the present moment can bestow unexpected boons if one is sufficiently receptive also pertains to our third inverse quality, restriction. We have seen that an 'excess' of freedom can perhaps be debilitating. However, we are not often given to imagining that limiting our freedom can be beneficial. Strangely enough though, such restrictions may paradoxically be liberating. Returning again to Buddhism, we encounter the insight that placing restrictions on choice can actually *create* freedom: one is alleviated from the burden of having to choose and is thus able to simply be present in the moment (Wright, 2008). It is for this reason that monastic life is strictly regulated by rigid routines, governing everything from sleep patterns to food intake. In restricting the body thus, the mind is liberated from the myriad of inconsequential but incessant choices that otherwise dominate daily existence ('Should I eat now or in 10 minutes? Or later? Pizza? Unhealthy. Tofu? Disgusting. Maybe, pizza . . .'). People are thus ennobled to 'step out of ordinary thought processes' and engage in the 'non-conceptual and focused' attention that is so valued by meditators (Wright, 2008, p. 14). The creation of such routines is not only beneficial in a spiritual context. Developing forces of habit that are strong enough to withstand the whims of our passing moods is central in other areas, from education to physical health. For instance, regular exercise requires us to commit to a pattern of activity regardless of whether we happen to feel like doing it at the time (Aarts et al., 1997). It is only by restricting our fleeting inclinations, and restraining our ability to make short-sighted choices, that we can pursue long-term goals – like health or obtaining qualifications – that are vital for flourishing.

So, in certain lights, we can find virtue in pessimism, humility and restriction. However, such analyses, while perhaps counterintuitive, are relatively uncontentious. What about more explicitly 'dark' qualities, like anger? Anger is often presented as a destructive emotion – for instance, Beck (1999) presents it simultaneously as a manifestation of hate, a form of 'warped' thinking and a root cause of evils such as war. But, is it always? In some respects, anger is the opposite of forgiveness: whereas both can be a response to being wronged, the former constitutes a form of acceptance, and the latter implies a lack of it. The question is, *should* certain things be tolerated, accepted or forgiven? As the saying goes, 'If you're not angry, you're not paying attention'! (This quote apparently first appeared as a car bumper sticker in the 1970s, not that this undermines the potency of its polemic; wisdom can be found in the most unlikely of places.) These sentiments have led to a re-evaluation of anger in some quarters, led by Tavris (1989), who argues that it is fundamentally a *moral* emotion, a response to an ethical or moral value being breached. This of course does not mean all incidents of anger are justified or proportionate – far from it. As Aristotle (2000/350 BCE) recognised, 'Anybody can become angry – that is easy, but to be angry with the right person and to the right degree and at the right time and for the right purpose, and in the right way – that is not within everybody's power'. Thus, as Haidt (2003) acknowledges, expressions of anger may often be both selfish and antisocial. However, 'the motivation to redress injustices can also be felt strongly in third-party situations, in which the self has no stake' (p. 856). Here we are getting close to the idea of anger as a moral reaction.

Thus, even if one has no 'ties to the victimized group', one can, and arguably *should*, feel outrage at iniquities such as oppression and so 'demand retaliatory or compensatory action' on behalf of the victims (Haidt, 2003, p. 856). Moreover, being among the victimised does not render one's anger selfish; on the contrary, it can lend it even greater moral force. These considerations raise searching questions about the nature of wellbeing and about the role of PP. We have enquired whether happiness could be a state of false consciousness, a fortuitous state which tranquilises us into accepting a societal status quo that is in fact profoundly invidious. Indeed, critics of PP have argued that in promoting 'happiness' activities that enable and even encourage individuals to accept this status quo, PP has not only often ignored the structural causes of suffering – from oppression to inequality – but may even be complicit in upholding it (Ehrenreich, 2009). We can ask, with so many people worldwide suffering untold torments, *should* we be happy? Should we even *want* to be happy? Are we in fact not closer to the spirit of wanting humanity to flourish if we are angry, despairing or protesting at the state of the world? And it is here that we can view anger as integral to flourishing but, crucially, not in an 'I'm all right' individualistic sense rather flourishing in a collective way. The great social movements of recent years, from civil rights to environmentalism, have been propelled by a righteous anger that the world should *and can* be better than it is (Siegel, 2009). One must not necessarily wish this kind of dysphoria away. As Ahmed (2010, p. 223) puts it, a 'revolutionary politics' – that is, movements to change the world for the better – must 'work hard to stay proximate to unhappiness'. Perhaps, then, a second wave PP will make room for anger as a moral emotion, recognising it as a vital motivational spur that compels us to agitate for a better world for all.

RESEARCH AND PRACTICE CASE STUDIES

The moral force of righteous anger has rarely been expressed more powerfully than by Dr Martin Luther King Jr., the civil rights leader who was assassinated in 1968. Preaching with almost unmatched eloquence, he articulated a vision of struggling for a better world, crucially though, without letting one's vision becoming poisoned by hate. As expressed in a sermon in 1958: 'As you press on for justice, be sure to move with dignity and discipline, using only the weapon of love. Let no man pull you so low as to make you hate him. Always avoid using violence in your struggle, for if you succumb to the temptation of using violence, unborn generations will be the recipients of a long and desolate night of bitterness. . . . So violence is not the way'. King realised that this meant taking the hard road: 'Honesty impels me to admit that such a stand requires willingness to suffer and sacrifice, so don't despair if you are persecuted for righteousness' sake'. However, echoing this point, King argued that one must not be lulled into settling for an easy, pleasant life: 'The end of life is not to be happy. The end of life is not to achieve pleasure and to avoid pain'. What then should we aim for? King was clear: 'Over the centuries men have sought to discover the highest good. . . . I have an answer. . . . It is love' (in King, 2007, pp. 344–345). These quotes perfectly encapsulate the dialectical message of this chapter and this book.

And yet, what if the world cannot be changed or at least cannot change as profoundly or as quickly as we would like? What then? There is the risk then that anger hardens and becomes hate, which is destructive, afflicting not only its target but also being corrosive inside the holder, as Martin Luther King, Jr. recognised. As the Buddha said: 'Holding on to anger is like grasping a hot coal with the intent of throwing it at someone else; you are the one who gets burned'. For this reason, the Dalai Lama (1997) urges compassion, of course for those suffering, but more challengingly, also for those causing this pain (partly to unburden oneself of hate but also on the grounds that such people, too, will ultimately be greatly pained as a result of their actions). One might ideally feel compassion even while fighting for a cause, as the Dalai Lama has shown in his struggle with China for Tibetan independence (Thurman, 2008). Even as we cultivate compassion, though, in the face of an implacable situation, anger may give way to sadness. Now, one would not wish sadness upon people, for it can truly be a heartbreaking state of mind. And yet, it may also be a profoundly *true* experience, one that we must not chastise people for feeling. In many ways, sadness may be the right, genuine response to a phenomenon, the very condition of caring. For instance, for most bereaved parents, intense experiences of grief are not a manifestation of disorder, but are an expression of love, and indeed a 'way to maintain a connection to a beloved deceased child' (Thieleman & Cacciatore, 2014, p. 6). As we asked in relation to anger, *should* one feel any differently in such a situation, or would one even *want* to? Would not happiness, or other positive states of mind, be profoundly inappropriate?

However, there is currently a danger – in PP and in society generally – of states such as sadness becoming viewed not as appropriate and genuine reactions to a troubling world but as dysfunctions to be alleviated. This danger, for our purposes here, is twofold. First, the encroachment of medical discourses in many areas of life means that we risk pathologising states like sadness, thereby condemning the dark side of life. For instance, Thieleman and Cacciatore (2014) discuss the construction of the recent edition of the APA's (2013) *Diagnostic and Statistical Manual of Mental Disorders* and the controversy over whether prolonged grief should be defined as a psychopathology ('persistent complex bereavement-related disorder'). Of course, therapeutic help should be given to people who want assistance to deal with such experiences; however, we enter troubling territory if we pathologise these dimensions of human existence. As Horowitz and Wakefield (2007, p. 225) put it, sadness is 'an inherent part of the human condition, not a mental disorder'. Unfortunately though, we see a creeping medicalization of existence, where ordinary aspects of being human are treated as diseases to be medicated away (Szasz, 1960). This is troubling on multiple levels. It alienates sufferers themselves, making them feel estranged from their suffering, and from humanity, as if there is something wrong with them. There can be more severe consequences too, such as the involuntary deprivation of freedom in psychiatric care (Matthews, 2000). As such, there are real ethical issues involved in the conceptualisation and treatment of 'unwanted' mental states, and PP must be wary of colluding in discourses that pathologise or otherwise condemn negative experiences such as sadness.

Even aside from these more extreme worries, there is a risk – milder and yet potentially more insidious and corrosive – that PP contributes to a culture in which states such as sadness are seen as somehow wrong. As we have seen, cultural expectations of happiness can have damaging consequences, from the 'tyranny of positive thinking' to the possibility that *seeking* wellbeing may actually foster unhappiness. Of course, it is to be welcomed that PP provides interventions that enable people, if they wish, to alleviate their distress and generate wellbeing. However, it is vital that PP does not imply that dysphoric states are inherently wrong. For one thing, this may well compound such distress, leading sufferers to feel bad about feeling bad. In Buddhism, this is known as the 'two arrows'; the initial distress (the first arrow) is wounding enough, but tormenting oneself over feeling distressed is a second arrow that exacerbates the suffering (Bhikkhu, 2013). Moreover, such states may bear important messages in which one may find value: they may show us how much we care and be a source of inspiration, or a font of meaning, and even transcendent beauty. Or they may not and may simply be distressing; but we need that to be OK, as simply another dimension of human experience that we allow ourselves to feel. In meditation, there is a wonderful metaphor designed to encourage people to listen to, and even value, ostensibly negative emotions, namely, the notion of respectfully welcoming these into the mind as if inviting guests into one's house. Even if these guests from the dark side are unexpected, or even unwanted, they may serve some purpose which we, in our current state, are unable to fathom or appreciate.

ART LINKS

The metaphor of respectfully 'welcoming' emotions into the mind was captured beautifully by the 13th-century Persian mystic–poet Rumi (1995, p. 109) in this timeless verse:

This being human is a guest house.
Every morning a new arrival.

A joy, a depression, a meanness,
some momentary awareness comes
as an unexpected visitor.

Welcome and entertain them all!
Even if they're a crowd of sorrows,
who violently sweep your house
empty of its furniture,
still, treat each guest honorably.
He may be clearing you out
for some new delight . . .

Be grateful for whoever comes,
because each has been sent
as a guide from beyond.

THE AESTHETICS OF DIALECTICS

We have painted a nuanced picture in which ostensibly positive qualities can be detrimental to wellbeing, whereas apparently negative ones may in fact have unanticipated virtues. Does this undermine the case for PP as its stated aim was to redress the 'negativity' of 'psychology as usual' by focusing on more positive dimensions of existence? If these concepts are contentious – if 'positive can be negative' and vice versa – does this not invalidate the very premise of PP? I would argue no. If PP is the antithesis to 'psychology as usual', if flaws are then discerned in this antithesis (as the two previous sections have highlighted), this does not compel us to scurry back to the thesis, back to psychology as usual. Rather, in this dialectical process, the next stage is ideally *synthesis*, in which the truths of both thesis and antithesis are preserved, and the flaws in their respective positions are overcome. And, I suggested, a second wave PP was beginning to emerge which represented just such a synthesis. In this, there is a movement away from a Manichean perspective – from a simplistic binary view that unreservedly views negative emotions as undesirable and positive ones as salutary – towards a more nuanced appreciation of the complexities of the good life. And it is this notion of *appreciating* these complexities that I shall focus on in this final section. First, I will argue that if we understand dialectics as the dynamic interplay between opposites (leaving aside for now the Hegelian notion of thesis–antithesis–synthesis), then human experience is inherently dialectical. I will do this by considering, as an example, perhaps the most elevated and sought-after of human emotions: love. I will then finish by drawing on aesthetic principles at the heart of Eastern philosophy that might offer us a model for how we can learn to appreciate these complexities.

Firstly then, let us consider the notion that human experience, including its most elevated states, is inherently dialectical (using this in a general sense to mean the interplay between opposites). This point has been recognized by scholars at the forefront of developing the second wave of PP (which remains concerned with flourishing but appreciates its ambivalent and complex nature). As Ryff and Singer (2003, p. 272) put it, the good life involves an 'inevitable dialectics between positive and negative aspects of living'. Likewise, Resnick et al. (2001) emphasise that dialectical opposites are conceptually codependent: the notion of 'positive' depends on the existence of 'negative' for its very meaning. As such, a key message underlying this second wave – and likewise this book – is that because the dark side (negative) is an inevitable dimension of life, our task in PP is to embrace it and allow it to be part of our experience of life. Going further, Lazarus (2003) suggests that many emotional states are 'co-valenced'. This means not only that it is difficult to characterise particular emotions as either positive or negative – because this appraisal depends on context, as this chapter has emphasised – but that specific mental states inherently involve complex, intertwined shades of light and dark. Lazarus offers various examples of this dialectical phenomenon. For example, hope involves a tantalising and fragile mix of yearning for a desired outcome, a degree of confidence that this outcome has at least some chance of occurring, and a gnawing anxiety that it will not. Perhaps nowhere is the dialectical nature of emotions revealed most strongly than by that most valorised of emotional states – love.

There are many ways of looking at love, a word that encompasses a multitude of emotional relationships. Drawing on distinctions elaborated at least as far back as classical Greece, Lee (1973) differentiates between six different 'types' of love: *eros* (romantic, passionate), *ludus* (flirtatious, playful), *storge* (filial, fraternal), *pragma* (rational, sensible), *mania* (possessive, dependent), and *agape* (unconditional, selfless). Such differentiations make us wary of generalising about love; nevertheless, arguably most, if not all, of these types – with the possible exception of *agape* – involve a dialectical blend of light and dark. There are many ways of viewing this dialectic, but all are essentially variations on the idea that, as C. S. Lewis (1971) so memorably put it, 'To love at all is to be vulnerable. Love anything and your heart will be wrung and possibly broken'. Love can be troubled and even ended by the vicissitudes of fate in all manner of ways, from heart-wrenching partings to the slow erosion of feelings over time. Even in the midst of love, one can be threatened by the fear of its loss, giving rise to complications in one's expressions of love, from anxiety to jealousy to anger. Spitzberg and Cupach (1998) – whose book *The Dark Side of Close Relationships* shows we are by no means the first to explore this murky territory – even go so far as to claim provocatively that 'love and hate are indeed impossible to disentangle' (p. xiii). Whereas this may not apply to all forms and instances of love – *storge*, *pragma* and *agape* all stand out as probable exceptions – it remains that love invariably encompasses, as an integral component, a spectrum of negative feelings that can be troubling to varying degrees.

However – and here is where we truly enter into dialectical thinking – the vulnerability we feel when we love is not an aberration of love but the very condition of it, the price tag, as it were. Love thus not only has an inevitable dark side, but this darkness is *inextricably* linked to the more beautiful and elevating dimensions of love. This is not to justify the complicated expressions already noted, such as anger or jealousy; these are indeed perversions of love, examples of 'love gone bad'. But the vulnerability that may potentially underlie these is, as Lewis (1971) recognised, the condition we have to enter into to be in love; they are inseparable, two sides of the same coin. This is because love, to an extent, means placing our hearts and our fates in the hands of the 'other', whose actions cannot be controlled and whose reciprocal love cannot be willed. This 'insurmountable duality of beings' creates what Levinas (1987, p. 88) calls 'the pathos of love': Love thus means entering into 'a relation with alterity, with mystery'. Indeed, as Bauman (2013, p. 7) phrases it, any attempt to 'tame' this mystery, to 'make the knowable predictable and enchain the free-roaming – all such things sound the death-knell to love'; thus, love means embracing the 'caprice of fate – that eerie and mysterious future, impossible to be told in advance'. Love is thus fundamentally dialectical, a transcendent blend of light and dark, joy and terror, safety and fear. As Bauman eloquently phrases it, 'to love means opening up to that most sublime of all human conditions, one in which fear blends with joy into an alloy that no longer allows its ingredients to separate'.

TRY ME

Music can be a powerful way of evoking complex emotions, creating mood states that can be hard to categorise as either positive or negative but which seem to involve mysterious blends of joy and sorrow. One particularly evocative song is the Simon and Garfunkel classic '7 O'Clock News/Silent Night'. As an exercise, please listen to this song, ideally at the following web link: http://vimeo.com/23100818. You could either listen mindfully with your eyes closed or watch the accompanying video (a thoughtful photo montage). You may find that the juxtaposition of words, melodies and photographs serve to create a poignant emotional state. After listening, take a few moments to reflect on how the exercise made you feel and what it teaches you about the complex dialectics of emotional experience.

Love teaches us that reaching some of the most profound, elevating experiences in life means taking risks; as King (2001, pp. 53–54) puts it, flourishing does not mean being a 'well-defended fortress, invulnerable to the vicissitudes of life', but appreciating and even embracing the complex and ambivalent nature of existence. Given this thought, do we have any models of how we might cultivate this kind of appreciation? Here, I would like to proffer one potential resource, namely, the aesthetics of Eastern philosophy. Whilst there are a dizzying array of different traditions and schools of thought under this umbrella, these share in common a deep appreciation of dialectics, as indeed does Eastern culture as a whole, if one might be permitted such a sweeping generalisation[3] (Schimmack et al., 2002). This appreciation is encapsulated in one of the archetypal symbols of the East, the yin–yang motif associated with Taoism, as is discussed further. As Sameroff (2010, p. 9) points out, this is the ultimate dialectic symbol, capturing in stark, beautiful simplicity the way that opposites – light and dark, positive and negative – are in a dynamic 'mutually constituting relationship'. It is beyond the scope of this chapter to do justice, in any way, to the richness and profundity of Taoism and Eastern philosophy more generally. Nevertheless, I shall attempt to provide a sense of the dialectical nature of Taoism before exploring various aesthetic principles based on this philosophy which may provide a guide for how we might go about appreciating the dialectical nature of existence.

The scriptural basis for Taoism is the *Tao Te Ching*, attributed to a sage and mystic named Lao Tzu (trans. 1937), who may have lived in the sixth century BCE in China, although his existence is disputed (Oldstone-Moore, 2003). The *Tao Te Ching* is a mysterious hybrid: partly treatise of governance, partly a mystical elucidation of the 'Tao', which Oldstone-Moore describes as a '[n]ameless, formless, all pervasive power which brings all things into being and reverts them back into non-being in an eternal cycle' (p. 6). (That said, the *Tao Te Ching*

FIGURE 1.1 Yin and Yang

is emphatic that the Tao cannot be captured in words. As Verse 1 puts it, 'The Tao that can be expressed is not the true Tao'.) The Tao is seen as operating through the dynamic inter-action of yin (negative and passive) and yang (positive and active). Thus, the very essence of Taoism is the dialectical 'mutual dependence of opposites' (e.g., the idea that 'positive' only makes sense if juxtaposed with 'negative', and light only exists as a concept because there is also darkness). As expressed in Verse 2: 'When all in the world understand beauty to be beautiful, then ugliness exists. When all in the world understand goodness to be good, then evil exists'. The key teaching of Taoism is thus the importance recognising the dialectical nature of existence and, moreover, living in harmony with it; as Inada (1997, p. 118) explains it: 'The enlightened or illumined (ming) life knows nothing positive or negative as such but everything in terms of fluid naturalness'.

Although appreciating the full mysterious profundities of Taoism would take at least a lifetime to master, we can nevertheless grasp some measure of its wisdom by consid-ering an especially effective vehicle for communicating its ideas: *aesthetics*. We shall here focus on one particular branch of Taoist-influenced aesthetics, namely Zen art. (When Buddhism was transmitted into China in the fifth century CE, it mingled with the indig-enous Taoist traditions to create *Chan* Buddhism, which was then pronounced *Zen* on its subsequent migration to Japan.) In Zen, the practice and appreciation of art, from painting to poetry, is elevated into a spiritual experience: at its highest, its art is a vehicle for expressing the spiritual insights of Zen; contemplation of this can ideally engender deep appreciation of these insights (in a way that discursive analysis would struggle to convey), thus facilitating spiritual development (Inada, 1997). In varied ways, Zen art attempts to communicate the dialectical character of existence as well as associated notions such as the fragile, fleeting nature of beauty and indeed of life itself. A wonderful elucidation of Zen aesthetics is provided by Parkes (2011), who identifies key concepts, including: *mono no aware* (the pathos of life), *sabi* (rustic patina), *wabi* (austere beauty), and *yūgen* (profound grace). We shall end here by briefly considering these, trying to get a sense for how these principles might help us find appreciation and even beauty in the dialectical nature of existence.

Firstly, *mono no aware* encapsulates the pathos (evocation of compassion or sorrow) derived from an awareness of the fleeting, impermanent nature of life. This is captured in the opening lines of the epic traditional folktale 'The Tale of the Heike': 'The sound of the *Gion shōja* bells echoes the impermanence of all things. . . . The proud do not endure, they are like a dream on a spring night'. Crucially, it is this very impermanence that endows these fleeting phenomena with their beauty, as expressed by Yoshida Kenkō (1283–1350 CE): 'If man were never to fade away like the dews of Adashino . . . how things would lose their power to move us! The most precious thing in life is its uncertainty' (cited in Keene, 1967, p. 7). This concept illuminates the terrifying power of phenomena like love: it is its very fragility that makes it so potent and poignant. However, in Zen, this type of aesthetic sensibility is *encouraged* as a profound sensitivity, one that allows us to be 'touched or moved by the world . . . inextricably intertwined with a capacity to experience the sadness and pathos that emanates from the transitory nature of things' (Woolfolk, 2002, p. 23). From a Buddhist perspective, the act of clinging resolutely to phenomena that are intrinsically subject to change is a fundamental cause of suffering. Much of Buddhism is thus about cultivating a deep, profound acceptance of impermanence and allowing ourselves to appreciate the flux of life without seeking futilely to arrest or capture it in its flow. To return to love, appreciating the transiency of life only serves to *enhance* our feelings of love. Thus, allowing oneself to cultivate the pathos of this 'tragic sense of life', rather than seeking to deny or escape from these truths, may actually be a doorway to some of the most elevated and transcendent states of existence.

Interestingly, this aesthetic sense of the transitoriness of life is counterbalanced by the second term, *sabi*, which captures the strange beauty of aged or ancient phenomena, the rustic or rusty patina that lends these gravitas and significance. Whereas mono no aware reflects the fleeting nature of phenomena, sabi reminds us that in this process of changing, a certain desolate beauty is nonetheless retained. Sabi thus distils the notion of aging well in the sense of 'ripe with experience and insight', together with the evocative senses of 'tranquility, aloneness' and 'deep solitude' that accompany the passage of time (Hammitzsch, 1979, p. 46). The appeal of sabi is captured well by Tanizaki (2001/1933) in his classic exposition of Zen aesthetics, *In Praise of Shadows*. He describes preferring a 'pensive lustre to a shallow brilliance, a murky light that, whether in a stone or an artifact, bespeaks a sheen of antiquity. . . . We love things that bear the marks of grime, soot, and weather, and we love the colors and the sheen that call to mind the past that made them'. Our sorrow at the passage of time might be transmuted if we could see it through such eyes.

The evocative concepts of *mono no aware* and *sabi* are augmented by *wabi* – 'austere' or 'understated' beauty. Here, appreciation of the impermanence of existence is reflected in the idea that we do injustice to life if we only value that which appears perfect and complete. Rather, we should endeavour to see the grace in all seasons, as it were. As Kenkō asks, 'Are we to look at cherry blossoms only in full bloom, at the moon only when it is cloudless? . . . Gardens strewn with faded flowers are worthier of our admiration' (cited in Keene, 1967, p. 115). This means we do not abhor phenomena for being imperfect but rather value their unique gifts. This aesthetic emerges in the art of the tea ceremony, where flawed utensils are more prized than 'perfect' ones; reaction to these is then illustrative of a person's understanding of life. As the 17th-century Sen no Rikyū put it, 'There are those who dislike a piece when it is even slightly damaged; such an attitude shows a complete lack of comprehension' (cited in Hirota, 1995, p. 226). This profound notion may be relevant as a model for cultivating deep acceptance of life and for not embarking on the 'quest' for happiness which, as already suggested, may be somewhat self-defeating. As Hirota (1995, p. 275) puts it, '*Wabi* means that even in straitened circumstances no thought of hardship arises. Even amid insufficiency, one is moved by no feeling of want. Even when faced with failure, one does not brood over injustice. . . . If you complain that things have been ill-disposed – this is not *wabi*'.

Finally then, we turn to *yūgen*, translated by Parkes (2011) as profound grace and described as the most 'ineffable' of aesthetic concepts: in philosophical texts it means 'dark' or 'mysterious', alluding to the unfathomable depths of existence and to the fundamental inability of the mind to comprehend these depths. Kamo no Chōmei (1968/1212; cited in Dyrness & kärkkäinen, 2008, p. 65) characterises *yūgen* thus: 'It is like an autumn evening under a colorless expanse of silent sky. Somehow, as if for some reason that we should be able to recall, tears well uncontrollably'. With *yūgen*, it is as if one is penetrating to the heart of existence, accessing the kind of profound, transcendental state described by Maslow (1972) as a 'peak experience' and by Wong (2009) as 'chaironic' happiness. Deeply profound and moving, such moments go far beyond mere hedonic pleasure or even eudaimonic meaning but shake the very core of our being. We have surpassed all concepts, entering the realm of awe, in which we are rendered speechless, powerless and even terrified by the mysterious power and grace of the universe (Keltner & Haidt, 2003). And, as such, this is perhaps the place to end this chapter: in discussing the dialectics of emotion, the fundamental point concerns the value of transcending narrow human constructs and categories (such as light and dark, positive and negative) and learning to appreciate the complex, nuanced nature of existence. As such, although in tentatively dipping our toe into Zen aesthetics, here we are barely scratching the surface of a deep ocean of wisdom; it may be enough to begin to cultivate an appreciation of the strange, mysterious, dialectical beauty of life.

SUMMARY – THIS CHAPTER HAS . . .

- Explained the emergence of second wave PP
- Introduced the concept of dialectics, including the idea of thesis–antithesis–synthesis
- Explored how seemingly positive qualities may be detrimental to wellbeing
- Examined the way ostensibly negative qualities can promote flourishing
- Shown how the dark side of life is inextricable entwined with its light side
- Discussed Taoism and Buddhist aesthetic principles
- Used these principles to cultivate appreciation for the ambivalent nature of the good life

RESOURCES AND SUGGESTIONS . . .

- For a clear explanation of the concept of dialectics, please visit www.csmt.uchicago.edu/glossary2004/dialectic.htm.
- For more on Buddhist aesthetics, please visit www.plato.stanford.edu/entries/japanese-aesthetics/.

NOTES

1   From here on, for aesthetic reasons, the terms positive and negative will not be enclosed in quotation marks. However, given that this whole chapter is problematizing and bringing into question the notions of positive and negative, please read all instances of these as if surrounded by appropriate scare quotes!

2   Emotions can be defined comprehensively as 'episodes of coordinated changes in several components (including at least neurophysiological activation, motor expression, and subjective feeling but possibly also action tendencies and cognitive processes) in response to external or internal events of major significance to the organism' (Scherer, 2000, pp. 138–139). However, I am also using the term 'emotions' generously here as a synecdoche to cover all subjective experience, including related concepts such as affect and feelings as well as cognitive constructs like self-esteem. It will be clear in the context of the text whether I am using the term in the narrow sense (as defined here) or the broad synecdoche sense.

3   That said, at the risk of being self-contradictory, please see Chapter 6 for consideration of why such generalisations about the East are problematic.

BIBLIOGRAPHY

Aarts, H., Paulussen, T., & Schaalma, H. (1997). Physical exercise habit: On the conceptualization and formation of habitual health behaviours. *Health Education Research, 12*(3), 363–374.

Ahmed, S. (2007). The happiness turn. *New Formations, 63*, 7–14.

Ahmed, S. (2010). *The promise of happiness*. New York: Duke University Press.

Aristotle. (2000/350 BCE). *Nicomachean Ethics* (R. Crisp, Ed.). Cambridge, UK: Cambridge University Press.

American Psychiatric Association. (2013). *Diagnostic and statistical manual of mental disorders* (5th ed.). Washington, DC: Author.

Batson, C. D., Klein, T. R., Highberger, L., & Shaw, L. L. (1995). Immorality from empathy-induced altruism: When compassion and justice conflict. *Journal of Personality and Social Psychology, 68*(6), 1042–1054.

Bauman, Z. (2013). *Liquid love: On the frailty of human bonds*. New York: John Wiley & Sons.

Baumeister, R. F., Smart, L., & Boden, J. M. (1996). Relation of threatened egotism to violence and aggression: The dark side of high self-esteem. *Psychological Review, 103*(1), 5–33.

Beck, A. T. (1999). *Prisoners of hate: The cognitive basis of anger, hostility, and violence*. New York: Harper Collins.

Bhikkhu, T. (2013, 30 November). *Sallatha Sutta: The arrow*. Access to Insight (SN 36.6).

Carver, C. S., & Scheier, M. F. (1990). Origins and functions of positive and negative affect: A control-process view. *Psychological Review, 97*(1), 19–35.

Chōmei, K. n. (1968/1212). An account of my hut (N. Soseki, Trans.). In D. Keene (Ed.), *Anthology of Japanese literature*. New York: Grove Press.

Crocker, J., & Park, L. E. (2004). The costly pursuit of self-esteem. *Psychological Bulletin, 130*(3), 392–414.

DasGupta, S. (2008). Narrative humility. *The Lancet, 371*(9617), 980–981.

Diener, E., Suh, E. M., Lucas, R. E., & Smith, H. L. (1999). Subjective well-being: Three decades of progress. *Psychological Bulletin, 125*(2), 276–302.

Dostoevsky, F. (1990/1880). *The brothers Karamzov* (R. Pevear & L. Volokhonsky, Trans.). San Francisco, CA: North Point Press.

Dyrness, W. A., & kärkkäinen, V.-M. (2008). *Global dictionary of theology*. Nottingham, UK: IVP Academic.

Ehrenreich, B. (2009). *Bright-sided: How positive thinking is undermining America*. New York: Metropolitan Books.

Friedman, H. S., Tucker, J. S., Tomlinson-Keasey, C., Schwartz, J. E., Wingard, D. L., & Criqui, M. H. (1993). Does childhood personality predict longevity? *Journal of Personality and Social Psychology, 65*, 176–185.

Garrett, H. J., & Schmidt, S. (2012). Repeating until we can remember: Difficult (public) knowledge in South Africa. *Journal of Curriculum Theorizing, 28*(1), 1–8.

Gerrard, M., Gibbons, F. X., Reis-Bergan, M., & Russell, D. W. (2000). Self-esteem, self-serving cognitions, and health risk behavior. *Journal of Personality, 68*(6), 1177–1201.

Gibran, K. (1996/1927). *The prophet*. Hertfordshire: Wordsworth.

Giltay, E. J., Geleijnse, J. M., Zitman, F. G., Hoekstra, T., & Schouten, E. G. (2004). Dispositional optimism and all-cause and cardiovascular mortality in a prospective cohort of elderly Dutch men and women. *Archives of General Psychiatry, 61*(11), 1126–1135.

Hadfield, C. (2013). *An astronaut's guide to life on Earth*. London: Macmillan.

Haidt, J. (2003). The moral emotions. In R. J. Davidson, K. R. Scherer & H. H. Goldsmith (Eds.), *Handbook of affective sciences* (pp. 852–870). Oxford, UK: Oxford University Press.

Hammitzsch, H. (1979). *Zen in the art of the tea ceremony* (P. Lemesurier, Trans.). New York: Arkana.

Harris, S. (2011). *The moral landscape: How science can determine human values*. New York: Simon and Schuster.

Hegel, G. W. F. (1969/1812). *Science of logic* (A. V. Miller, Trans.). London: George Allen & Unwin.

Held, B. S. (2002). The tyranny of the positive attitude in America: Observation and speculation. *Journal of Clinical Psychology, 58*(9), 965–991.

Held, B. S. (2004). The negative side of positive psychology. *Journal of Humanistic Psychology, 44*(1), 9–46.

Hirota, D. (Ed.). (1995). *Wind in the pines: Classic writings of the way of tea as a Buddhist path*. Fremont, CA: Asian Humanities Press.

Horowitz, A. V., & Wakefield, J. C. (2007). *The loss of sadness*. Oxford, UK: Oxford University Press.

Inada, K. K. (1997). A theory of oriental aesthetics: A prolegomenon. *Philosophy East and West, 47*(2), 117–131.

Iyengar, S. S., & Lepper, M. R. (1999). Rethinking the value of choice: A cultural perspective on intrinsic motivation. *Journal of Personality and Social Psychology, 76*(3), 349–366.

Jost, J. T. (1995). Negative illusions: Conceptual clarification and psychological evidence concerning false consciousness. *Political Psychology, 16*(2), 397–424.

Kabat-Zinn, J. (2003). Mindfulness-based interventions in context: Past, present, and future. *Clinical Psychology: Science and Practice, 10*(2), 144–156. doi: 10.1093/clipsy.bpg016

Keene, D. (1967). *Essays in idleness: The Tsurezuregusa of Kenkō*. New York: Columbia University Press.

Keltner, D., & Haidt, J. (2003). Approaching awe, a moral, spiritual, and aesthetic emotion. *Cognition & Emotion, 17*(2), 297–314.

Kierkegaard, S. (1957/1834). *The concept of dread* (W. Lowrie, Trans., 2nd ed.). Princeton, NJ: Princeton University Press.

King, L. A. (2001). The hard road to the good life: The happy, mature person. *Journal of Humanistic Psychology, 41*(1), 51–72.

King, M. L. (2007). The papers of Martin Luther King. Volume VI: Advocate of the social gospel, September 1948–March 1963. Berkeley: University of California Press.

Lacan, J. (2006). *Ecrits* (B. Fink, Trans.). New York: W.W. Norton.

Lama, H. H. t. D. (1997). *The heart of compassion*. Twin Lakes, WI: Lotus Press.

Lamotte, É. (1981). The Gārava-Sutta of the Samyutta-nikāya and its Mahāyānist developments. *Journal of the Pali Text Society, 9*, 127–144.

Lazarus, R. S. (2003). Does the positive psychology movement have legs? *Psychological Inquiry, 14*(2), 93–109.

Lee, J. A. (1973). *The colors of love: An exploration of the ways of loving*. Don Mills, Ontario: New Press.

Levinas, E. (1987). *Time and the Other and other essays* (R. A. Cohen, Trans.). Pittsburgh: Duquesne University Press.

Lewis, C. S. (1971). *The four loves*. New York: Houghton Mifflin Harcourt.

Linley, P. A., & Joseph, S. (2004). Applied positive psychology: A new perspective for professional practice. In P. A. Linley & S. Joseph (Eds.), *Positive psychology in practice* (pp. 3–12). Hoboken, NJ: John Wiley and Sons.

Lykken, D., & Tellegen, A. (1996). Happiness is a stochastic phenomenon. *Psychological Science, 7*(3), 186–189.

Marx, K. (1975/1844). A contribution to the critique of Hegel's philosophy of right: Introduction (R. Livingstone & G. Benton, Trans.). In L. Colletti (Ed.), *Karl Marx: Early writings* (pp. 243–257). London: Penguin.

Maslow, A. H. (1972). *The farther reaches of human nNature*. London: Maurice Bassett.

Matthews, E. (2000). Autonomy and the psychiatric patient. *Journal of Applied Philosophy, 17*(1), 59–70.

Mauss, I. B., Tamir, M., Anderson, C. L., & Savino, N. S. (2011). Can seeking happiness make people unhappy? Paradoxical effects of valuing happiness. *Emotion-APA, 11*(4), 807–815. doi: 10.1037/a0022010

McMahon, D. M. (2006). *Happiness: A history*. New York: Atlantic Monthly Press.

McNulty, J. K., & Fincham, F. D. (2011). Beyond positive psychology? Toward a contextual view of psychological processes and well-being. *American Psychologist, 67*(2), 101–110.

Merriam-Webster. (2014). Dialectic. Retrieved from http://www.merriam-webster.com/dictionary/dialectic

Mill, J. S. (1863). *Utilitarianism, liberty and representative government*. London: Dent & Sons.

Mill, J. S. (1960/1873). *Autobiography*. New York: Columbia University Press.

Mills, J. (2000). Dialectical psychoanalysis: Toward process psychology. *Psychoanalysis & Contemporary Thought, 23*(3), 20–54.

Norem, J. K. (2001). *The positive power of negative thinking*. New York: Basic Books.

Oldstone-Moore, J. (2003). *Taoism: Origins, beliefs, practices, holy texts, sacred places*. Oxford, UK: Oxford University Press.

Parkes, G. (2011, October 10). Japanese aesthetics. *Stanford Encyclopedia of Philosophy*. Retrieved from http://plato.stanford.edu/entries/japanese-aesthetics/

Peterson, C. (2000). The future of optimism. *American Psychologist, 55*(1), 44–55.

Post, S. G. (2005). Altruism, happiness, and health: It's good to be good. *International Journal of Behavioral Medicine, 12*(2), 66–77.

Prilleltensky, I. (2008). The role of power in wellness, oppression, and liberation: The promise of psychopolitical validity. *Journal of Community Psychology, 36*(2), 116–136.

Reed, G. L., & Enright, R. D. (2006). The effects of forgiveness therapy on depression, anxiety, and posttraumatic stress for women after spousal emotional abuse. *Journal of Consulting and Clinical Psychology, 74*(5), 920.

Resnick, S., Warmoth, A., & Serlin, I. A. (2001). The humanistic psychology and positive psychology connection: Implications for psychotherapy. *Journal of Humanistic Psychology, 41*(1), 73–101.

Rowatt, W. C., Ottenbreit, A., Nesselroade Jr, K. P., & Cunningham, P. A. (2002). On being holier-than-thou or humbler-than-thee: A social-psychological perspective on religiousness and humility. *Journal for the Scientific Study of Religion, 41*(2), 227–237.

Rowatt, W. C., Powers, C., Targhetta, V., Comer, J., Kennedy, S., & Labouff, J. (2006). Development and initial validation of an implicit measure of humility relative to arrogance. *The Journal of Positive Psychology, 1*(4), 198–211.

Rumi, J. a.-D. M. (1995). *The essential Rumi* (C. Barks, Trans.). San Fransisco: Harper.

Ryan, R. M., & Deci, E. L. (2000). Self-determination theory and the facilitation of intrinsic motivation, social development, and well-being. *American Psychologist, 55*(1), 68–78.

Ryff, C. D. (1989). Happiness is everything, or is it? Explorations on the meaning of psychological well-being. *Journal of Personality and Social Psychology, 57*(6), 1069–1081.

Ryff, C. D., & Singer, B. (2003). Ironies of the human condition. Well-being and health on the way to mortality. In L. G. Aspinwall & U. M. Staudinger (Eds.), *A Psychology of Human Strengths* (pp. 271–287). Washington, DC: American Psychological Association.

Sameroff, A. (2010). A unified theory of development: A dialectic integration of nature and nurture. *Child Development, 81*(1), 6–22.

Sartre, J.-P. (1952). *Existentialism and humanism* (P. Mairet, Trans.). Paris: Methuen.

Scherer, K. R. (2000). Psychological models of emotion. In J. C. Borod (Ed.), *The neuropsychology of emotion* (pp. 137–162). Oxford: Oxford University Press.

Schimmack, U., Oishi, S., & Diener, E. (2002). Cultural influences on the relation between pleasant emotions and unpleasant emotions: Asian dialectic philosophies or individualism-collectivism? *Cognition & Emotion, 16*(6), 705–719.

Schwartz, B. (2000). Self-determination: The tyranny of freedom. *American Psychologist, 55*(1), 79–88.

Seligman, M. E. P. (1990). *Learned optimism*. New York: Pocket Books.

Siegel, A. (2009). Justice Stevens and the Seattle schools case: A case study on the role of righteous anger in constitutional discourse. *UC Davis Law Review, 43*, 927–937.

Spitzberg, B. H., & Cupach, W. R. (1998). *The dark side of close relationships*. London: Routledge.

Szasz, T. S. (1960). The myth of mental illness. *American Psychologist, 15*(2), 113–118.

Tangey, J. P. (Ed.). (2005). *Humility*. New York: Oxford University Press.

Tanizaki, J. (2001/1933). *In praise of shadows*. New York: Random House.

Tavris, C. (1989). *Anger: The misunderstood emotion*. New York: Touchstone.

Tedeschi, R. G., & Calhoun, L. G. (2004). Posttraumatic growth: Conceptual foundations and empirical evidence. *Psychological Inquiry, 15*(1), 1–18.

Thieleman, K., & Cacciatore, J. (2014). When a child dies: A critical analysis of grief-related controversies in DSM-5. *Research on Social Work Practice, 24*(1), 114–122.

Thurman, R. (2008). *Why the Dalai Lama matters: His act of truth as the solution for China, Tibet, and the world*. New York: Simon and Schuster.

Trzesniewski, K. H., Donnellan, M. B., Moffitt, T. E., Robins, R. W., Poulton, R., & Caspi, A. (2006). Low self-esteem during adolescence predicts poor health, criminal behavior, and limited economic prospects during adulthood. *Developmental Psychology, 42*(2), 381–390.

Lao-Tzu. (1937). *Tao Te Ching* (C. u. Ta-Kao, Trans.). London: George Allen & Unwin.

Voltaire, F. (1759). *Candide, ou L'Optimisme*. Genève: Cramer.

Weinstein, N. D., Marcus, S. E., & Moser, R. P. (2005). Smokers' unrealistic optimism about their risk. *Tobacco Control, 14*(1), 55–59.

Wong, P. (2009). Positive existential psychology. In *Encyclopedia of Positive Psychology* (pp. 345–351). Oxford, UK: Blackwell.

Wong, P. T. P. (2011). Positive psychology 2.0: Towards a balanced interactive model of the good life. *Canadian Psychology/Psychologie Canadienne, 52*(2), 69–81.

Woolfolk, R. L. (2002). The power of negative thinking: Truth, melancholia, and the tragic sense of life. *Journal of Theoretical and Philosophical Psychology, 22*(1), 19–27.

Worthington, E. L. (2007). *Humility: The quiet virtue*. New York: Templeton Foundation Press.

Wright, D. S. (2008). Introduction: Rethinking ritual practice in Zen Buddhism. In S. Heine & D. S. Wright (Eds.), *Zen Ritual: Studies of Zen Buddhist theory in practice* (pp. 3–20). Oxford, UK: Oxford University Press.

2

Positive development – our journey of growth

'We rarely set out to age well. Positive ageing is what happens when we are doing other things. The challenge and question for us is to understand what those things might be, and to choose our personal expression of them'.

Lesley Lyle

Learning objectives – at the end of the chapter you will be able to do the following:
- Summarise four primary theories of lifespan development
- See periods of transition as representing a tension between potentially positive and negative outcomes
- Identify ways in which PP perspectives might be used to support lifespan development periods of transition

List of topics:
- Erik Erikson's life cycle theory
- Daniel Levinson's eras of development
- George Vaillant's aging well
- Dan McAdams' life stories
- The potential application of these theories to PP

The chapter will review four theories of developmental psychology and then relate specific ideas or aspects to PP. After this, reflective questions will be provided to support individual use or exploration. The 'dark side' in this chapter refers to challenging experiences, thoughts, emotions and behaviours which trigger discomfort in us as our lives develop and change over time. Such discomfort is frequently avoided as it carries an engagement with fear, pain, distress, uncertainty or confusion in the face of what is happening or changing at the time. However, engaging with challenge and discomfort has great potential for growth, healing, insight and transformation in our journey of development. In other words, the chapter describes human development through the lens of the 'dark side' while emphasising the potential positive impact of this process. The four developmental theories described in this chapter include the following:

- Erik Erikson's life cycle theory
  - This provides us with an understanding of the stages of life.
  - The theory also helps us identify positive and negative polarities that life may involve and understand a 'strength' that may emerge from it.
- Daniel Levinson's 'seasons' of a man's and woman's life
  - The 'seasons' provide further articulation of the phases of life that alternate between stability and transition and change.
  - They also illustrate for us the decisions we make that constitute our 'life structure' and how these may be revisited over time.
- George Vaillant's descriptions of social maturation and the development of mature defense mechanisms that occur as we age.
  - This work illustrates for us many positive things we might do over time to influence the quality of our aging.
  - This work also illustrates for us four adaptive coping or defense mechanisms that are the means by which we may deal with the often difficult experiences of aging. Perhaps ironically, they appear to be one source of positive ageing.
- Dan McAdams' theories and research regarding how our identity is based on stories we construct about ourselves
  - Through these theories we can see characteristics of the stories we may create to explain our lives, which in turn give us the opportunity to explore which PP interventions might contribute to change.

These theories are intended to offer or create a mosaic of understanding or different perspectives of human development. They might be seen or used individually by readers or in conjunction with each other. Erikson, Levinson, Vaillant and McAdams each assume that an individual progresses through a series of stages or tasks during life in which the structure and experience of identity may change according to the issues being experienced and addressed at the time. However they each infer a different developmental and growth experience. Additionally, they propose that identity and personality are shaped, developed and influenced by interactions with society over time. They look at the psychosocial experience of the lifespan. Many of these developmental experiences and transitions can feel uncertain or unknown to us and press us to change in ways that may feel uncomfortable and uncertain. This reflects the 'dark side' feelings that are the basis of this book. Understanding these four theories will allow you to investigate you own personal developmental process of change and growth through the years.

ERIK ERIKSON – THE LIFE CYCLE THEORY

Erikson's (1958/1980) theory of the life cycle is arguably the most comprehensive of the lifespan theories covering childhood through old age. His theory was the first major developmental perspective offered in modern times. Some may consider this dated, yet more recent work, for example, the Grant Study of Adult Development (Vaillant, 1977, 2002), has appeared to prove this structure empirically and finds it adds to our understanding of complex experience over time.

Erikson's theory originated through his psychoanalytic work, his work with healthy adolescents and with the Sioux and Yurok American Indian tribes. It is a theory that is meant to encompass both sexes and to be cross-cultural. Possible criticisms of this theory will be examined later in this section.

Erikson (1988) saw the life cycle as containing eight discrete and sequential stages through which eight basic strengths may emerge 'each the outgrowth of a time-specific developmental confrontation' (p. 74). Each stage is characterised as a 'crisis' by Erikson that comes from the conflict of two opposing forces or trends at that particular time of life. This tension, or pressure of 'opposing forces' may feel like the 'dark side' pressing in on us. A positive outcome to the crisis led, in Erikson's view, to the development of a virtue or strength. This immediately offers an unexpected and unusual link to more recent theories of human strength in PP and also reflects Wong's (2011) proposal that our discipline must involve a dialogue between positive and negative experiences. The resolution of the tension of the opposites is not either–or but a balance between the two.

Erikson's use of the word 'crisis' did not imply a possible disaster but a turning point, an opportunity and that the resolution of the conflict of the two opposing forces could direct individual development in positive or negative directions. The nature of the resolution achieved, or the failure to confront its needs, will affect each subsequent life stage, which potentially illustrates to us how the 'dark side' experiences may guide and develop our lives (Perlmutter & Hall, 1992). Erikson conceived of growth and development as occurring through an integration of the conflicting forces at each stage and not succumbing to alienation (Roazen, 1976). He believed that a person would interpret and experience this pattern through his or her own particular traits and character, a style unique to each. A key practical part of this theory is that the individual faces holding the tension between the two opposing forces from that point on through life, with the goal being that the positive tendency or force, on balance, is primary. This illustrates to us how difficult or 'dark side' experiences may bring about a change in our insight and understanding of the life that follows. Joan Erikson made clear that a failure to achieve balance, or the favouring of the negative tendency, could be redressed later in life (Erikson, 1988).

To summarise, here are the stages (Erikson, 1980; Berk, 1998; Bee, 1998; McAdams, 1985):

Stage 1: basic trust versus mistrust with an emerging strength of 'hope'

This occurs in an approximate age range from birth to approximately 12 to 18 months. The stage is focused on the food and support needs of the baby and the experience that they can be consistently met. The baby will seek the 'world' to both respond and care. The balance includes both the quality and quantity of care. The caregiver's own emotional state and experiences will obviously influence what is provided. If positive care is received, on balance, Erikson proposes that 'basic trust' emerges.

Stage 2: autonomy versus shame and doubt with an emerging strength of 'will'

This occurs in an approximate age range from 12 to 18 months to 3 years. This stage occurs as the child enters a period of early muscle use and mobility. There is a capacity to explore the environment and exercise some personal choice. The stage is focused on whether the caregiver will support the development and exploration or whether there is a constraint or limitation that the child may experience as shame or lack of choice. The positive outcome is where a child is supported in his or her early stages of choice and independent actions. If successful, this stage will support the early development of 'will'.

Stage 3: initiative versus guilt with an emerging strength of 'purpose'

This occurs between approximately 3 and 5 years of age. The child is experiencing increasing muscle and physical capability and the use of language. There is an increasing capacity to explore physically and via imagination. This age range may involve early time at school, which in turn involves socialisation and restrictions. 'Initiative' occurs when children can experience choice or influence and a sense of purpose or direction. 'Guilt' may emerge if they acquire a sense of their efforts being wrong or 'bad'.

Stage 4: industry versus inferiority with an emerging strength of 'competence'

This occurs between approximately 6 and 12 years of age. This stage takes place during early stages of schooling and where influence happens outside and inside the home and reflects surrounding social and cultural norms. The child is experiencing learning and a growth of ability in knowledge and skills valued or seen as needed in surrounding society. A sense of 'industry' emerges with positive experiences and 'inferiority' with failures in this area.

Stage 5: identity versus identity confusion with the emerging strength of 'fidelity'

This stage occurs during adolescence, approximately 12 to 18 years of age. The young person knows he or she is in a transition between a 'childhood' self and a self that is moving towards the adult world. This may involve questioning or seeking experiences that influence his or her present world and beliefs or who he or she may become in their future. McAdams (1985) described this as involving the forming of a story of who we have been, who we are and who we may be becoming. This implies a decision of whom or what we are within our social context. If this can involve a commitment, a movement towards a goal that may be personal, occupational, ideological and more, this will be an 'identity' which we now know may be reshaped and revisited over the year. A failure or inability to commit may involve compromises, such as taking on the norms of others rather than our own.

Stage 6: intimacy versus isolation with the emerging strength of 'love'

Authors quote different age ranges for this stage, which could be approximately 19 to 20 to 40 years old. This is initially the time of further education, moving away from the family home, early work choices and committing to a partner. This involves further steps of choice and commitment that may be tentative at first or revised over this phase. This stage is about relationship and intimacy; an experience that will be explored is the willingness, or otherwise, to fuse or join with another without also fearing the loss of self. Vaillant (2002) advocated that this phase was not detailed enough in its expression and includes the tasks of finding and growing work-related interests. This phase, given its length, is about making and adjusting major life decisions over this time period.

Stage 7: generativity versus stagnation with the emerging strength of 'care'

The approximate age range for this stage would be 40 to 65 years old. The stage involves an attention and commitment given to care and support for a new generation, more widely than that in the family home. Personal goals and objectives may involve things that will outlive us and into the next generation. With this attention, there is an implied increase of awareness of our own mortality and in turn what we may wish to contribute to society now and to leave behind for others. The emerging strength of 'care' might be expressed materially, in work left behind, or relationally. The choice emerges from the individual's own sense of what 'care' means.

Stage 8: ego integrity versus despair with the emerging strength of 'wisdom'

The age range for this stage is 65 years and upwards. This stage involves an individual coming to a realisation and sense of his or her life as it is. It may be a time in which the shape of an individual life, its wholeness and the way in which events came together over time can be evident to an individual. A positive outcome involves a sense of responsibility for the life that exists and has been lived. The negative outcome, despair, may involve the fear of death, the sense of time being limited or lost and the wish for another chance to experience or change aspects of life.

It is important to consider the dynamics of these stages together. Erikson saw each stage as emerging from and dependent on its predecessor. Each stage is seen as 'grounded' in all the ones preceding it, and the achievement of the emerging strength is expected to give new connotations to all the ones that had been experienced to date (Erikson, 1982; Genter & Stevens, 1983). For example, the capacity for us to learn some skills when 'playing' (Stage 3) may in turn give us the confidence to learn further skills during school days (Stage 4). However, our ability to learn may be revisited and reshaped repeatedly over time. This suggests a process that is evident in Vaillant's findings: we continue to process and re-understand our experiences over time. The timing of each stage is, according to Erikson, based on the earliest practical time it could be developmentally experienced and the latest moment it would need to give way or yield to the next crisis and strength (Erikson, 1982).

Joan Erikson (1997) furthered the work of her husband and herself, extending the life cycle to include a ninth and unnamed stage prompted by increasing life spans and longevity. The Eriksons had developed these theories from clinical and research work and then elaborated their theory though their experience of living through each particular stage of the life cycle. Acknowledging the extension to longevity experienced in both their lives (writing at the age of 97), Joan Erikson described a ninth stage (which appears to have been ignored in modern psychology textbooks) as the experience of living a simple, sometimes limited life in the physical frailty of advanced years. This increased age brings with it 'new demands, re-evaluation, and daily difficulties' (p. 105). It involves living with uncertainties as 'it is impossible to know what emergencies and losses of physical ability are imminent' (p. 105–106). In contrast to the other eight stages, the ninth has the negative possibilities placed first. She describes a process of another review of each of the prior stages and a re-evaluating and experiencing their qualities through the physical frailties and limitations of advanced age.

Erikson's theories are hard to evaluate and have been criticised. The complexity and time encompassed by Erikson's theory make it very hard to test. For example, the early non-verbal stages of life are probably beyond verification or refutation (Roazen, 1976). Neither the terms used nor the concepts employed are precisely defined by Erikson, a situation that may lead to ambiguity in using the framework in a study such as this (Bee, 1998; Perlmutter & Hall, 1992; Roazen, 1976).

Erikson put forward his theory as cross-cultural and universal; yet others (e.g., Perlmutter & Hall, 1992; Genter & Stevens, 1983) acknowledge that its focus on individualism make it oriented to Western culture, and the generality of the research which originated these theories makes such claims at best still unproven. This said, the work of the Grant Study of Adult Development and George Vaillant (2012), cited next, argued that these stages are seen in empirically collected data.

In considering the applicability of these theories to women, there is some questioning, for example, whether the stage of intimacy (the sixth stage) would precede the stage of identity (e.g., Genter & Stevens 1985). Erikson discussed these questions in later life (e.g., Erikson & Erikson, 1981). His perspective remained that these theories were 'only a tool to think with, and cannot be a prescription to abide by' (Erikson 1980, p. 243) – therefore, not an absolute definition but a tool through which to explore.

APPLICATION OF ERIKSON'S WORK TO POSITIVE PSYCHOLOGY AND THE 'DARK SIDE'

Erikson's theories illustrate that life is comprised of polarities in our experience:

- Basic trust versus basic mistrust (with a resulting virtue/strength of hope)
- Autonomy versus shame (with a resulting virtue/strength of will)
- Initiative versus guilt (with a resulting virtue/strength of purpose)
- Industry versus inferiority (with a resulting virtue/strength of competence)
- Identity versus identity confusion (with a resulting virtue/strength of fidelity)
- Intimacy versus isolation (with a resulting virtue/strength of love)
- Generativity versus stagnation (with a resulting virtue/strength of care)
- Integrity versus despair (with a resulting virtue/strength of wisdom)

Our lives are not one side of these polarities and experiences or the other. Life is a balance of both, one we must seek to actively influence. Erikson illustrated that a particular strength may emerge from the tensions and the 'dark side'. PP interventions are a potential resource for this. The dialogue between polarities, between the positive and negative, the 'dark side' we must face, was proposed by Wong (2011) as part of the needed development of PP.

The proposed outcomes of the stages, virtues and strengths add to the current positive psychology theorising on this subject. It suggests not only a personal strengths profile but a generic or developmental profile to be considered and explored further. This suggests that these virtues and strengths will be seen alongside others we possess, interpreted in the context of the traits, characteristics and lives of individuals.

REFLECTION

In your life to date, do you see your development as involving these stages?

Do you recognise the description of 'polarity'?

Do you see the outcome of the stage as one of your strengths or virtues?

What does the inclusion of these developmental strengths or virtues have on your overall perception of your strengths profile?

DANIEL LEVINSON – 'THE SEASONS OF A MAN'S AND A WOMAN'S LIFE'

Levinson's works were different to those of Erikson's in that they were empirically (rather than clinically) derived. Levinson's theories were generalisations formed from in-depth biographical interviews with 40 men and 45 women and provide detailed descriptions of development from late adolescence through to middle age – with theoretical perspectives added for the years following this period. Levinson's studies were conducted over two periods of approximately 13 to 14 years – the men's study between 1965 and 1978 and the women's study between 1979 and 1994. In both cases interviews were conducted in the early part of the study. The remaining time was devoted to analysis and writing. Levinson and Levinson (1996) accepted these were not representative or statistical samples. Yet they were detailed studies which he argued contributed to an overall understanding of adult development, a view which appears to be borne out by the extent to which his studies are referred to in other literature.

The men represented four occupational groups and were 35 to 45 years old at the time of the interviews in 1968. The women came from three groups but were presented as two groups for the purposes of the study – traditional homemakers and career women. The women were 30 to 45 years old at the time of interview. Further data was gathered from analysing 14 biographies, plus fiction, drama and poetry in the men's study and questionnaires to other groups in the women's study.

The following descriptions of adult development represent material from the men's and women's studies. Levinson updated some of his earlier findings (e.g., descriptions for developmental periods) on the basis of experience gained in the women's study. Levinson and Levinson (1996) presented three primary findings:

- *Eras* which form the underlying structure of the human life course
- *Developmental periods* which are the structure of each era
- *The individual 'life structure'* within these eras and periods, based on the choices and priorities of the person

(The eras and developmental periods are portrayed in the table overleaf.)

The finding of eras within the human life was described by Levinson as an underlying order within the life through which we would all pass. Reflecting the names of Levinson and Levinson's (1996) books, they are 'seasons'. This order, flow or sequence does, however, permit expression and variations that reflect what must be countless combinations of gender, race, culture and social context. Levinson and his colleagues saw the eras as lasting approximately 25 years. The eras overlap, so as one ends the next is starting – and this ending and beginning are embraced in a transitionary period (Levinson, Darrow, Klein, Levinson, & McKee, 1978). The eras are the broad structure of the life cycle, and within them are contained developmental periods. Each era was seen as having its own biological, psychological and social character that adds to the overall development in the life cycle (Levinson & Levinson, 1996). The sequence was found to be the same for men and women.

Each era had within it developmental periods – an alternating pattern of periods of building and maintaining a life structure and periods of transition in which aspects of a life structure are terminated and individuals move towards a new one. Developmental tasks and goals applying to each age period were pursued within the life structure chosen and constructed – with outcomes questioned and new choices made during the periods of transition (Perlmutter & Hall, 1992).

Levinson and Levinson (1996) saw a further primary contribution of this work as providing a language and detail to the nature and structure of this experience and age in adulthood. Even at that relatively recent time of writing (1996), he argued that adulthood is still the least understood period of life development in contrast with childhood and old age. Table 2.1 portraying the eras of the life cycle and the development periods is portrayed overleaf.

Levinson found that the eras and developmental periods each began at an average age (shown in Table 2.1), with a range of variation two years above and below this average. The era of childhood, or 'pre-adulthood', was not covered as part of these studies.

The concept of the 'life structure' was also central to Levinson's findings, and he is credited with being the first person to propose it. He defined the life structure as the small number of key choices that form of our lives over time (Levinson & Levinson, 1996; Levinson et al., 1978). He saw a person's life as having many components (e.g., occupation, relationships, marriage and family, relationship to self and roles in social contexts). The choices and decisions associated with these components and the balance between them change through time, reflecting the importance accorded to them by the individual. These components and the decisions about them formed the 'fabric of one's life' and the relationships between the self and the surrounding world (Levinson et al., 1978, p. 42). This concept mirrors or reflects ideas on 'meaning' subsequently described in Wong (2012) portraying ways in which we give priorities to core aspects of our lives. Levinson proposed that those parts of our lives accorded the greatest priority are also the central components that will influence the unfolding of our lives (Levinson et al., 1978). When one or more components of the life structure are given priority, Levinson argued, by implication, other aspects of life would not receive so much attention and

TABLE 2.1 The eras of the life cycle and the developmental periods within them

Era	Ages	Phase	Age
Early Adulthood	Approx. 17–45	Early adult transition	17–22
		Entry life structure for early adulthood	Approx. 22–28
		Age 30 transition	Approx. 28–33
		Culminating life structure for early adulthood	
Middle Adulthood	Approx. 40–60	Midlife transition	Approx. 40–45
		Entry life structure for middle adulthood	Approx. 45–50
		Age 50 transition	Approx. 50–55
		Culminating life structure for middle adulthood	Approx. 55–60
Late adulthood transition and life eras were not researched by Levinson.			

may eventually be perceived as unfulfilled. Additionally, the choices made in a life structure by an individual would inevitably have flaws, and dissatisfaction would be felt with them. The choices made, experiences of their effects and personal wishes for change or difference form the focus for any alteration to the life structure. The concept of the life structure and the changes in personal emphasis or choice found within it will be examined biographically through time in this research project.

The life structure, he proposed, would evolve and change through the orderly sequence of eras and developmental periods in the adult years. What follows is an overview of the eras and developmental periods described in Levinson and Levinson (1996) and Levinson et al. (1978).

Era: early adulthood, age range approximately 17 To 45

This era has the potential to display the greatest energy of our lives. Our physical peak will occur in the 20s and 30s. In this time we will probably explore society's expectations of us to create a relationship, build a family, choose work or a career and develop our skills.

Developmental period: early adult transition, age range approximately 17 to 22

This is a period of time where 'childhood' ends and a young person transitions into early adulthood. This is likely to be a time of uncertainty, when the sense of ourselves entering the adult world may be unclear. Yet Levinson introduced one of his most important concepts here, that of the 'dream', this period being the early stage of its formation, possibly with the support of a mentor.

Developmental period: the entry life structure for early adulthood, age range approximately 22 to 28

Levinson described this period with a comforting humanity and understanding of the experience of a young person. Provisional choices are being made about the structure of adult life. These may include an occupation, a partnership, a place to live that may or may not be near the family of origin and a personal lifestyle. The provisional choices may be re-evaluated in this time period and adjusted. If the young person is fortunate, his or her sense of personal dream may get clearer and stronger, possibly via the presence and help of a mentor.

Developmental period: age 30 transition, age range approximately 28 to 33

One of the most moving and powerful outcomes of Levinson's research, particularly in the context of this book, was that our lives have periods of stability and transition when change occurs. A transition may be uncertain, and through this, the feelings of the qualities of the 'dark side' are present. This transition is a period when we may re-evaluate the choices made that form the life structure and, through this, change ones that may not be working, or develop new possibilities.

Developmental period: the culminating life structure for early adulthood, age range approximately 33 to 40

In this period an individual may be consolidating and developing the choices that comprise the life structure. This may have qualities expected or mirrored by society, such as the development of occupational skill and career and home and family.

Developmental period: the midlife transition, age range approximately 40 to 45

Levinson described this as the transition from early to middle adulthood. In this period we are reappraising personal perspectives, the choices and achievements made as what might be seen as 'youth' ends, and we are both young and more mature. The reappraising is likely to reflect a sense that time is becoming more limited. The work of George Vaillant, reviewed next, suggested this period is one where our own 'voice', perhaps less socialised and more individual, emerges. This reflects the Jungian concept of 'individuation', becoming more individual, undivided and who we truly are.

Era: middle adulthood, age range approximately 45 to 65

Our physical peak has passed, and a slow decline may have begun. However, creative and productive time remains and occurs in this era. Reflecting Erikson's life stages, there is the recognition that our sphere of attention and care may broaden and mature in this era, and our contribution may affect a wider society and the following generation.

Developmental period: the entry life structure for middle adulthood, age range approximately 45 to 50

Reflecting Levinson's powerful and valuable concept of life being structured and shaped by choices, this is the period where a new structure may emerge and be shaped. Individual priorities may be adjusted or changed and reflect in the choices and structure that is created.

Developmental period: the age 50 transition, age range approximately 50 to 55

In Levinson's transitions the life structure is reappraised. The possibly tentative decisions made in the 40s may be revisited. We continue to explore our sense of self in the world of an older generation. Levinson proposed a cautionary note in his work which suggested that crises were common for individuals who limit changes or perhaps do not reappraise.

Developmental period: the culminating life structure for
middle adulthood, age range approximately 55 to 60

In this period the culminating life structure for the era has been achieved, and through this aspirations and goals are explored and achieved.

Developmental period: the late adulthood transition,
age range approximately 60 to 65

This transition closes the era or middle adulthood and forms the move into late adulthood. Reflecting recurring themes in Levinson's work, this involves the reappraisal of life experiences and choices and an adjustment or changed life structure for the future.

Levinson reported a core aspect and development of these phases as being the 'individuation' of the person. This is a concept found in Jungian psychology and in Carl Rogers' 'actualising tendency', arguing that we grow into the fullness of who we are. We draw more fully on our inner resources (desires, values, talents and archetypal potentials). Given that these overlap with the focus of PP, it could be argued that the discipline is supporting or resourcing the individuation process. Levinson made a point, however, of saying that this was not a description of what happened within the individual alone – that it was a process that occurred in relationship and in contact with the world in which the individual existed. This reflects the recent work of Biswas-Diener, Kashdan, and Minhas (2011), implying our development of strengths, and presumably other aspects of ourselves, occurs in context and within relationships.

The descriptions provided are generalised comments on the experiences of both men and women. There is a strong possibility, in the lapse of time since Levinson's writing, that his comments on the differences in the experiences of women may have been subject to social change. The writer has repeatedly presented these findings to undergraduate psychology students in the last five years to ask their views of their accuracy. Their opinions have always been divided – some saw society as very different now; others didn't.

Levinson's work has obvious limitations. He is clear that his studies involved relatively small numbers of people in geographically defined areas and that they capture information at a point in time for the individuals and the cultures in which they are found. Culturally at least, given that the men were interviewed in the 1960s and the women in the 1980s, the influences on them have almost certainly changed since these dates. While acknowledging his results should be seen in the context of their time, Levinson proposed a universality of these results. Levinson backed up the information from participants with data from biographies and questionnaires, so he had taken into account other factors. It needs to be acknowledged, however, that the universality has not been much tested in other times and cultures. The work does, however, offer a level of detail on early and middle adulthood absent from Erikson's sixth and seventh stages covering the same period (Levinson & Levinson, 1996, p. 17) and is therefore particularly valuable in understanding the experiences of these life phases. Levinson's work also reflects and reinforces the conclusions of Erikson's sixth and seventh stages, for example, attention to family formation, intimacy, and so on (stage six) and subsequently moving on to focus on the development of the next generation (stage seven).

The work of Vaillant (1977, 2002, 2012), to be reviewed next, provides endorsement for Levinson's findings from different study groups using different research methods. If, as Levinson asserted in the 1996 study, there are still comparatively few studies on adult development, then his work offers a language and a structure through which to anticipate and examine the experience of adulthood.

APPLICATION OF LEVINSON'S WORK TO POSITIVE PSYCHOLOGY AND THE 'DARK SIDE'

As mentioned, arguably Levinson's work adds articulation and detail to the time periods proposed by Erikson. As such, it provides us with an orientation to our own experiences or those of individuals or groups we might work with as PP practitioners.

Levinson's concept of the 'life structure', based on three or four key decisions which shape our lives, allows us to see and explore what may have been given priority at a particular point in individual development, usually in the mid or late 20s. This concept may reflect more recent thinking in positive psychology, for example, Wong (2012) on the differing types of 'meaning' we may seek and how this appears in our lives.

Following Levinson's thinking, a decision made or priority given may also indicate a decision that was *not* made or chosen, a part of life that was *not* chosen. It is possible that the decision not to live a certain way may have been taken out of a 'dark side' experience of tension or uncertainty. Levinson proposed that decisions made and not made return to be reconsidered at times of transition between eras of our lives, particularly in the late 30s. A priority chosen indicates a decision to live a particular part of our experience potentially at the cost or exclusion of another. In a subsequent transition we may choose to revisit or return to aspects of our life not yet lived. This is a moving and hopeful insight which suggests an opportunity for further exploration of our lives, perhaps supported by PP interventions.

The way in which Levinson highlights our lives being periods of stability followed by transition or change into a new era of our lives illustrates how each of us may anticipate or expect a normality of change occurring. The 'transitions', albeit a key part of our stages of growth, may have the quality of the 'dark side' in being uncertain, unexpected and new directions that we may or may not have wanted. This uncertainty may create tension, anxiety or fear. Yet Levinson illustrates for us how these are key to our growth. Transitions may be uncertain and stressful. Some may face them drawing on belief and courage, or some may not, potentially halting growth. Can we encourage ourselves and others to see them as a creative possibility and move towards them, not away (Emmons, 2003)?

If we see strengths, for example, as being contextual, and we change our life structure or context, then our use of strengths may also evolve and change (Biswas-Diener, et al., 2011). If we accept Levinson's argument for 'individuation', life being a journey in which we become more fully who we are, then implicitly he was also arguing that eudaimonic experiences and happiness may also change and take on a greater priority as our lives proceed.

REFLECTION

Where are you within Levinson's eras of life? Do you recognise his descriptions in your own experience?

If you are experiencing a transition between phases of life, is there a PP perspective or intervention that may help you shape your decisions or choices?

What three or four primary decisions have shaped your life structure to this point? Is there any aspect of your being you chose not to make part of your life structure? Do you wish to revisit that decision?

GEORGE VAILLANT (1977, 2002, 2012) – 'ADAPTATION TO LIFE' AND 'AGING WELL'

Vaillant's works represent a reporting of a prospective longitudinal study of male participants named the Grant Study of Adult Development that had originated in 1938. Two further studies/cohorts were drawn upon for a period of time to add to the data achieved. An inner-city cohort of 456 males (delinquent and non-delinquent) was involved to provide a perspective on those with less-advantaged backgrounds to the Grant Study participants. Ninety women were involved from a parallel study of 1,500 individuals, named the Stanford (Terman) Study of Gifted Children (Vaillant, 2002).

The Grant Study men were followed from their college days via questionnaires every 2 years, physical examinations every 5 years and interviews every 15 years to the present day. They were men perceived as physically healthy, to be of independent attitude and of good academic standing, located within a competitive liberal arts college in the United States. The participant group was 268 males chosen from college classes between 1939 and 1944.

Vaillant is a psychiatrist, and his work often demonstrates that perspective. He noted that after decades of study, none of his participants had a solely positive life; all encountered some kind of challenge. Vaillant recognised the difficulty of defining what 'health' meant in the context of the participants and life generally. He explored physical and psychosocial health. With some innovative work on defence mechanisms of psychoanalytical theory, these were seen as means by which we as humans cope and adapt to the circumstances of life (Vaillant, 1977). The fascination that Vaillant did not grasp in his initial involvement in the 1960s is that in following participants over time, we learn how adaptation to life changes and develops. This offers us a deeply hopeful perspective illustrating growth along with change and inevitable physical loss that occurs through life.

Vaillant, writing initially before the publication of Levinson et al.'s 1978 study, said that the Grant Study data tended to confirm the adult life patterns proposed by Erik Erikson. Vaillant's results confirmed Erikson's suggestion that life stages were generally, but not always, passed in sequence and that a life stage is rarely achieved unless its predecessor had been mastered. Yet within the Grant Study results, Vaillant suggested that the step between Erikson's sixth and seventh life cycle stages, intimacy and generativity, was too wide. A significant focus of work in between, for the men, was on career consolidation – a finding reflected in Levinson's books (Levinson et al., 1978, 2002).

In the follow-up period of work on early adulthood, Vaillant confirmed a finding of Levinson et al. (1978), that the men 'became lost in conformity' (p. 217); that is, for all their newfound freedom in adulthood, these men used their energy to follow the norms of others, particularly employers. However, this is something we can do and that does emerge from Worth (2010). Also echoing research on the exceptional creative individual and Levinson et al.'s (1978) study, the location of and relationship with a mentor in this period tended to make a central contribution to an individual's success.

Vaillant (1977) reported that the 40s became a decade where energy focus shifted from hectic work activity to an exploration of our inner world. Vaillant believed that the suggestion that this may arise from an awareness of personal mortality was too simplistic. He argued that it became a time when the men became more alert to the social influences and pressures shaping their lives and began to be uncertain of themselves again. He suggested that this decade was a transition period through which new and personal answers (rather than externally dictated ones) must be found. Through this transition, however uncertain or with 'dark side' qualities, we are potentially moving further towards our uniqueness and authenticity. The transition remained a period where individuals continued to pull themselves from parental and external restrictions and, like Levinson's revisiting of the 'life structure', one where change would occur.

Vaillant (2002) also argued for a further stage of development occurring between Erikson's seventh and eight stages (generativity vs. stagnation and integrity vs. despair). He believed there was a further task to be addressed that he termed 'Keeper of Meaning' (p. 48). His justification of this idea does not appear detailed or particularly clear. However, he argued for a task, that of conservation and preservation of the collective past products and cultural achievements of his social context. He saw the role of an older person as guiding others in this preservation while in turn facilitating the unfolding of them as people. Vaillant's presentation of results appears to have two distinct themes: life 'through time' and 'in the moment of time'.

Through the life cycle of time

Vaillant saw the study as providing empirical evidence for the adult life cycle stages proposed by Erik Erikson (1958/1980). However, he identified two additional stages (in italics): identity, intimacy, *career consolidation*, generativity, *keeper of meaning*, and integrity.

Vaillant (1977) saw these as tasks to be lived rather than stages and believed that the quality of meeting each task by an individual was a predictor of aging. Generativity (the nurturing of the younger generation) was the strongest predictor of a happy marriage and positive aging. Giving and receiving joyously and learning to be grateful were observed behaviours in positive aging. In retirement Vaillant also believed we need to rediscover learning, play and creativity. All of these have clear links to PP. The descriptions have a quality that suggests the priority of engagement, responsiveness, adjustment and flexibility – the 'meeting' of life, not being 'subject' to it.

In the moment of time in which we live

Vaillant (1993) also proposed that a range of behaviours that are seen in the moment and in the day also reflected positive aging. Examples follow:

- Be willing to give and receive love and to do so over time (Fredrickson, 2013).
- Use a creative process such as poetry or art to explore and process emotional experiences (e.g., Pennebaker, 1990).
- Develop a vital reaction to change in ourselves or the environment.
- Seek to draw upon transcendent emotions – joy, love and awe – all of which may link us to meaning and purpose in which we transcend ourselves (Fredrickson, 2013).

While indicating the overlaps between Erikson and Levinson, it is Vaillant's (1993) additional focus on how as individuals we 'socially mature' and draw on specific involuntary coping mechanisms to help us in the face of difficult experiences that provides a further perspective for this chapter.

Vaillant (1993) used the lens of Freudian ego 'defences' as one basis to examine the life stories of these men. He wrote a tour de force exploration in 1993 of the appearance of these defence or coping mechanisms in lives.

In the context of this writing the idea of 'ego' must be seen in a specific way, which may contrast with simpler or culturally influenced perspectives. The 'ego' is our conscious sense of self, in a moment of time, and through time. Vaillant (1993), along with most psychologists, acknowledge the presence of an unconscious mind, along with socially influenced expectations and norms that we tend to absorb often outside our awareness and which become habits affecting our behaviour. The ego is our sense of self and is the place in which rational thought occurs and in which cognitions such as hope and positive emotions occur. The Grant Study of Adult Development (Vaillant, 2012) argued that healthy development includes developing ego strength then letting it go and using it in support of the next generation in the phase of generativity outlined by Erikson.

Vaillant and others acknowledged that pressures arising from within us and externally may place the ego under pressure or tension. The qualities of his descriptions relate to the 'dark side' feelings described in this chapter and book. He saw these coping mechanisms as akin to the body's immune system, protecting us by finding ways of seeing or responding to circumstances, that filters pain (Vaillant, 1993).

Vaillant (1977) argued that four mature adaptive or coping mechanisms develop and show in us over time. He believed these happen outside our awareness, involuntarily, and become a means of coping. They are summarised here:

- 'Sublimation' is a form of transformation or, in Vaillant's words, 'psychic alchemy', further echoed in his own analysis of the need to involve ourselves in creative work as we age and in the research outcomes of James Pennebaker (1990). We process our emotional and psychological understanding of difficult experiences into something more positive for us to bear.
- 'Altruism' reflects our willingness to offer care to others, often care we seek for ourselves.
- 'Humour' in the face of adversity allows us to look at a serious or uncomfortable experience and transform (trans-form, or change the form) of pain.
- 'Suppression', while initially concerning, Vaillant translated our understanding of this to 'stoicism' in the face of difficulty.

Vaillant (2002) proposed that these behaviours may be seen as emergent 'virtues', something again which often adds to and expands our strengths.

Vaillant's work suggests our adaptive or defence styles change and mature with time. We all have the opportunity to become more conscious of our behaviour, which gives us 'choice' in how we 'cope' or adapt. While these adaptive behaviours may seem surprising concepts to propose, Vaillant argued that this tempering or moderation of adult behaviour can be seen in different developmental studies and findings.

Vaillant acknowledged (in a similar way to other researchers' quoted) that this study, based on a male, healthy, academically able group of individuals from socioeconomically privileged backgrounds, was not representative. He suggested that the sample equated to Terman's longitudinal study of 1,000 gifted children from California schools. Like Levinson, Vaillant argued that so little, relatively, was known of the period of adult development that the use of a specific group to explore this field was an appropriate contribution to knowledge.

APPLICATION OF VAILLANT'S WORK TO POSITIVE PSYCHOLOGY AND THE 'DARK SIDE'

Vaillant appears to argue that positive development and aging occurs through a combination of 'through time' (our developmental tasks and phases) and 'in time' behaviours (what we do in any moment of time) illustrated earlier. At the same time he implied that positive aging is what happens while we are doing other things, what we are describing as 'in time' behaviour, described earlier. The unanticipated and surprising characteristic of this prospective study was that it illustrated how we have a capacity to change, adapt and grow over time, even while our bodies are ageing.

Vaillant, similarly to Erikson, proposed the coping process (mechanisms) as 'virtues'. Perhaps these, too, add to our understanding of strengths we possess and to the overall profile of our personal strengths.

REFLECTION

When you review the developmental stages, phases or eras described earlier in this chapter, how would you assess yourself as facing or meeting these developmental tasks?

Do you recognise these adaptive or defence mechanisms in your life as they are at present?

Do you see these as adaptive or positive behaviours? Do you see them as virtues or strengths? How does this influence your perspective on your own strengths?

Which of these four is the strongest or most positive behaviour for you?

If you could choose to develop another, which has the best fit for you? How might you develop this behaviour further?

IDENTITY AND LIFE AS 'STORY' – DAN P. MCADAMS

Dan McAdams has provided a milestone contribution to psychology in his theoretical and research-based work on personality and identity as life 'story'. Different disciplines within psychology, for example, developmental and counselling, have begun to use concepts and structures of story and narrative to explore the coherence and meaning of individual experience and life (McAdams, 2001).

McAdams (1985, 1993, 2001) drew on the fifth Eriksonian stage of development in which identity, an integrated sense of self, is believed to form for the first time. He argued that the individual, in teenage years, is exploring his or her talents and strengths, social context, possible roles and motivation into a sense of self and direction in the adult world. It is at this stage that McAdams argued that we make sense of ourselves and our past, present and possible future through self-defining stories. Implicitly, this making-sense-of-self task never stops through life.

This is illustrated in this time period, and over time, by research indicating we have an autobiographical memory that is a resource to our sense of self and may be used to sustain or change the self (Conway & Pleydell-Pearce, 2000). In the act of reflecting on and describing our biographical experiences, even from an early age, we display and use the features of stories and their structure (McAdams, 2001). While research suggests this occurs from an early age, Erikson and McAdams argue that it is in the teenage years that this constitutes identity formation.

If life events are seen, made sense of, as story then it is a natural extension that individuals will infer causal links within these stories. This, in turn, may mean we explain our traits, talents, strengths, beliefs and attitudes via these stories (Mc Adams, 2001). Habermas and Bluck (2000) suggested these causal links go further to a sense of coherence in our sense of self in the areas of time, context and specific themes. As we form and reform these stories over time, our identity is a life journey and potentially our biggest creative task (Csikszentmihalyi, 1996). By describing it in this way, Csikszentmihalyi links this act of 'identity creation' to our strengths, positive experiences and emotions, finding meaning and a meaningful life.

Having made an argument for the place and presence of personal story and life narrative, let us now turn to summarise the characteristics we may find within them. These are summarised, from McAdams (1985, 1993, 2006) and Adler and Paulin (2009).

Story characteristic: thematic lines

These are the main 'themes' showing in the story, the motivational forces within the individual: their *needs, drives,* and *incentives.*

McAdams (1985) argued for two primary themes being apparent in stories: 'agency' and 'communion'. 'Power' and 'intimacy' are comparable words he used. Agency or power implies ability, asserting oneself, particularly on one's surrounding environment. These words imply *a recurrent preference or readiness for experiences of having impact and feeling strong (potent) in the environment. These themes may involve words which indicate strength, impact, action and achieved status.* Communion or intimacy implies *reciprocal dialogue, reciprocity, harmony, concern for others, 'being', and 'a recurrent preference or readiness for experiences of warm, close, communicative exchange. This may imply sharing or relinquishing of control. These themes may involve words which indicate communion or sharing, friendship or love, sympathy or touch'.* These motivational themes or lines were seen by McAdams as a predictor of certain content being contained in story patterns.

Story characteristic: nuclear episodes

These 'episodes' comprise the core structure of our story. They are likely to be associated with our feelings at certain times. These episodes may be critical or formative and, as we experience them, define who we are. They may be positive or negative. They may have transformative qualities or act as confirming the stability or sameness in our lives.

The episodes may include early memories: peak or nadir or 'flow' experiences. Bear in mind that the feeling of these episodes may be our interpretation of events rather than their factual content. Episodes of continuity may confirm or indicate a link to our past, our origins. Episodes of transformation may involve turning points, such as the ending of a life phase or a reconstruction of our perceptions.

Story characteristic: 'imagoes' or characters

McAdams (2001) suggested that the characters that populate our lives reveal indications of our identity. He drew on the Jungian concepts of characters as 'archetypes', *patterns of behaving and experiencing* that may reflect polarities of experience within our lives. Within his earlier research McAdams found that the characters in the stories of those motivated by power and agency, or intimacy and communion with others, commonly represented characteristics of those two states. They represented, to McAdams, *idealised and personified images* of the self the individual seeks to be.

Story characteristic: setting

The setting of a story will often have a quality, reflective of an individual's culture, values and/or beliefs. The setting reflects a 'time and space' of the individual's story and within which the actions find sense and meaning.

Story characteristic: narrative tone

McAdams (2001) proposes that the narrative tone of a story is both pervasive and reflective of a storyteller's view of the world. In more recent research and writing, McAdams described two embracing tones within stories, those of redemption and contamination. 'Redemption' is described as a capacity to find positive meaning, benefits and growth within difficult circumstances. 'Contamination' is defined as being negatively affected by events with an inability to control them.

Story characteristic: generativity

McAdams (1995) made a startling development in Erikson's thinking of 'generativity' as a stage of development; he proposed that it is a larger aspect of our identity in which we form a view of our generative future. What are we going to do to have a generative future, to leave a legacy for others? What are we going to create, produce or institute in the future? McAdams sees this as a general sense we may have over time and then particularly in mature adulthood where we may be motivated by caring for others and a younger generation.

McAdams (2006, 2006a) took a bold step in asserting that our stories and life narratives represent one of the primary ways in which we can reach an integrated understanding of personality and meaning. The readjusting or rethinking of our life stories over time may reflect the very act of responding to and reconsidering the darker experiences of our lives.

APPLICATION OF MCADAMS' WORK TO POSITIVE PSYCHOLOGY AND THE DARK SIDE

This raises the importance of looking at PP and its links to story.

Maybe an individual's 'story' and its characteristics will give us an indication of which PP intervention might be most valuable? In the priority given to short-term PP interventions, is PP overlooking a 'through-time' or longitudinal element or perspective to its possible contributions?

REFLECTION

Can you identify the characteristics of your own story? For example, What are the nuclear episodes of your story? Its primary characters? The setting? The narrative themes and tone that appear in your story?

In what way, if any, do they surprise you?

Consider using some PP perspectives to revisit and explore your story? For example, contemplate the following:

What memory might you savour more deeply? What strengths did you demonstrate in different nuclear episodes of your life? Does this insight surprise you? Have these strengths stayed consistent or changed in circumstance and time?

Could you undertake a gratitude exercise where you review characters, episodes or themes in your life and notice what you might be grateful for that you have not yet been aware of?

OVERALL APPLICATION OF THESE THEORIES TO POSITIVE PSYCHOLOGY

Figure 2.1 is intended to highlight key parts of the four theories and to support you in seeing these in overview.

This diagram is intended to summarise key aspects of the four theories. Each illustrates that our experiences over time may include tensions between the positive and negative, the known and the unknown or uncertain. Each implies directly or indirectly that our unfolding or growth occurs in these steps into the unknown that are a natural and inevitable part of our growth and development. In this, the writer believes, that our developmental journey is one of unfolding growth which carries us, consciously or unconsciously, more closely to our uniqueness and individuality.

SUMMARY – THIS CHAPTER HAS

• Summarised four theories of adult development
• Proposed the links these theories have with PP
• Offered reflective questions to support the reader in exploring these topics
• Offered resources for following up these ideas in other literature

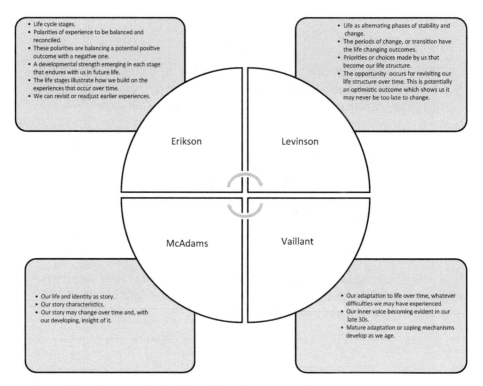

- Life cycle stages.
- Polarities of experience to be balanced and reconciled.
- These polarities are balancing a potential positive outcome with a negative one.
- A developmental strength emerging in each stage that endures with us in future life.
- The life stages illustrate how we build on the experiences that occur over time.
- We can revisit or readjust earlier experiences.

- Life as alternating phases of stability and change.
- The periods of change, or transition have the life changing outcomes.
- Priorities or choices made by us that become our life structure.
- The opportunity occurs for revisiting our life structure over time. This is potentially an optimistic outcome which shows us it may never be too late to change.

Erikson

Levinson

McAdams

Vaillant

- Our life and identity as story.
- Our story characteristics.
- Our story may change over time and, with our developing, insight of it.

- Our adaptation to life over time, whatever difficulties we may have experienced.
- Our inner voice becoming evident in our late 30s.
- Mature adaptation or coping mechanisms develop as we age.

FIGURE 2.1 Key Aspects of the Four Theories

RESOURCES

If you wish to follow up the ideas in this chapter, the work of Levinson and Levinson (1996), Levinson et al. (1978), Vaillant (2002, 2012) and McAdams (1995) are particularly readable and positive in outlook.

BIBLIOGRAPHY

Adler, J.M., & Poulin, M.J. (2009). The political is personal: Narrating 9/11 and psychological well-being. *Journal of Personality, 77*(4), 903–932.

Bee, H. (1998). *Lifespan development* (2nd ed.). Harlow, England: Longman.

Berk, L.E. (1998). *Development through the lifespan*. London: Allyn and Bacon.

Biswas-Diener, R., Kashdan, T.B., & Minhas, G. (2011). A dynamic approach to psychological strength development and intervention. *The Journal of Positive Psychology, 6*(2), 106–118.

Conway, M.A., & Pleydell-Pearce, C.W. (2000). The construction of autobiographical memories in the self-memory system. *Psychological Review, 107*(2), 261–288.

Csikszentmihalyi, M. (1996). *Creativity: Flow and the psychology of discovery and invention*. London: Harper Collins.

Emmons, R. A. (2003). Personal goals, life meaning and virtue: Wellspring of a positive life. In C. L. M. Keyes & J. Haidt (Eds.), *Flourishing: Positive psychology and the life well-lived*. New York: American Psychological Association.

Erikson, E. H. (1958/1980). *Identity and the life cycle*. New York: Norton.

Erikson, E. H. (1963). *Childhood and society* (2nd ed.). New York: Norton.

Erikson, E. H. (1974). *Dimensions of a new identity: The 1973 Jefferson lectures in the humanities*. New York: Norton.

Erikson, E. H. (1980). On the generational cycle: An address. *International Journal of Psychoanalysis, 61*, 213–223.

Erikson, E. H. (1982). *The life cycle completed: A review*. New York: Norton.

Erikson, E. H. (1985). *The life cycle completed*. New York: Norton.

Erikson, E. H. (1997). *The life cycle completed* (Rev. ed.). J. M. Erikson (Ed.). New York: Norton.

Erikson, E. H., & Erikson, J. (1981). On generativity and identity: From a conversation with Erik and Joan Erikson. *Harvard Educational Review, 51*(2), 249–269.

Erikson, E. H., Erikson, J. M., & Kivnick, H. Q. (1986). *Vital involvement in old age*. New York: Norton.

Erikson, J. M. (1988). *Wisdom and the senses: The way of creativity*. New York: Norton.

Fredrickson, B. L. (2013). *Love 2.0*. London, Hudson Street Press Ltd.

Gentner, D., & Stevens, A. (1983). *Mental models: Cognitive science series*. New Jersey: Lawrence Erlbaum.

Habermas, T., & Bluck, S. (2000). Getting a life: The emergence of life story in adolescence. *Psychological Bulletin, 126*(5), 748–769.

Levinson, D. J., Darrow, C. N., Klein, E. B., Levinson, M. H., & McKee, B. (1978). *The seasons of a man's life*. New York: Ballantine Books.

Levinson, D., & Levinson, J. (1996). *The seasons of a woman's life*. New York: Alfred Knopf.

McAdams, D. P. (1985). *Power, intimacy, and the life story: Personological inquiries into identity*. New York: Guilford.

McAdams, D. P. (1988). *Power, intimacy and the live story: Personological inquiries into identity*. London: Guildford.

McAdams, D. P. (1993). *The stories we live by: Personal myths and the making of the self*. New York: Morrow.

McAdams, D. P. (1995). *The stories we live by: Personal myths and the making of the self*. London: Guildford.

McAdams, D. P. (2001). The psychology of life stories. *Review of General Psychology, 5*(2), 100–122.

McAdams, D. P. (2006). A new big five: Fundamental principles for an integrative science of personality. *American Psychologist, 61*(3), 204–217.

McAdams, D. P. (2006a). *The person: A new introduction to personality psychology* (4th ed.). London: John Wiley and Sons.

McAdams, D. P. (2006b). *The redemptive self: Stories Americans live by*. Oxford, UK: Oxford University Press.

Pennebaker, J.W. (1990). *Opening up: The healing power of expressing emotions*. London: Guildford.

Perlmutter, M., & Hall, E. (1992). *Adult development and aging* (2nd. ed.). New Jersey: John Wiley & Sons.

Roazen, P. (1976). *Freud and his followers* (3rd ed.). New York: Alfred A. Knopf.

Roberts, P., & Newton, P. M. (1987). Levinsonian studies of woman's adult development. *Psychology and Aging, 2*(2), 154–163.

Rogers, C. R. (1963). The actualizing tendency in relation to "motive" and to consciousness. In M. Jones (Ed.), *Nebraska symposium on motivation* (pp. 1–24). Lincoln: University of Nebraska Press.

Vaillant, G. E. (1977). *Adaptation to life*. Boston: Little, Brown.

Vaillant, G. E. (1993). *Wisdom and the ego*. Cambridge, MA: Harvard University Press.

Vaillant, G. E. (2002). *Aging well*. Boston: Little Brown.

Vaillant, G. E. (2012). *Triumphs of experience: The men of the Harvard grant study*. Cambridge, MA: Harvard University Press.

Wong, P. T. P. (2011) Positive psychology 2.0: Towards a balanced interactive model of the good life. *Canadian Psychology, 52*(2), 69–81.

Wong, P. T. P. (2012) *Towards a dual system model of what makes life worth living*. In P. T. P. Wong (Ed.), *The human quest for meaning*. London: Routledge.

Worth, P. (2010). *Four questions of creativity: Keys to a creative life*. Bloomington, IL, Trafford.

Worth, P., & Lyle, L. (2014). *Positive ageing*. Poster presentation at the Conference of the Canadian Positive Psychology Association, Toronto, Canada.

3
The dark side of meaning in life

'A man who becomes conscious of the responsibility he bears toward a human being who affectionately waits for him, or to an unfinished work, will never be able to throw away his life. He knows the "why" for his existence, and will be able to bear almost any "how"'.

Victor Frankl

Learning objectives – at the end of the chapter you will be able to do the following:

- Define and explain the concept of meaning
- Differentiate between meaning and purpose
- Contemplate the relationship between the 'dark side' and authenticity
- Understand the sources of meaning and look into different ways to measure meaning
- Investigate the relationship between authenticity, meaning and the 'dark side'
- Grasp the relationship between meaning and wellbeing
- Distinguish between the presence of meaning and the search for meaning
- Investigate the search for meaning, the interactions it has with the 'dark side' and its potential effects
- Understand the variety of sources of meaning
- Discuss the changes in meaning and their potential dark side
- Understand the depth of meaning and its relationship with self-transcendence

List of topics:

- Meaning
- Purpose
- Wellbeing
- Presence of meaning
- Search for meaning
- Purpose in life sub-scale
- Authenticity

- Sources of meaning
- Personal meaning profile
- The 'dark side' of meaning
- Malfunctioning goals and purposes
- Meaning meditation
- Depth of meaning

Meaning in life is a prominent PP variable that greatly interests many scholars. It is mainly associated with enhanced wellbeing, and yet under certain circumstances, some of its aspects may prove to be difficult. The 'dark side', in the context of this chapter, refers to challenging experiences, thoughts, emotions and behaviours relating to mean-ing and purpose, which trigger discomfort in us. We tend to avoid such discomfort as it leads to an experience of confusion and distress which are involved with our search for meaning and purpose. The search for meaning could be a challenging journey. However, engaging with this challenge and discomfort leads to greater authenticity, growth, and deeper meaning in life. In this chapter we will explore the meaning of meaning, under-stand its relationship with wellbeing, be introduced to different levels of meaning, and engage with its dark side to allow for a more comprehensive understanding of meaning in life.

WHAT IS MEANING IN LIFE?

The psychological study of meaning in life has been neglected for many years because of the philosophical connotations of the question 'What is the meaning of life?, which explores the role human beings play in their own lives on a global, non-personal, level. This question could indeed be a theological or a philosophical one and therefore out of bounds for modern science. However, this very question has great psychological impor-tance when it is asked in a personal, subjective way, referring to one's personal meaning in life. When this is the case, we can theorise, measure, compare and conceptualise meaning in a psychological context. Different models and theories exist that attempt to answer the question of meaning and its role in our lives. Researchers argue that mean-ing is based upon, and supported by, goal-directed behaviour (Ryff & Singer, 1998); that it is all about making sense of life (Battista & Almond, 1973); that it has a central, affective quality to it (Reker & Wong, 1988); that it is linked with transcendent or spiritual concerns (Emmons, 2003; Mascaro, Rosen, & Morey, 2004; Reker, 2000); and finally, that it is derived from factors such as a sense of self-worth and self-justification (Baumeister, 1991). Accordingly, the definitions of meaning incorporate these different dimensions. For example, Steger (2009, p. 680) states that meaning 'enables people to interpret and organize their experience, achieve a sense of their own worth and place, identify the things that matter to them, and effectively direct their energies'. Reker and Wong (1988) offer a parallel definition, stating that meaning is based upon our capacity to perceive order and coherence in our existence, pursue our goals, and feel the fulfil-ment that follows these achievements. It would appear then that researchers consistently distinguish between cognitive and action-based aspects of meaning. To understand why this distinction is necessary we must decipher the difference between meaning and purpose.

MEANING AND PURPOSE

The concepts of meaning and purpose refer to different aspects of our understanding and experience of meaning in life. Meaning refers to understanding-based cognitive expe-rience, where we make sense of life and our roles in it (Steger, 2012). We all carry a series of schemas that are part of our self-concept. They help us make sense of the self, the world around us, and the role of the self within this world. This is a narrative, a life story that is built upon a coherent grouping of the schemas we carry. Purpose, on the other hand, refers to aspirations that motivate our activities (Emmons, 2003). Perhaps the most inspiring work that highlights the role of purpose is Frankl's (1963) theory, which determined that each of us has a unique purpose or some meaningful aim in life. To live fully we must pursue this unique purpose, and this choice creates deep satisfaction and a sense of fulfilment in life. In essence, the difference between meaning and purpose could be summarised as the difference between theory and action. While meaning provides us with a theoretical context, an understanding of the *why* in life, it is purpose that traces for us the required corresponding action, the *how* in life. That is why the approaches applied to define meaning are often multidimensional. One approach defines meaning in life as cognitive in nature (significance-centred definition); another approach refers to it as mainly motivational (purpose-centred definition). The first approach corresponds to content and understanding, while the second approach corresponds to purpose and action. Wong (1998), offering a prominent theoretical framework for meaning, according to which three components participate in producing an experience of meaning:

1   *A motivational/behavioural component*: This is an active component, replete with the pursuit of goals seen as valuable and worthy. According to Wong (1998), a meaningful life is never passive, and the activity involved in it signifies the most valuable aspects of one's existence.
2   *A cognitive component*: This component, which is part of our thinking, is in charge of making sense of life. The individual's way of thinking attaches significance to his or her life, cognitively giving it meaning.
3   *An emotional component*: This is a feeling of deep satisfaction that accompanies one's involvement with the cognitive and motivational components. When individuals feel their lives make perfect sense, and live in pursuit of what they consider worthwhile goals, they are filled with positive emotions and feelings of fulfilment.

Another dimension of meaning and purpose in life is that they are multifaceted (Reker & Wong, 1988). You could have an overarching sense of meaning and purpose in your life and at the same time experience varying levels of meaning and purpose in different areas such as work, romantic relationships, friends, family and leisure time. In other words, it is usually not possible to determine meaning and purpose by simply lumping together all aspects of life. One should rather take into account the multifaceted nature of life and be ready to find different levels of meaning and purpose in each of its areas.

The interrelation between meaning and purpose is quite clear. Without purpose, meaning risks generating a feeling of cognitive dissonance as our understanding of our self and the way it is applied are not synchronised. This might stem from lack of courage to apply our meaning and could lead to frustration and dissatisfaction (Ruffin, 1984). The dissonance seems no less problematic when it is regarded from the opposite direction: purpose without meaning could clash one's aims or actions with the schemas that define one's place in the world. This could result from being unable to formulate a clear narrative and understanding of meaning and then making choices that are not based on the theoretical foundation of a clear narrative (Prince, 1991). Such a dissonance, and its relationship with the 'dark side', could be understood most clearly as part of our experience of authenticity.

AUTHENTICITY, MEANING, AND THE 'DARK SIDE'

Existential philosophy regards authenticity as a central human feature and defines it as the experience of being faithful to one's true self (Harter, 2002). Obviously, you cannot escape being yourself, and whenever you make a choice or take action, the one who is doing these things is yourself. However, it may happen that some of your thoughts, decisions and actions are not in line with whatever feels right for you and therefore do not actually reflect who you are. Being authentic means living according to your own desires, beliefs, motives and ideals rather than those of someone else. To be authentic, these motives and beliefs must be reflected in your actions and behaviours. Living this way warrants for much desired autonomy and control. Trilling (1971, p. 14) explains that the word 'authentic' comes from Greek, where *authenteo* means 'to have full power'. An authentic individual becomes 'the master of his or her own domain'. In humanistic psychology, authenticity is considered a fundamental aspect and a necessary condition of wellbeing (May, 1960; Rogers, 1961). Humanistic psychology scholars place authenticity at the heart of healthy functioning.

Meaning and purpose in life walk hand in hand with authenticity. Two of the most important themes in the experience of authenticity are awareness and behaviour (Barrett-Lennard, 1998). Awareness means recognizing one's own motives and desires; for example, being familiar with one's personal values. Behaviour refers to acting according to one's own preferences and needs, as opposed to acting blindly or to please others. We all ask ourselves questions about our values and beliefs. This is the role of the awareness component of authenticity that helps understand better the meaning in our life. To translate our true values, beliefs and priorities into meaning, we must be aware of what they are. This engagement with our own beliefs is liable to trigger difficulty and confusion. As you observe yourself to determine which beliefs and choices are in line with your deepest values, you have to extract your own true beliefs from 'false' ones, namely, ones that are not truly part of you. This process tends to be painful and challenging, and as such it is an aspect of the 'dark side' of meaning in life. Letting go of irrelevant values and admitting they are not truly yours is not easy, but once we have succeeded, we are rewarded by greater awareness, deeper authenticity, and clearer meaning in life.

A similar facet of the 'dark side' has to do with the behavioural aspect of authenticity, namely, the way your purpose in life is manifested. Even if you are aware of your personal meaning in life, is your authenticity strong enough to apply it, to act accordingly? This choice is not easy to make. For many of us this behavioral dimension of authenticity requires making difficult changes. Living our innermost purposes could mean letting go of comfortable circumstances where life feels safe and secure. Frequently, giving life to your purposes requires great courage. The 'dark side' of meaning and purpose is reflected again in this process as this conflict between your comfort zone and the application of purpose might be unsettling. You may also have to stand up for your principles against others and be criticised for doing so. And yet, typical of the 'dark side', devoting yourself to this process and embracing it would take you through a journey of transformation that would bring you closer to experiencing purpose.

REFLECTION

Given that meaning and purpose are closely associated with different variables of wellbeing, the discussion, which has so far been objective, must now turn into a personal, subjective investigation. Personal reflection helps you understand your own relationship with meaning and purpose. In addition, such an exercise allows you to engage with your own personal 'dark side' of meaning with greater awareness, thereby finding ways to embrace these challenges and find deeper meaning and purpose. All you need for this reflection exercise is pen, paper, and a quiet moment alone. When you are ready, answer the following question:

- What is the personal meaning and purpose of your life?

The question may seem overwhelming or complicated, and yet it is well worth your time. You may feel that you need some time to answer it; reflect on it for a while today, write whatever comes out easily, and get back to your writing when you feel you are able to expand your answer. By increasing your awareness of what you see as the meaning and purpose in your own life, you will find it easier to lead a life that best matches this meaning and purpose – an authentic life.

MEANING RESEARCH

A significant body of work carried out over years of research has demonstrated that there is a correlation between higher levels of meaning in life and enhanced levels of certain wellbeing variables. Greater meaning in life has been associated with love, joy and vitality (Steger et al., 2009); higher self-esteem and morale (Ryff, 1989); ego development (King & Hicks, 2007); hope, optimism and productive coping skills (Steger, 2012); life satisfaction (Steger et al., 2008); positive affect (Hicks & King, 2009); engagement with work (Bonebright et al., 2000; Steger & Dik, 2010); and psychological adjustment (Thompson et al., 2003). Greater meaning in life also seems to be associated with resilience in the face of maladaptive psychological dimensions: participants report lower levels of depression and anxiety (e.g., Debats, Van Der Lubbe, & Wezeman, 1993), lesser negative affect (e.g., Chamberlain & Zika, 1988), and decreased need for therapy (Battista &

Almond, 1973). This also works the other way around: poor meaning in life is associated with mental health disorders and addiction problems (Kinnier et al., 1994). The interrelation between lack of meaning and addiction is worth contemplation as it illustrates the importance of attaining personal meaning in life. Lack of meaning creates a deep feeling of discomfort, which is sometimes dealt with by seeking an external substitute to meaning that would cover up this discomfort and provide temporary relief. Drugs, alcohol and other dependencies are often regarded as capable of dissociating suffering individuals from the pain of meaninglessness (Newcomb et al., 1987).

RESEARCH AND PRACTICE CASE STUDIES

A study by Littman-Ovadia and Steger (2010) explored the potential relationship between strengths and meaning. The study demonstrated that when individuals endorsed character strengths, they were more likely to experience a sense of meaning. To measure the relationship between these two aspects of wellbeing, the participants completed a questionnaire intended to establish the extent to which they felt they exhibited certain character strengths and were also asked to complete a measurement of meaning. The findings indicated that the endorsement of strengths was positively associated with meaning. This association was replicated in paid and voluntary workers as well as in a general population of adolescents and adults. The implications of these data are interesting. They suggest that by endorsing their strengths, individuals naturally relate to life in a more meaningful manner as their actions are strength based. They also suggest that stronger meaning may encourage one to apply one's prominent strengths and utilise them in life.

MEANING: PRESENCE VERSUS SEARCH

In the past 40 years, the research of meaning has become revitalised, focusing on the issue of the presence of meaning (Steger et al., 2008). Even though meaning has different dimensions, the investigations have focused on the levels of meaning in peoples' lives and on the outcomes of having a weaker or stronger presence of meaning. So far, our discussion of meaning in this chapter has focused on the presence of meaning. Considering that one of the most important and influential texts dealing with meaning is Viktor Frankl's (1963) *Man's Search for Meaning*, it is fascinating to observe that the search for meaning has been almost completely neglected over the 40 years of meaning research. Frankl's work has been said to be crucial to the emergence of meaning as an important psychological construct (Wong & Fry, 1998), and yet until recently, the search for meaning has not been taken up in contemporary research. Frankl was not the only one to focus on the search for meaning; Maddi (1970), for example, claimed that the search for meaning is one of the most important human motivations. Each and every one of us has a different capacity and interest in that search, defined by Steger and colleagues as the 'strength, intensity, and activity of people's desire and efforts to establish and/or augment their understanding of the meaning, significance, and purpose of their lives' (Steger et al., 2008, p. 200).

PSYCHOMETRIC SCALES

In PP, the most popular tool for measuring meaning is the Meaning in Life Questionnaire (MLQ) devised by Steger et al. (2006). The MLQ makes a clear distinction between scores of the presence of meaning and scores of the search for meaning.

Please take a moment to think about what makes your life and existence feel important and significant to you. Please respond to the following statements as truthfully and accurately as you can and also please remember that these are very subjective questions and that there are no right or wrong answers. For each question choose a number between 1 (absolutely untrue) and 7 (absolutely true). Please choose the number that best describes your present agreement or disagreement with each statement.

1   I understand my life's meaning.

2   I am looking for something that makes my life feel meaningful.

3   I am always looking to find my life's purpose.

4   My life has a clear sense of purpose.

5   I have a good sense of what makes my life meaningful.

6   I have discovered a satisfying life purpose.

7   I am always searching for something that makes my life feel significant.

8   I am seeking a purpose or mission for my life.

9   My life has no clear purpose.

10   I am searching for meaning in my life.

Scoring: Final scores for presence and search are obtained in the following manner:

Presence = 1, 4, 5, 6, and 9 (reverse coded)

Search = 2, 3, 7, 8, and 10

SEARCHING FOR MEANING: PLANTING THE SEEDS OF THE 'DARK SIDE'

What is the impact of the search for meaning? Is it beneficial or harmful? Does it actually result in greater meaning or lead to confusion and difficulty? According to Frankl (1963) and Maddi (1970) the search for meaning is an important motivational aspect of being human. The search for meaning, therefore, is a natural and productive experience, encouraging us to seek new challenges and grow. However, other scholars offer a different perspective, claiming that the search for meaning has both a positive and a negative foundation – and could therefore be beneficial or harmful, respectively. Reker (2000), for example, stipulates that the search for meaning could have positive, life-affirming, motivational roots or negative, deficit-based ones. Similarly, Steger et al. (2008) suggest that the search for meaning could arise from different motivations and may therefore be associated with very different consequences. An important example of this could be the difference between an individual's motivation to seek positive experiences, growth and change against the motivation of another individual to try and avoid negative experiences (Carver et al., 2000). As part of their search for meaning, the first group of individuals seeks positive experiences, while the second group avoids negative experiences (Elliot & Tharash, 2002). In the group of *seekers of positive experiences*, the search for meaning would correlate positively with the presence of meaning; a more vigorous search would increase the presence of meaning in their lives. Those who *avoid negative experiences*, however, would find that searching for meaning correlates negatively with the presence of meaning; a more vigorous search would result in a decreased presence of meaning in life.

SOURCES OF MEANING

We are able to understand the presence of meaning and the search for it, but the sources of meaning remain unknown. What is it that brings meaning to our lives? Obviously, the sources of meaning are extremely subjective and might be specific to one's personal circumstances. Nevertheless, theory and research indicate that we experience and emphasise certain themes in our lives as sources of meaning. Wong (1998) describes seven such central sources:

1   *Relationships:* Supporting others and being supported by others is a source of great satisfaction and therefore a powerful source of meaning. This includes friendships and membership in clubs or organisations that are part of the community.
2   *Intimacy:* Meaning is derived from sharing one's intimate and most personal feelings, desires, goals, thoughts, triumphs and failures with a special person, such as a friend, a lover, or a relative with whom one has a deep and meaningful connection.
3   *Self-transcendence:* This source derives meaning from focusing on causes, responsibilities and pursuits that exist outside the self and transcend it.
4   *Achievement:* Pursuing and achieving one's goals is an important source of meaning. This regards the fulfilment of both large-scale life goals and smaller-scale projects.

5 *Self-acceptance:* Learning self-acceptance provides you with a foundation for personal meaning in life. It is easier [...] with the person you are. Simil[...] [...]ore difficult for you to feel the[...]

6 *Fairness/Respect:* For certain [...] and respect are powerful sourc[...]

7 *Religion/Spirituality:* Engagin[...] [...]ine being, god or higher powe[...]

Another perspective on sourc[...] who extracted eight themes from mate[...] The information was obtained from c[...] m- ples of what was most meaningful [...] ng the meaning individuals derive f[...] ib- ing the desire of individuals to h[...] us, political and sociological beliefs; [...] res expressed by some; 'growth', acc[...] nt and for a greater understanding [...], comprising physical and mental health; 'life work', describing those who derived meaning from their occupations; and finally, 'pleasure', perceiving pleasure or happiness as generally meaningful. Evidently, the themes of Wong (1998) and Ebersole (1998) are quite similar. This similarity corresponds to a number of studies that attempt to determine the most important sources of meaning (e.g., DeVogler & Ebersole, 1980; Fiske & Chiriboga, 1991; Hedlund & Birren, 1984; Klinger, 1977; Levi, 1996; Reker, 1988). According to Prager (1998), the sources that were found to be most central were relationship (interpersonal orientations); personal growth (gaining more knowledge about self and perfection of personal potentials); materialism (concrete possessions); expression and creativity (arts, athletics, music and writing); altruism (providing services and helping others); and hedonism (pleasure in daily life). The issue of sources of meaning is highly relevant to the continuous changes that eventually occur in the experience of meaning. These potential changes lie at the heart of an impending dark side of meaning, as the next section explores.

REFLECTION

What are your personal sources of meaning in life?

Do you find that certain sources of meaning are more prominent and influential than others? Recognise the most central ones.

MEANING CHANGES: A 'DARK SIDE' OF MEANING

The sources and experiences of meaning in life are based upon the development of a coherent sense of self and identity (Heine et al., 2006). This identity gives life to the mosaic of schemas that structure the cognitive understanding of personal meaning. In other words, the schemas that underlie our self-concept are not random ones; they are derived from our personal sense of identity. The sense of identity keeps changing and growing over the years, and therefore the process of meaning making via personal schemas also keeps changing throughout life (Fry, 1998). The emergence of meaning is therefore linked with individual development, relating to the maturity of identity, to relationships, and to goals (Steger et al., 2009). Personal meaning is therefore prompted by the values people live by and the themes that take part in forming their self-concepts (Prager, 1998). These themes, which are flexible and changeable (Kaufman 1986), come together to create personal meaning. Consequently, research shows, people experience different levels of meaning at different ages (Ryff & Essex, 1992). Several studies have indicated that the levels of meaning in life generally increase as we get older (Reker, 2005; Reker, Peacock, & Wong, 1987; Van Ranst & Marcoen, 1997). The only meta-analysis conducted in this field (Pinquoart, 2002) depicts a more specific picture, indicating that people of 69 or above have reported increased meaning, while for those age 70 and above, meaning decreased.

The levels of presence are not the only ones to change throughout life; the sources of meaning change as well. Yalom (1980) stated that the sources of meaning could change over a lifetime; as the years go by, meaning may spring from different dimensions of one's life. Jung (1963) expressed similar views when he suggested that in our later years, a developmental shift occurs from instrumental values toward inner-directed ones. To test these ideas, Ebersole (1998) applied the eight themes he had formulated based on data collected from college students to a sample of middle-age adults (mean age of 45) and a sample of older adults (mean age of 75). Significant differences were found between these two groups in the sources of meaning. Zika and Chamberlain (1992), who studied a group of young mothers and a group of older participants, also found that the sources of meaning changed over one's lifetime. These differences across age groups were also apparent in a study performed by Reker (1988) on a Canadian sample ranging between 18 and 63 years of age. Reker developed for the study a Sources of Meaning Profile (SOMP) which was made of 16 statements the participants were required to grade on a seven-point scale. The statements mirrored the themes formulated by Ebersole (1998), for example: 'engaging in personal relationships with family and/or friends' or 'being of service to others'. Reker reported a pattern where the older participants graded the more inwardly centred statements higher than the younger participants. Reker's study was based on the work of Neugarten (1968), who posited that a typical change occurred in the later stages of life, whereby orientation shifted from the outer world to the inner world. Finally, research data suggests that meaning could change in the course of life in correlation with individual developmental stages and the transition between stages (Prager, 1996; Reker, 1991).

The concept of change reveals the experience of meaning and purpose to be dynamic. As we have seen, during our lifetime, both the presence and sources of meaning fluctuate and change. Lifespan theorists describe shifts in values and beliefs that lead to greater introspection (Jung, 1971), deeper experience of faith (Fowler, 1983), greater integration (Erikson, 1963) and increasing interiority (Neugarten, 1964). At certain points in life we may experience high levels of meaning with clear, applicable goals and purposes. For a certain period of time, we feel that this process is accompanied by deep fulfilment and satisfaction. This period of time may last just a few days, or it may continue for dozens of years, and yet at some point, a shift is bound to occur. Our personal schemas may change, changing with them our individual narratives of meaning and purpose. This is a difficult point for many, as we might miss the change and therefore get stuck with irrelevant goals, meaning, and purpose, or alternatively, we could be aware of the change and reject it in panic, holding onto the old patterns of meaning and purpose. Whatever the reason, awareness and self-knowledge are crucial to maintaining personal meaning and purpose that match the ongoing narrative of one's self-concept. The 'dark side' of meaning includes the engagement with changes of meaning's source in our lives. This is frequently a difficult engagement as it might require letting go of the known and movement towards uncharted territories, and yet, as it is with the 'dark side', embracing the call for such a change would lead to great transformation and positive growth. Primarily, embracing the 'dark side' under these circumstances would ensure the alignment of our current sources of meaning with our purposes.

As we grow and change through life, meaning naturally changes as well. When the transition is a healthy one, the different developmental stages invite changes to identity, which in turn lead to restructuring our schemas, giving rise to new sources of meaning (Prager, 1996; Reker, 1991). However, when the transition is not clear-cut, and the new sources of meaning are not assimilated into one's modified self-concept, an existential crisis risks to be triggered (Yang et al., 2010). As we go through life, our environment, narrative and schemas change; with each of these changes, the question is whether or not we are able to gain a sense of meaning or purpose in life as we adapt to the new environment. Failure to achieve this would trigger a search for meaning, to fill the existential void (Wong, 2009). The 'dark side' of meaning includes this search for meaning and could involve great discomfort due to the mismatch between our current identity and schemas and the goals and purposes we set for ourselves. According to Klinger (1998), a life of inadequate goals leads to distress and psychopathology. If the purposes of an individual are not aligned with his or her developmental stage, the existing set of inadequate goals and purposes would lead to 'desultory, apathetic activity, to much inactivity, and to reduced reactivity to environmental events' (p. 47). Under these circumstances, says Klinger, an individual would go through a process of self-examination, asking questions about personal meaning and purpose, trying to identify an adequate set of purposes that would be relevant to the newly formed identity. If this process fails, and the individual is unable to find such purposes, he or she is likely to try and remedy the situation by artificially manipulating affect, through substance abuse, for example (Lukas, 1972). The resulting lifestyle is likely to be characterised by isolation, alienation and depression. These circumstances link with the discussion of the potential dark side of the search for meaning and the different approaches to this search (Elliot & Tharash, 2002). Your experience of the 'dark side' depends on the way you approach the search: if during the search the individual's motivation is to *avoid* the negative challenges of time, the search will probably lead to decreased presence of meaning and wellbeing. However, if the change is embraced, and one's motivation is to accept the change and grow, the searching individual will find an adequate purpose and therefore raise the levels of meaning and wellbeing.

In essence, the answers to the questions 'who am I' and 'why am I here' must match. Understanding one's self-identity at a given moment should give rise to meaning and purpose in life. If the meaning and purpose being applied at a certain moment belong to a self-concept and self-identity that no longer exist, the goals, meaning and purpose being experienced would be inadequate. This would impair wellbeing. Carnegie (1981, p. 147) said, 'Are you bored with life? Then throw yourself into some work you believe in with all your heart, live for it, die for it, and you will find happiness that you had thought could never be yours'. So many people choose to do this only to find themselves deeply disappointed, feeling deflated in the face of a cause they have fully invested themselves in without achieving the anticipated fulfilment. The reason for this is simple: they had neglected to apply the quote's words *believe in with all your heart*. Meaning is not the outcome of an isolated idea or action; it springs from the close relationship between one's identity and these ideas and actions. Only when the identity, one's heart, is in line with one's ideas and actions will one live through a relevant and meaningful experience.

TRY ME

Ivtzan et al. (2015) created an eight-week mindfulness intervention program, where each week combines a prominent PP factor with mindfulness meditation. The intervention is titled Positive Mindfulness Programme (PMP). The sixth week of the program focuses on ways to increase meaning in life. The intervention created for that week combines ideas from the 'best possible self' intervention (King, 2001) with mindfulness meditation practice. Over the week, the participants meditate daily and carry out daily practice to enhance meditation. The protocol for both follows. You can practice this as a one-off or follow the full week structure that could enhance the impact of the meditation as a practical exercise.

Introduction: Welcome to the daily meditation practice for Week 6. This session will focus on becoming more aware of the things in life you find most meaningful. Please dedicate 10 minutes to the exercise.

- Begin by sitting comfortably, let your body relax, and bring your full awareness to your breath.

- For a few minutes inhale deeply and exhale fully while concentrating on the flow of air as it enters and leaves your body.

- From this place of relaxation, begin to visualize yourself in the future . . . take yourself to a place and time where you see yourself living a meaningful life.

- You have achieved everything you wished to achieve and have done everything you set out to do.

- Visualize a scenario that illustrates vividly this meaningful life: imagine people you meet, interactions, situations and anything else that embodies what you visualize as a most meaningful life.

- This future vision of yourself is the best possible legacy you could leave behind. . . . Breathe deeply. . . and connect fully to the experience.

- Try not to hold onto any thoughts about how you got there – simply imagine it as vividly as you can, and feel the emotions this vision evokes.

- Take all the time you need to visualize all aspects of this future life. . . . Breathe . . . and observe.

- Bring your awareness into your body; feel the sensations that arise in your body as you witness the experience of living a meaningful life.

- Gradually shift from imagining your best possible legacy to the actual sensations that are triggered in your body.

- Breathe in . . . and out. . . . Scan your body, and find the most prominent sensations.

- Breathe into these sensations. Feel them. Explore them. Do nothing about these sensations – simply observe them.

- These bodily sensations arise from contemplating your meaningful life.

  Notice what you are feeling in your body. . . . Appreciate the sensations you

  notice. . . . Watch them with kindness and acceptance.

- When you feel ready, let your awareness spread through your whole body and then over the room around you. Slowly open your eyes, and feel the effects of the meditation.

Daily Practice:

During the day, we invite you to take action and support your best possible legacy. Become mindful of your behaviour and notice your actions. Ask yourself if you are choosing words that align with this vision of your life. Ask yourself if you are choosing to participate in activities that you think are meaningful. Consider ways to introduce more meaningful actions into your daily life. Don't be under pressure to change your current situation; just observe and bring your awareness to building up meaning in your life.

PRACTICE ESSAY QUESTIONS

- What are the building blocks of meaning and purpose?

- Describe the process by which meaning is deepened towards self-transcendence, and specify what might go wrong along the journey.

DEPTH OF MEANING

A powerful example of adjusting self-identity, and the changing concept of meaning, is provided by the question of depth of meaning. As we strive to engage with the potentially dark side of meaning and take up its productive aspects, we must address the important question of how we should approach meaning in life so that we can experience it in depth and derive from it the greatest satisfaction and fulfilment. To answer this question we have to address meaning at different levels, progressing from the most basic to the deepest transformative ones. Baumeister (1991) argues that meaning begins with the particular, the self, and gradually grows and reaches an integrative, all-encompassing level. Depth of meaning refers to the *quality* of an individual's experience of meaning (Reker, 2000, p. 9): 'Is the experience of meaning shallow, fragmented, and superficial or is it deep, integrated, and complex? We need to be able to differentiate between these seemingly different levels of meaning and to assess the extent to which they contribute to an overall sense of fulfilment'. To fully conceptualise and operationalise meaning, Rokeasch (1973) developed a hierarchical system that comprised four levels of meaning:

1   The lowest, basic level is that of *self-preoccupation*, where meaning is rooted in hedonistic pleasures and personal comforts.
2   The second level comprises resources that focus on the *realisation of personal potential*.
3   In the third level, meaning is derived from resources that are *beyond the realm of self-interests*, involving services to others and commitment to a larger social or political cause.
4   The final and highest level includes values that *transcend the self and others* by incorporating cosmic meaning and ultimate purpose.

These levels do not stand for a judgmental approach to meaning but rather reflect one's personal stages of development and identity building. Each of the levels serves as a unique background against which meaning is created and discovered. Each individual experiences depth of meaning corresponding to his or her stage of personal development, identity focus and schemas that accompany these two. The real challenge is to succeed in truly matching the depth of meaning with who we are at that particular stage in life. This is important because it enables dealing with the contradictions, conflicts and challenges of life by coupling them with their relevant, authentic levels of meaning (Prager, 1998).

Frankl (1963) was convinced that the only way to embrace the full meaning of life is by transcending self-interests. He maintains that such transcendence would occur when people shift their sources of meaning outwardly, away from their own needs, directing more love, hope, compassion and generosity at others. Frankl is not the only one to propose this progressive understanding of meaning; Wong (2009) and Seligman (2002) agree with Frankl that using our strengths to serve a greater good is a path to deeper fulfilment. The perspectives of Wong and Seligman reflect Rokeach's (1973) four levels of depth of meaning. All these scholars are of the opinion that deeper meaning would offer greater benefits to the individual. These claims also find support in Reker (1991), who concluded that individuals deriving meaning from the sources of level 3 and 4 are more fulfilled and satisfied with life than those who derive meaning from levels 1 and 2.

Reker and Wong (1988) define depth of meaning as the degree to which self-transcendence is realised; a greater depth of meaning requires higher levels of self-transcendence. This definition links this chapter with the previous one, which dealt with spirituality and the 'dark side' of self-awareness. Spirituality and meaning are frequently said to be interlinked (Emmons, 2005; Ivtzan et al., 2011; Mascaro, Rosen, & Morey, 2004), with meaning being at the heart of the spiritual experience. In both chapters the reader sees how engagement with potential self-transcendence may turn out to be hazardous under certain circumstances. In the case of spirituality, self-transcendence requires self-awareness which sometimes leads to psychological discomfort. The experience of meaning growing deeper and advancing towards self-transcendence may result in a mismatch between meaning and existent self-concepts, thereby triggering dysfunctional goals and purposes. But at the same time, the path towards self-transcendence has a high potential for joy and fulfilment. As long as self-awareness is approached with acceptance and compassion as part of the spiritual journey, and meaning deepens by maintaining relevant and authentic sources of meaning, self-transcendence has the potential of radically changing our lives in a manner that allows flourishing to be our most prominent psychological experience.

SUMMARY – THIS CHAPTER HAS ACCOMPLISHED THE FOLLOWING

- Described the concept of meaning and its interrelation with wellbeing
- Delineated meaning and purpose and their relationship with the 'dark side'
- Discussed the difference between the presence of meaning and the search for it

- Contemplated the changing sources of meaning during one's lifetime
- Discussed the relationship between authenticity and meaning while contemplating the impact of the 'dark side'
- Investigated the potentially dark side of meaning that stems from changes in meaning
- Explained the depth of meaning and its different levels
- Offered a practical meditative exercise to deepen the experience of meaning in life

RESOURCES AND SUGGESTIONS

- One of the most inspiring books relating to meaning and purpose is Viktor Frankl's *Man's Search for Meaning* (1963). This is an account of Frankl's struggle to survive in Nazi concentration and death camps and his incredible experience of finding meaning in the midst of these horrors.
- Dr Michael Steger is the leading researcher of meaning in PP. To read more about his work and the *laboratory for the study of meaning and quality of life*, you may wish to visit his website: http://www.michaelfsteger.com/.
- Paulo Coelho's (2011) book *Like the Flowing River: Thoughts and Reflections* is an inspiring collection of short stories. One story in particular, 'The Pianist in the Shopping Centre', embodies the heart and soul of meaning in life.

BIBLIOGRAPHY

Barrett-Lennard, G.T. (1998). *Carl Rogers' helping system: Journey and substance.* London: Sage.

Battista, J., & Almond, R. (1973). The development of meaning in life. *Psychiatry, 36,* 409–427.

Baumeister, R.F. (1991). *Meanings of life.* New York: Guilford.

Bonebright, C.A., Clay, D.L., & Ankenmann, R.D. (2000). The relationship of workaholism with work–life conflict, life satisfaction, and purpose in life. *Journal of Counseling Psychology, 47,* 469–477.

Carnegie, D. (1981). *How to win friends and influence people.* New York: Simon & Schuster.

Carver, C.S., Sutton, S.K., & Scheier, M.F. (2000). Action, emotion, and personality: Emerging conceptual integration. *Personality and Social Psychology Bulletin, 26,* 741–751.

Chamberlain, K., & Zika, S. (1988). Religiosity, life meaning, and wellbeing: Some relationships in a sample of women. *Journal for the Scientific Study of Religion, 27,* 411–420.

Coelho, P. (2011). *Like the flowing river: Thoughts and reflections.* New York: Harper.

Crumbaugh, J.C., & Maholick, L.T. (1964). An experimental study in existentialism: The psychometric approach to Frankl's concept of nöogenic neurosis. *Journal of Clinical Psychology, 20,* 200–207.

Debats, D. L., Van Der Lubbe, P. M., & Wezeman, F. R. A. (1993). On the psychometric properties of the Life Regard Index (LRI): A measure of meaningful life. *Personality and Individual Differences, 14,* 337–345.

Devogler, K. L., & Ebersole, P. (1980). *Categorization of college students' meaning of life. Psychological Reports, 46,* 387–390.

Ebersole, P. (1998). Types and depth of written life meaning. In P. T. P. Wong & P. S. Fry (Eds.), *The human quest for meaning: A handbook of psychological research and clinical application* (pp. 237–259). Mahwah, NJ: Erlbaum.

Elliot, A. J., & Thrash, T. M. (2002). Approach-avoidance motivation in personality: Approach and avoidance temperaments and goals. *Journal of Personality and Social Psychology, 82,* 804–818.

Emmons, R. A. (2003). Personal goals, life meaning, and virtue: Wellsprings of a positive life. In C. Keyes & J. Haidt (Eds.), *Flourishing: Positive psychology and the well-lived life* (pp. 105–128). Washington, DC: American Psychological Association.

Emmons, R. A. (2005). Striving for the sacred: personal goals, life meaning, and religion. *Journal of Social Issues, 61,* 731–745.

Erikson, E. H. (1963). *Childhood and society.* New York: Norton.

Fiske, M., & Chiriboga, D. A. (1991). *Change and continuity in adult life.* San Francisco: Jossey-Bass.

Fowler, J. W. (1983). Stages of faith: PT conversation with James Fowler. *Psychology Today, 17,* 56–62.

Frankl, V. E. (1963). *Man's search for meaning.* New York: Washington Square Press.

Fry, P. S. (1998). The development of personal meaning and wisdom in adolescence: A reexamination of moderating and consolidating factors and influences. In P. T. P. Wong & P. S. Fry (Eds.), *The human quest for meaning: A handbook of psychological research and clinical application* (pp. 91–110). Mahwah, NJ: Lawrence Erlbaum.

Harter, S. (2002). Authenticity. In C. R. Snyder & S. J. Lopez (Eds.), *Handbook of positive psychology* (pp. 382–394). Oxford, England: Oxford University Press.

Hedlund, B., & Birren, J. E. (1984). Distribution of types of meaning in life across women. Paper presented at the Gerontological Society of America, San Antonio, Texas, November.

Heine, S. J., Proulx, T., & Vohs, K. D. (2006). The meaning maintenance model: On the coherence of social motivations. *Personality and Social Psychology Review, 10,* 88–110.

Hicks, J. A., & King, L. A. (2009). Positive mood and social relatedness as information about meaning in life. *Journal of Positive Psychology, 4,* 471–482.

Ivtzan, I., Chan, C. P. L., Gardner, H. E., & Prashar, K. (2011). Linking religion and spirituality with psychological wellbeing: Examining self-actualisation, meaning in life, and personal growth initiative. *Journal of Religion and Health, 51,* 13–30.

Ivtzan, I., Young, T. K., Jeffrey, A. D., Martman, J. L., Hart, R., & Eiroa-Orosa, F. J. (2015). Integrating mindfulness into positive psychology: A randomised controlled trial of an eight-week positive mindfulness programme. Manuscript submitted for publication.

Jung, C. G. (1963). *Modern man in search of a soul*. New York: Harcourt Brace and World.

Jung, C. G. (1971). The stages of life. In R. F. C. Hill (Ed.), *The portable Jung*. New York: Viking.

Kaufman, S. R. (1986). *The ageless self*. New York: Meridian.

King, L. A. (2001). The health benefits of writing about life goals. *Personality and Social Psychology Bulletin, 27*, 798–807.

King, L. A., & Hicks, J. A. (2007) Whatever happened to 'What might have been'? Regrets, happiness, and maturity. *American Psychologist, 62*(7), 625–636.

Kinnier, R., Metha, A., Keim, J., Okey, J., Adler-Tapia, R., Berry, M., & Mulvenon, S. (1994). Depression, meaninglessness, and substance abuse in 'normal' and hospitalised adolescents. *Journal of Alcohol and Drug Education, 39*(2), 101–111.

Klinger, E. (1977). *Meaning and void*. Minneapolis: University of Minnesota Press.

Klinger, E. (1998). The search for meaning in evolutionary perspective and its clinical implications. In P. T. P. Wong & P. S. Fry (Eds.), *The human quest for meaning: A handbook of psychological research and clinical application* (pp. 27–50). Mahwah, NJ: Lawrence Erlbaum.

Levi, D. (1996). *Determining sources of meaning in life using focus groups of Israeli aged*. Unpublished master's theses, Bob Shapell School of Social Work, Tel Aviv University.

Littman-Ovadia, H., & Steger, M. F. (2010). Character strengths and well-being among volunteers and employees: Towards an integrative model. *Journal of Positive Psychology, 5*, 419–430.

Lukas, E. (1972). Zur Validierung der Logotherapie [Toward the validation of logotherapy]. In V. Frankel (Ed.), *Der Wille zum Sinn: Ausgewählte Vorträge über Logotherapie. [The will to meaning: Selected lectures on logotherapy]* (pp. 233–266). Bern, Switzerland: Huber.

Maddi, S. R. (1970). The search for meaning. In M. Page (Ed.), *Nebraska symposium on motivation* (pp. 137–186). Lincoln: University of Nebraska Press.

Mascaro, N., Rosen, D. H., & Morey, L. C. (2004). The development, construct validity, and clinical utility of the spiritual meaning scale. *Personality and Individual Differences, 37*, 845–860.

May, R. M. (1960). The emergence of existential psychology. In R. May (Ed.), *Existential psychology* (pp. 11–51). New York: Random House.

McDonald, M. J., Wong, P. T. P., & Gingras, D. T. (2012). Meaning-in-life measures and development of a brief version of the Personal Meaning Profile. In P. T. P. Wong (Ed.), *The human quest for meaning: Theories, research, and applications* (2nd ed., pp. 357–382). New York: Routledge.

Neugarten, B. L. (1968). Adult personality: Toward a psychology of the life cycle. In B. L. Neugarten (Ed.), *Middle age and aging*. Chicago, IL: University of Chicago Press.

Neugarten, B. L. (1964). *Personality in middle and late life*. New York: Atherton.

Newcomb, M., Bentler, P., & Fahey, B. (1987). Cocaine use and psychopathology: Associations among young adults. *International Journal of the Addictions, 22*, 1167–1188.

Pinquart, M. (2002). Creating and maintaining purpose in life in old age: A meta-analysis. *Ageing International, 27*, 90–114.

Prager, E. (1996). Exploring personal meaning in an age-differentiated Australian. Sample: Another look at the Sources of Meaning Profile (SOMP). *Journal of Aging Studies, 10*, 117–136.

Prager, E. (1998) Observations of personal meaning sources for Israeli age cohorts, *Aging & Mental Health, 2*(2), 128–136.

Prince, G. (1991). Narratology, narrative, and meaning. *Poetics Today, 12*, 543–552.

Reker, G. T. (1988). Sources of personal meaning among middle-aged and older adults: A replication. Paper presented at the Annual Meeting of the Gerontological Society of America, San Francisco.

Reker, G. T. (1991). Contextual and thematic analyses of sources of provisional meaning: A life-span perspective. Paper presented at the Biennial Meeting of the International Society for the Study of Behavioral Development, Minneapolis, MN.

Reker, G. T. (1992). *Manual of the life attitude profile – revised*. Peterborough, ON: Student Psychologists Press.

Reker, G. T. (2000). Theoretical perspective, dimensions, and measurement of existential meaning. In G. T. Reker & K. Chamberlain (Eds.), *Exploring existential meaning: Optimizing human development across the life span* (pp. 39–58). Thousand Oaks, CA: Sage.

Reker, G. T. (2005). Meaning in life of young, middle-aged, and older adults: Factorial validity, age, and gender invariance of the Personal Meaning Index (PMI). *Personality and Individual Differences, 38*, 71–85.

Reker, G. T., Peacock, E. J., & Wong, P. T. P. (1987). Meaning and purpose in life and well-being: A life-span perspective. *Journal of Gerontology, 42*, 44–49.

Reker, G. T., & Wong. P. T. P. (1988). Aging as an individual process: Toward a theory of personal meaning. In J. E. Birren & V. L. Bengston (Eds.), *Emergent theories of aging* (pp. 214–246). New York: Springer.

Rogers, C. (1961). *On becoming a person: A therapist's view of psychotherapy*. Boston: Houghton MiZin.

Rokeach, M. (1973). *The nature of human values*. New York: Free Press.

Ruffin, J. (1984). The anxiety on meaninglessness. *Journal of Counseling and Development, 63*, 40–42.

Ryff, C. D. (1989). Happiness is everything, or is it? Explorations of the meaning of psychological well-being. *Journal of Personality and Social Psychology, 57*, 1069–1081.

Ryff, C. D., & Essex, M. J. (1992). The interpretation of life experience and well-being: The sample case of relocation. *Psychology and Aging, 7*, 507–517.

Ryff, C. D., & Singer, B. (1998). The contours of positive human health. *Psychological Inquiry, 9*, 1–28.

Seligman, E. P. (2002*). Authentic happiness*. New York: Free Press.

Shin, J. Y., & Steger, M. F. (2014). Promoting meaning and purpose in life. In A. Parks (Ed.), *Positive psychology interventions*. Chicago, IL: Wiley.

Steger, M. F. (2009). Meaning in life. In S. J. Lopez (Ed.), *Oxford handbook of positive psychology* (2nd ed., pp. 679–687). Oxford, UK: Oxford University Press.

Steger, M. F. (2012). Making meaning in life. *Psychological Inquiry, 23*, 381–385.

Steger, M. F., & Dik, B. J. (2010). Work as meaning. In P. A. Linley, S. Harrington, & N. Page (Eds.), *Oxford handbook of positive psychology and work* (pp.131–142). Oxford, UK: Oxford University Press.

Steger, M. F., Frazier, P., Oishi, S., & Kaler, M. (2006). The Meaning in Life Questionnaire: Assessing the presence of and search for meaning in life. *Journal of Counseling Psychology, 53*, 80–93.

Steger, M. F., Kashdan, T. B., & Oishi, S. (2008). Being good by doing good: Daily eudaimonic activity and well-being. *Journal of Research in Personality, 42*, 22–42.

Steger, M. F., Oishi, S., & Kashdan, T. B. (2009). Meaning in life across the life span: Levels and correlates of meaning in life from emerging adulthood to older adulthood. *Journal of Positive Psychology, 4*, 43–52.

Thompson, N. J., Coker, J., Krause, J. S., & Henry, E. (2003). Purpose in life as a mediator of adjustment after spinal cord injury. *Rehabilitation Psychology, 48(2)*, 100.

Trilling, L. (1971). *Sincerity and authenticity.* Cambridge, MA: Harvard University Press.

Van Ranst, N., & Marcoen, A. (1997). Meaning in life of young and elderly adults: An examination of the factorial validity and invariance of the Life Regard Index. *Personality and Individual Differences, 22*, 877–884.

Wong, P. T. P. (1998). Spirituality, meaning, and successful aging. In P. T. P. Wong & P. S. Fry (Eds.), *The human quest for meaning: A handbook of psychological research and clinical applications* (pp. 359–394). Mahwah, NJ: Lawrence Erlbaum.

Wong, P. T. P. (2009). Positive existential psychology. In *Encyclopedia of positive psychology*. Oxford, UK: Blackwell.

Wong, P. T. P., & Fry, P. S. (1998). *The human quest for meaning: A handbook of psychological research and clinical application.* Mahwah, NJ: Erlbaum.

Yalom, I. D. (1980). *Existential psychotherapy.* New York: Basic Books.

Yang, W., Staps, T., & Hijmans, E. (2010). Existential crisis and the awareness of dying: The role of meaning and spirituality. *Omega, 61*, 53–69.

Zika, S., & Chamberlain, K. (1992). On the relation between meaning in life and psychological well being. *British Journal of Psychology, 83*, 133–145.

...d
...th

> ...e thing: the last of the human free-
> ...et of circumstances, to choose one's

Viktor Frankl

...to do the following:

(PTG)

List of terms:

- ... building resilience
- ...sustaining resilience
- ...Recovery, challenge and reconfiguration
- ...The six competencies
- Cognitive behavioural techniques
- Physical resilience

- ...cept of trauma
- ...l growth
- ...atic growth (PTG)
- Relationship between PTG and posttraumatic stress
- Models of PTG
- PTG interventions

As we progress through this life, we will inevitably encounter difficult times, necessitating the scientific understanding and applications of resilience and transformational growth research. This chapter will review the evidence supporting the possibility of individuals' capacity to stand strong in the face of adversity, bounce back after trauma and even thrive alongside suffering. More specifically, this chapter will review the differing definitions and perspectives of resilience throughout the lifespan as well as current applied programmes aimed at fostering these skills. The second part of this chapter will deconstruct the concept of transformational growth following trauma, with a particular emphasis on PTG. Thus, the 'dark side' is conceptualised within this chapter as those adverse or traumatic experiences we encounter, across the lifespan, that can evoke great discomfort, fear, pain, distress and confusion. However, when we engage with the 'dark side', there is great potential for growth, healing, insight and transformation. Thus, similar to the other chapters presented within this book, this one will argue that the 'dark side' contains the seed for a potential positive outcome, even when the path towards this outcome is testing.

PRACTICE ESSAY QUESTIONS

- Critically discuss the differences and similarities between the three main definitions of resilience.

- Critically debate the recent developments of PTG programmes.

THE INEVITABILITY OF LOSS AND SORROW

The inescapable difficulties that one encounters across the lifespan may be experienced during early childhood (e.g., poverty or abuse) or later on during adolescent development (e.g., heartbreak or bullying) and even well into adulthood (e.g., personal loss, serious illness). And yet, despite common preconceptions that we are doomed to crumble in the face of adversity, many of us are actually more resilient than we have been led to believe (Bonanno, 2004; Bonnano et al., 2002; Wilson & Gilbert, 2005). Overall, the 'dark times' that we will encounter can also provide us with the possibility of learning from our struggles to become psychologically stronger and ultimately grow as humans. Resilience is one way that we can try and understand how individuals can confront the 'dark side' successfully. This next section will review the current conceptualizations within this field of study as well as common measurement tools to assess the complexity of the discipline area and its links to the 'dark side'.

REFLECTION

Before every lecture I present on this topic, I ask the audience to think about how they would define the overly used term 'resilience'. At first, this task seems juvenile and even futile – everyone knows what resilience is. And yet, as we feed back the differing group definitions of resilience, the room turns from collective understanding to fierce debate. Students are offered differing perspectives and challenging notions of resilience that they had not previously considered. They are struck by the variations, and this chaotic reaction to such a seemingly simple question personifies the field of resilience research – a smorgasbord of differing, competing and complementary definitions, measurement tools and overall conceptualisations of what seems, at first, to be a relatively accepted term from the outside (Windle, 2011).

A HISTORY OF RESILIENCE

Psychological resilience may now exist as a cornerstone of PP; however, research into this phenomenon started many decades ago within the area of developmental psychology. Indeed, the amount of research dedicated to unravelling the intricacies of this seemingly simple construct has increased rapidly over the past 20 years (Windle, 2010). Early researchers were interested in studying how at-risk children survived and even thrived[1], against identified risk factors (e.g., birth complications, perinatal stress, poverty, uneducated parents, alcoholic parents or parent with mental health difficulties) as well as focusing on child, family and community protective factors (Werner, 1993, 1996; see Lomas et al., 2014 for full review). Later, researchers started to become interested in not just childhood resilience to difficult early environments (and/or cumulative risk) but general adult resilience to single and/or chronic negative life events (e.g., bereavement, illness or accidents) (Bonnano, 2004; Vanderbilt-Adriance & Shaw, 2008). Due to the vastness of this research area, we have chosen to narrow the focus of this chapter to predominantly reflecting upon the research and complexity experienced during the latter circumstances.

DEFINING RESILIENCE

Resilience is indeed a notoriously difficult concept to define. For example, a recent literature search on psychological resilience found 122 different definitions (Meredith et al., 2011, p. 20). On the whole, researchers have attempted to separate these differing definitions into three accepted types of resilience[2]. The first is 'resistance resilience', which reflects when someone has the strength to stand strong (maintains equilibrium) in the face of stressful or adverse situations. If using the analogy of a tree, the roots are firmly planted in the ground, and the tree weathers the storm arguably undisturbed as it might have been expected to. Other research has labelled this type of resilience the 'basic definition' and conceptualises resilience as 'a process or capacity that develops over time' (Meredith et al., 2011, p. 20). 'Recovery resilience' is displayed when one is able to bounce back or recover to previous (baseline) levels of functioning before the adverse event occurred. In this case, the tree does indeed bend and sway during the storm, however returns to its previous position once the storm has passed. Alternatively labelled as 'adaptation', this definition perceives resilience as akin to the notion of 'bouncebackability'. 'Reconfiguration resilience' is a third type of resilience and argues that something has changed since experiencing an adversity or traumatic event and is related to the concept of PTG (Lepore & Revenson, 2006). Also sometimes labelled as 'growth definitions', these infer that there was additional psychological or emotional growth following the event(s). Overall, recovery (adaptation) definitions of resilience (ability to bounce back) seem to be the most popular characterization of resilience in the research literature (Meredith et al., 2011).

Another hot topic within the resilience research is the contention that there is a 'resilient personality'. Although used in common language, the research suggests that there is no resilient personality per se but that it is more of a 'process of adjustment after experiencing significant adversity' and is therefore amenable to skills-based training

(Meredith et al., 2011; Revich & Shatte, 2002). Thus, resilience is not necessarily something you have or you don't have (Britt, Sinclair & McFadden, 2013). It is a dynamic process and will be experienced differently across the lifespan (Windle, 2010). Although some researchers have identified personality traits positively associated with resilience outcomes such as extraversion, contentiousness and hardiness (Sinclair, Waitsman, Oliver, & Deese, 2013), it is not clear whether these researchers believe that it is a 'single trait, collections of traits or an outcome of these traits' (p. 34). For example, researchers have focused on identifying personality traits or 'clusters' of personality traits associated with resilience and argue that these personality traits may be 'antecedents' of resilience (Sinclair et al., 2013, p. 22) and not actually components of resilience per se. Overall, the majority of researchers are reticent to label resilience as a stable personality trait (although there are tools to measure as such) as it may divide individuals into survivors and victims, implying 'that a person who does not have this attribute is somehow a failure' (Windle, 2010, p. 156).

MEASURING RESILIENCE: WHAT DOES RESILIENCE LOOK LIKE?

Now that we have categorised the different types of resilience, we need to think about what resilience actually *looks* like. How do we know when we have 'achieved' resilience? It is thus extremely important to reflect upon how resilience researchers operationally define resilience in terms of observable outcomes in their assessment of contextual and intervention research. In reality, resilience is what you want it to be. Or more specifically, resilience is how the researcher defines it. Thus, researchers need to be clear on how they are operationally defining resilience and what resilience 'looks' like to proclaim change. For example, in earlier PP research, resilience was conceptualised as the absence of depression or presence of optimism (Gillham et al., 2006). Within early development research, resilience was defined as 'meeting of societal expectations and behaviors, the absence of undesirable behaviors, mental illness, emotional distress, criminal behaviors, risk taking; and the meeting of developmental markers (e.g. social milestones) (Masten, Herbers, & Reed, 2009, p. 118). Thus, you could arguably have one researcher defining resilience as increased positive emotions, another as reduced depression and a third as being socially intimate with others. Indeed, how you define and measure resilience will depend on the type of resilience you are trying to show exists.

There are however, several specifically identified 'resilience scales' in the current academic literature. Windle, Bennett, & Noyes (2011) conducted what is arguably the most rigorous review of the level of quality within resilience measurements, a review of commonly used 'resilience scales', as they were concerned that these tools varied considerably in their acceptance within academia. After isolating 15 scales for review, they concluded that the Connor-Davidson resilience scale (CD-RISC) (Connor & Davidson, 2003), the resilience scale for adults (RSA) (Friborg et al. 2003) and the brief resilience scale (Smith et al., 2008) scored highest amongst the 15; however, they were all considered of modest quality overall. These scales were also tested with and for adult populations only. The measures were further criticised for not being culturally sensitive, arguing that resilience might look like something different depending on the culture one finds oneself in (especially if the criteria for assessing resilience has been labelled as meeting socially determined milestones; e.g., Masten et al., 2009). Indeed, the concept of resilience may not even be 'comparable across cultures' (Windle, et al. 2011, p. 15). Overall, there is no one 'gold-standard', agreed-upon tool that assesses resilience, and so researchers need to include valid measurement tools that adhere to their theoretical approach and population chosen. Indeed, this incredible variability across researchers, context and populations can make cross comparison of findings extremely difficult (Meredith et al., 2011).

FOSTERING RESILIENCE

Despite these methodological issues, there have been several successful resilience programmes created that have focused on developing core resilience skills. Effective and evidence-based resilience programmes have been found to include variables that not only focus on decreasing negative psychological and physical functioning in the face of stress and adversity but also increasing positive functioning in day-to-day life. Meredith et al. (2011) identified 20 factors[3] that were associated with promoting resilience. They found that individual-level resilience factors were the most often utilised in resilience programmes and the top three components with moderate[4] and strong[5] evidence supporting them including: *positive coping, positive affect* and *positive thinking* (followed by realism and behavioural control; see Table 4.1).

Overall, the majority of PP resilience (preventative-approach) programmes tend to include these evidence-based individual factors and focus heavily on facilitating and fostering these top-three resilience factors (Brunwasser et al., 2009; Reivich & Shatte, 2002). The next section will delve deeper into the overarching key component within these programmes, perception and cognition, and their role in resilient functioning.

TABLE 4.1 Resilience Factors (Adapted from Meredith et al., 2011, p. 21)

Level	Resilience Factor	Example
Individual	Positive coping	*Offering skills in adaptive coping such as problem-focused coping*
	Positive affect	*Increasing exposure to positive emotions, optimism, hope, and so on*
	Positive thinking	*Positive reframing, goals training*
	Realism	*Learning to have understanding of locus of control, self-efficacy and self-worth*
	Behavioural control	*The inclusion of activities to increase self-regulation and self-discipline such as monitoring techniques*

REFLECTION

If you were to create your own resilience programme for your chosen population, what would it look like?

- What would it include?

- How long would it run for?

- What format would it take (e.g., weekly sessions, homework, in class)?

- What would you want the outcome to be?

- How would you know when you have achieved this?

COGNITIVE BEHAVIOURAL PSYCHOLOGY: BUILDING RESILIENCE

As previously stated, several PP resilience programmes are underpinned by cognitive behavioural psychology, which stems from cognitive behavioural therapy (CBT), a recognized therapeutic intervention. CBT emerged in the 1960s as a form of psychotherapy that identified thought distortions as the reason for depression (Beck, 2011). Since then, there have been several successful adaptations of this approach (e.g., rational emotional behaviour therapy [REBT]), and some would argue that we are now on to the third wave of CBT approaches (e.g., mindfulness and acceptance).

The main premise of CBT is that 'when people learn to evaluate their thinking in a more realistic and adaptive way, they experience improvement in their emotional state and their behavior (sic)' (Beck, 2011, p. 3). There have been several hundred studies conducted on CBT showing successful outcomes on a range of physical and psychological issues ranging from general mood improvements to addressing severe psychological disorders (Beck, 2011). These techniques have been used successfully on a variety of participants ranging from small children to war veterans (Stallard, 2003). The techniques are short term and time limited, and the process is collaborative and owned by the participants.

The cognitive model that underpins this approach argues that thinking affects how a person feels (emotionally and physiologically) and what they then do (behaviourally). The model also highlights the multi-directional ways in which thinking, feeling and doing (behaviors) are linked. The point of this model is not to prescribe rigidly to one mode of direction being stronger or 'better' than another but to bring awareness to these links and how they can affect subsequent areas in our life. By becoming aware of how our thinking affects our feelings and behaviors as well as the other directional influences, we are arguably better able to step back, look at situations rationally, find more appropriate solutions and enable the chance to increase our psychological resilience and wellbeing.

REFLECTION

'For there is nothing either good or bad, but thinking makes it so'

(Shakespeare, *Hamlet*, Act 2, Scene 2, p. 11).

What do you think of this statement? Do you have any personal experience or examples that support or contradict this statement?

It is important to note that cognitive behavioural techniques can and have been used successfully within various settings outside of therapy. For example, PP resilience programmes tend to be aimed at teaching attendees to identify, evaluate and where appropriate, change their negative thinking patterns. These programmes also tend to engage only at the surface to intermediate level. They are not usually aimed at challenging attendees to discuss or dissect their core beliefs as this is more appropriately tackled over time and with a trained professional. Participants of resilience programmes can become aware of their automatic thoughts, which are manifestations of their core and fundamental beliefs (Beck, 2011). By doing this at a superficial level, individuals can identify distorted ways of thinking but not necessarily aim to modify the core ways they think about themselves, others and the world. This has been deemed as much more achievable in the early stages of engaging with the cognitive model (Beck, 2011). Finally, these resilience programmes tend not to deal with real adversities, although the topics and tools within them can certainly help build the psychological skills and resources required to help buffer the effects of future adversity and stress (Fredrickson et al., 2003). In sum, they offer techniques to identify maladaptive thought patterns and are to be used in the following situations:

* Reactions to events are not in proportion with the event.
* Individuals are confused about their reactions.
* Individuals realise their reactions are draining them.
* They wish to find another, more adaptive way of reacting.

EXERCISES TO TRY . . . ABCS (BECK, 2011)

Activating events are everyday occurrences that really 'get to you'; they can push your buttons and demonstrate **consequences** (feelings and behaviours) that are out of proportion to the event itself. These will be very unique to you. When teaching this model, it is easier to teach in an A–C couplet as we tend to think something happens – and we respond. But there is something going on in the middle, a **belief** that is causing the maladaptive reaction. This is what cognitive behavioural

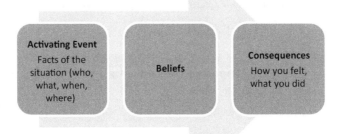

FIGURE 4.1 The ABC Process

techniques aim to bring awareness to – the belief – to bring about adaptive change.

So let's try out an ABC exercise . . .

Acknowledge your own activating events

Please think about events that happen that really get you going. Is it being cut off in traffic? Children not taking out the bin? Make a note as to how much they get to you. You may find you have more or less in certain areas of your life.

Activating event 1:

Activating event 2:

Activating event 3:

Now think of the **consequences** of these actions:

How did they make you *feel*?

What did you *do*?

Now we will step back and reflect upon the **belief:**

What was going through your mind?

Challenging and creating alternative interpretations

Is there a way to challenge your belief? For example, is this interpretation 100 percent true?

What and where is the evidence? Note down examples the support or contradict your beliefs. When you reflect on the list, what is the evidence supporting?

Creating alternative interpretations

If you find that your list is skewed, you can try and delve deeper and create others ways of interpreting the event. What information are you missing? What else could be influencing the situation?

PHYSICAL RESILIENCE

Finally, last, but not least, researchers have proposed that the body can play a role in improving individual's psychological resilience. The somatopsychic principle (Harris, 1973) argues that physical activities that engage and improve the physical functioning of the body can have a reciprocal effect on the positive functioning on the mind. Thus, we can build strong and psychologically healthy individuals via a strong and healthy body (*Mens sana en corpore sane*, or healthy body equals a healthy mind) (Faulkner, Hefferon, & Mutrie, 2015; Hefferon, 2013). For example, decades of research has shown that engaging in acute and chronic sessions of physical activity has been linked to increased positive emotions (Reed & Buck, 2009; Reed & Ones, 2006); increased positive body image and self-perception (Ginis, Bassett-Gunter, & Conlin, 2012); reduced depression (Babyak et al., 2000; Blumenthal et al., 1999, 2007) and reduced anxiety (Petruzzello, 2012). Physical activity also has been lauded as an important component of resilience programmes (Meredith et al., 2001) and is included in the programmes that we, the authors, create and promote for a holistic approach to optimal functioning (please see Hefferon, 2013, for a full review).

TRANSFORMATIONAL GROWTH[6]

The next section will shift from the focus on bouncing back or standing strong in the face of adversity and take a closer look at how some individuals report positive changes and transformational growth from confronting the 'dark side' – their adverse experiences. Throughout millennia, societies have held versions of the same message, albeit told or portrayed in different ways: The experience of difficult and painful times can lead to positive transformation. Many religions, such as Christianity and Judaism, as well as philosophical writings (e.g., Nietzsche and Yalom) and more recently psychological research (e.g., Tedeschi & Calhoun, 1995) have attempted to link and understand the complex relationship between adversity and subsequent growth. Today, this line of research could be argued to fall under the umbrella term of 'adversarial growth', coined by Linley and Joseph (2004) to encompass a collection of terms that focus on positive changes following trauma, including: 'posttraumatic growth, stress-related growth, perceived benefits, thriving, blessings, positive by-products, positive adjustment, and positive adaptation' (p. 11). The differences between these topics of study have been debated, and although they are typically used interchangeably, they have been found to be independent constructs (Jansen et al., 2011)[7]. Positive changes from adversity have been found across a variety of different traumas ranging from cancer to combat to sexual assault (Joseph et al., 2005).

At the present moment, the most widely researched construct underneath the adversarial growth umbrella is PTG and thus will be the focus for the rest of this chapter. Although there is a general lack of clarity regarding definitions within the discipline area, PTG is commonly defined as 'the experience of positive change that the individual experiences as a result of the struggle with a traumatic event' (Calhoun & Tedeschi, 2013, p. 6). The underlying premise here is 'the possibility that positive change could be set in motion by the encounter with difficult life situations' (p. 6). It is extremely important to note that the focus is not to advocate suffering as a situation worth striving for but rather to examine how engaging with the 'dark side', experiencing suffering and grief, can also co-exist with enlightenment and growth (Linley & Joseph, 2004). PTG is actually much more common than many people assume, ranging from 30 to 90 percent of a variety of traumas reporting at least some elements of PTG (Calhoun & Tedeschi, 2013). Research into PTG has been conducted across several continents including North and South America, Australia, Europe, Asia and Africa, demonstrating the possibility of this transformative experience having cross-cultural existence (Calhoun & Tedeschi, 2013; Weiss & Berger, 2010).

REFLECTION

What are your thoughts on the differences between PTG and resilience? Tedeschi, Addington, Cann, & Calhoun (2014) suppose that this relationship between the two constructs is indeed complex. Although a person may require resilience skills (e.g., adaptive coping) at the start of the process of PTG, the authors contend that ultimately, PTG leads to resilience. What do you think?

DEFINING TRAUMA

The first question we need to tackle when attempting to understand the links between the 'dark side' (trauma and adversity) and the potential for growth is how one defines trauma. There are several perspectives and models within PTG research using differing definitions of what trauma actually means. The majority of these models use the original work of Janoff-Bulman's (1992) Shattered Assumptions Theory, which claims that at the core of our inner world or personal narrative, there are fundamental assumptions of a sense of safety and security. Trauma occurs when these assumptions are tested and our sense of security is 'shattered': '*At the most fundamental level of our inner world, we believe that who we are and how we act determine what happens to us: if we are good people (justice) and we engage in appropriately precautionary behaviours (control) bad things will not happen to us*' (Janoff-Bulman, 2004, p. 33).

Tedeschi and Calhoun have previously defined 'trauma' as 'those events that have a seismic impact on the individuals assumptive world' (Calhoun & Tedeschi, 2013, p. 16), where the event creates a sense of 'before and after', is unexpected and out of the ordinary, creates long-lasting problems and substantially interrupts a person's narrative (Tedeschi & Calhoun, 1995, 2006). PTG is therefore defined as the process of engaging with painful realisations of reality (the 'dark side'), rebuilding around the traumatic experience and thus acknowledging the trauma in a non-anxious way.

REFLECTION

What are some issues that you can see with the aforementioned definitions of 'trauma'? One difficulty that emerges is when we contemplate situations where there is no one defined trauma or multiple or secondary traumas (e.g., cancer). Indeed, there is a dire lack of longitudinal, multi-method PTG research that attempts to understand how people experience trauma(s) and positive change over time. This is an exciting and necessary area of inquiry for PTG researchers.

CONCEPTUALISING PTG

There are currently two main theoretical perspectives within PTG. The first stems from the originators of the concept, Tedeschi and Calhoun (1995). This perspective contends that there are five main areas of change reported by survivors and assessed by the main questionnaire in use. These areas are identified as: *personal strength, relating to others, new possibilities in life, appreciation of life and spirituality*. These can cluster further into three overarching areas of change, including: *a changed sense of oneself, a changed sense of relationship with others* and *a changed philosophy in life*.

The first domain, 'personal strength', refers to reported changes to the self. This tends to represent narratives such as feeling stronger in the self, the belief that if the person can get through such an adverse situation, then they are better prepared for future stressors and adversity. They also report feeling more authentic, a deeper and 'better' self, having gone through their adverse experience. Individuals also can discuss becoming more open and empathetic to others, especially those who have gone through similar situations. For individuals who experience trauma at an early age, some can report maturing faster than their peers. Trauma also can bring a sense of humility via the recognition that we cannot control everything in our lives and we are not as invincible as we may believe (Calhoun & Tedeschi, 2013; see Hefferon et al., 2009, for review).

The second domain, 'relating to others', refers to the reporting of changed and most often, closer relationships with family members and/or friends. Following trauma, individuals have relayed instances where neighbours would rise up to help and support the family. They can also report newfound bonds with fellow trauma survivors. One potentially distressing element can be that individuals report losing friends; although this is difficult at the time, they discuss benefits in finding out who their true friends really are (Calhoun & Tedeschi, 2013; Hefferon et al., 2009). This identification of closer relationships is important when considering the next domain, 'changed philosophy in life', which encompasses an individual's increased appreciation for life, most often due to heighted existential awareness. Reflections on one's own mortality (the 'dark side') can cause one to start to think about the meaning in life as well as the limited amount of time they have left and with whom and how they want to spend it (see Chapter 5 for a review of the transformational benefits of mortality). This links to the 'changed priorities' domain, in which individuals discuss altering their previously held extrinsic priorities to become more intrinsic (e.g., money and appearance tend to shift to more simple things such as time, health, nature, etc.) as well as goals (e.g., some reports changes to life goals such as returning to school to study or retrain in a new skill).

Finally, following trauma, an individual can undertake the questioning of spiritual matters, such as the concepts and roles of the universe, nature, a god, religion, and so on. Although often taken as a religious component to PTG, this domain refers more widely to spirituality changes and can occur outside of organised religions. The strengthening of spirituality is a contentious element of the overall model and is found more often in the bereavement literature. Furthermore, the importance and existence of this domain differs across cultures and genders (Tedeschi et al., 2010). Overall, research has shown it is possible that by confronting the difficult and uncomfortable questions and circumstances – the dark side – that arise following trauma, there is the potential for transformation and growth across a variety of life domains.

CAVEATS OF PTG

Despite this potential for growth following trauma, there are important things to note with regard to this conceptualisation of PTG. The first is in relation to the five main domains. These are not presented in any sequential or hierarchal order, nor do you need to have all five domains to 'grow'. You could identify with one, two or more as well as report significant decreases in other domains. The second point is that PTG is not a state of 'hedonic happiness' or denial of the trauma experience. Indeed, PTG can co-exist with distress (discussed further later); '[p]osttraumatic growth is not necessarily an experience that leads people to feel less pain from tragedies they have experienced, nor does it necessarily lead to an increase in positive emotions' (Calhoun & Tedeschi, 2013, p. 21). Thirdly, researchers clearly state that PTG does not arise from the trauma itself but the personal struggle following the trauma; "[i]t is through this process of struggling with adversity that changes may arise that propels the individual to a higher level of functioning than which existed prior to the event' (Linley & Joseph, 2004, p. 11). This gives power back to the individual and not the traumatic event as something worth 'wishing for'. Finally, PTG is not a universal phenomenon and should not be expected of all trauma survivors (e.g., tyranny of positive thinking). Furthermore, from my own research experience, I would like to highlight that these domains may not encompass the entirety of the PTG experience (e.g., health behaviour changes and corporeal awareness); Hefferon et al., 2009) and the original authors have acknowledged that there may be other reported changes not mentioned, especially according to trauma type and experience (Calhoun & Tedeschi, 2013).

> ## REFLECTION
>
> What do you think of Tedeschi and Calhoun's conceptualisation of PTG?
> Is there anything you feel is missing?

The second main PTG perspective stems from researchers Stephen Joseph and Alex Linley, who have presented an alternative model, the organismic valuing theory of PTG, which situates PTG as an increase in eudaimonic (versus hedonic) wellbeing (Joseph, 2013). PTG is conceptualised as potential positive changes that are akin to psychological growth as defined by Ryff (1989): self-acceptance, personal growth, autonomy, purpose in life, environmental mastery and positive relations with others. Thus, the organismic valuing theory model posits that all humans are geared towards growth and that traumatic situations (the 'dark side') can catapult a person into engaging with this growth process. Under this model, PTG is therefore conceptualised as a journey, not necessarily a destination (Joseph, 2013).

> ## REFLECTION
>
> Recently there have been additional conceptualisations regarding what
> PTG actually is. For example, it could be considered as the cognitive
> restructuring of a person's life story (Pals & McAdams, 2004) or even
> more recently proposed – a personality change (Jayawickreme & Blackie,
> 2014) – focused on assessing the malleability of personality change in the
> aftermath of trauma or significant events. What do you think of these
> alternative conceptualisations?

PROCESS OF PTG

Again, both of the aforementioned main models have proposed differing models on the process of approaching the 'dark side' and eventual positive transformation and growth, according to their own perspectives. The next section will review these models as well as the measurement tools used to assess them.

The transformational model (Tedeschi & Calhoun, 1995; Groleau, Calhoun, Tedeschi, & Cann, 2013) is the most widely used model of PTG (although many do not realise they are ascribing to this model when undertaking research using the posttraumatic growth inventory [PTGI]) and proposes that PTG mainly results from excessive rumination (or cognitive processing) following a seismic event. The model begins with the person pre-trauma: they exist with their own characteristics, such as personality traits, gender, assumptions about how the world works and current life goals. Following this seismic event, their assumptive world is shattered and requires them to re-evaluate their core beliefs. To do so, they engage in a series of stages aimed at managing excessive rumination. At first, rumination about the event and the circumstances surrounding it is automatic, intrusive and unwelcome and encompasses a person's life world. As the person moves through the model, this automaticity slows down, becoming more deliberate and focused, and there is an attempt to garner meaning from the event. Thus, it is at this point we see how engaging with the 'dark side' can transform into positive experience, such as meaning in this case. It is also during this time that the model purports that engaging in social support (proximal and distal) as well as self-disclosure and self-analysis are important to the growth process (Tedeschi & Calhoun, 2006). From this discursive stage, individuals then become more able to reflect in deliberate and constructive rumination that eventually leads to acceptance of their 'changed world' and PTG (Calhoun & Tedeschi, 2013, p. 17). The model also purports that one's life narrative has become more complex, and there may be an increase in wisdom along with wellbeing and adjustment. Finally, the model accepts that throughout this process, emotional distress arising from the struggle of engaging with shattered assumptions can co-exist. Overall, this model places a heavy emphasis on the role of cognitive processing and its positive role in the recovery and growth process (Janoff-Bulman, 1992).

The organismic valuing theory stems from a person-centred approach and states that all humans are oriented towards growth (Joseph & Linley, 2005). This model focuses primarily on how people rebuild their previous assumptions following a traumatic event. The authors argue that how a person incorporates traumatic events into his or her world view (either via accommodation or assimilation) will dictate whether an individual returns to his or her previous baseline (albeit more fragile than before) and arguably more susceptible to depression and/or helplessness or goes on to experience positive growth. Assimilation occurs when a person keeps his or her 'old world view' and does not alter his or her pre-trauma schemas (Joseph & Linley, 2008). Assimilation can therefore cause individuals to become potentially more vulnerable to future stressors as they have not attempted to renegotiate their assumptive world. Thus, not engaging with the 'dark side' can lead to negative or harmful consequences. Accommodation on the other hand, is when an individual engages with this new, yet difficult, reality and uses this information to rebuild assumptions. A wonderful analogy of this process of growth is *the theory of the shattered vase* (Joseph, 2012): when a vase shatters into many pieces, one can try and put all the pieces back together with glue. From afar, the vase might look like it used to, but up close, you will see that it is riddled with tiny cracks and any slight knock will cause it to shatter again (assimilation). However, you could decide to take those pieces and make something different, like a mosaic. Thus, you might create something altered but potentially more beautiful than what was once there (accommodation). Overall, this model aims to explain why some may or may not experience growth and aligns the outcome of PTG to a form of eudaimonic wellbeing.

MEASURING PTG

To date, the most commonly used approach to PTG measurement is through self-report questionnaires. The most widely used tool is the PTGI (Tedeschi & Calhoun, 1998). The PTGI is a retrospective, self-report tool that asks individuals to reflect on their experiences and identify how much they have changed as a result of their identified traumas. The PTGI has 'good to excellent' internal consistency and test–re-test reliability scores (Calhoun & Tedeschi, 2013, p. 14). The authors of the scale report that social desirability does not play factor in the com- *La* pletion of the questionnaire and has found that changes have been corroborated by close others (Calhoun & Tedeschi, 2013; Shakespeare-Finch & Enders, 2008)[8]. The PTGI consists of 21 items across five domains. The scale ranges from a score of 0 to 105; however, it is important to note that one may have an overall score that is low but may score high in one particular domain (Calhoun & Tedeschi, 2013). Finally, the researchers state that the PTGI was created for research purposes only and was not intended for clinical use (Calhoun & Tedeschi, 2013).

As there are differing perspectives on what PTG actually is, there are several other commonly used scales to assess PTG and positive changes from trauma including, but not limited to, world assumptions scale (Jannoff-Bulman, 1989); core beliefs inventory (Cann et al., 2010); stress-related growth scale (SRGS) (Park, Cohen, & Murch, 1996); psychological wellbeing – posttraumatic changes questionnaire (PWB-PTCQ) (Joseph et al., 2012); changes in outlook questionnaire (CIOQ) (Joseph, Williams, & Yule, 1993); silver lining scale (Sodergren & Hyland, 2000) and benefit finding scale (BFS; Antoni et al., 2001; Park & Lechner, 2006). It is important that researchers understand the benefits and limitations of each tool, as well as their theoretical and practical backgrounds, when choosing the appropriate scale to use for their own research purposes.

Finally, at present, the majority of PTG research is cross-sectional and retrospective in nature, and thus methodological concerns regarding the use of these tools has been raised when interpreting the current set of literature (please see Jayawickreme & Blackie, 2014, plus open commentary reports for further discussion). Furthermore, longitudinal and prospective designs are required to assess change over time and from trauma experiences. Although this type of research design is extremely difficult to engineer, there are examples of such designs in practice (e.g., Bonnano et al., 2002; Frazier et al., 2009; Manne et al., 2004). Finally, the introduction of biomarkers will help advance the understanding of positive outcomes beyond subjective reports of growth.

REFLECTION

As far as the authors are aware, there is only one study to date exploring the neural correlates of PTG using electroencephalography. Rabe, Zöllner, Maercker, and Karl (2006) analysed the brain activity of survivors (n = 82) of severe motor accidents. Their analysis drew on Davidson's (2000) theory that individual differences in asymmetric activation of the prefrontal cortex (PFC) is linked to affective style, with greater left-sided activation (relative to right-sided activation) being associated with 'approach behaviour' and higher levels of self-reported subjective wellbeing. As predicted, the authors found that PTG was associated with increased left PFC activation, even after controlling for dispositional positive affect. What are your thoughts on these findings? How else do you think we could assess PTG from a biological perspective?

IS PTG A 'GOOD THING'?

As mentioned in the opening section on adversarial growth, the research field is a complex mix of constructs and outcomes linked to PTG. In the early days of inquiry, researchers were concerned with the identification, prevalence and associated variables of positive change following adversity and trauma (Jayawickreme & Blackie, 2014). It was during this time that research began to show that the existence of benefits finding and accounts of positive change in the aftermath of tragedy had positive outcomes above and beyond the reports themselves (e.g., less distress, less depression and increased wellbeing; Helgeson, Reynolds, & Tomich, 2006). Furthermore, if we conceptualise PTG as an increase in eudaimonic wellbeing (Joseph, 2012), then this is arguably a 'positive' outcome in itself as research has shown the links between higher levels of eudaimonic wellbeing and positive mental health (Joseph, 2012).

However, at the present time, one of the most interesting developments within the research field has been the paradoxical positive association between posttraumatic stress and PTG; the two seem to 'go hand in hand' (Joseph, 2012, p. 91). Indeed, individuals are likely to feel negative emotions such as sadness, fear, anxiety or guilt as well as experience intrusive ruminations regarding the adverse events. However, posttraumatic stress ranges along a continuum, and whilst most people exhibit distress in immediate aftermath, only a small minority will go on to experience a psychiatric diagnosis of posttraumatic stress disorder (PTSD) (Calhoun & Tedeschi, 2013). Calhoun et al. (2010) urge readers to think about PTG and pain or distress along two independent dimensions, where 'changes in one will not necessarily be related to changes in the other" (p. 20). Furthermore, these natural reactions may actually kick-start the process of PTG (Joseph, 2012).

Thus, in the initial aftermath of trauma, PTG and posttraumatic stress symptoms have been found to be positively associated, arguably due to intrusive rumination and shattering of assumptions (Engelhard, Lommen, & Sijbrandij, 2014). Shakespeare-Finch and Lurie-Beck (2014) conducted a meta-analysis on 42 papers and concluded that there was indeed a significant linear relationship between PTG and PTSD; however, there was stronger evidence of a curvilinear relationship, in that high levels of PTSD were associated with higher levels of PTG. This became detrimental once a certain critical point was reached with regard to the severity of symptoms. Furthermore, the analyses showed that this relationship was moderated by trauma type and age such that civilians in conflict zones and natural disasters demonstrated the strongest association. There was a weak and non-existent relationship between the two variables for traumas such as illness (of the self or others), carers and health professionals. The relationship was seen to be stronger for children versus adults; however, there were noted issues with small samples (n = 2 studies) and trauma type (civilians of conflict) that may have confounded the findings. Overall, Shakespeare-Finch & Lurie-Beck (2014) urge researchers to note that the small statistical findings between the association found within their meta-analysis be taken with caution as 'just because the relationship between PTG and PTSD is significant statistically, does not mean the relationship found is significant practically or psychologically' (p. 227). Above all, they contend that therapists and researchers must continue the search for understanding what can help the survivor first and foremost.

APPLYING PTG: THE RISE IN PROGRAMMES

Although research into PTG has been underway since the mid-1990s, the possibility of attempting to facilitate this phenomenon was deemed potentially inappropriate given the already existing pressures individuals experience in the aftermath of trauma. Furthermore, the area was very adamant that it did not want to perpetuate the 'tyranny of positive thinking' (Ehrenreich, 2010; Held, 2003). However, the recent decade has seen the development and testing of several variations of PTG programmes (e.g., clinical practice, online and self-help options and group-based interventions), which this last section will now review.

PTG IN CLINICAL PRACTICE

In 2008, there was the emergence of the first, structured guidelines on facilitating PTG by the original researchers Tedeschi and Calhoun (2008). Their acknowledgement and facilitation of PTG in clinical practice has been offered not as an 'alternative' to other therapeutic techniques and approaches but rather to add to and enhance 'best practice' (Calhoun & Tedeschi, 2013, p. 2).

Their approach purports the role of the therapist as the 'expert companion' (Calhoun & Tedeschi, 2013, p. 2). The stance one is guided to take is one of non-judgement as a way of trying to help clients create a narrative that attempts to makes sense of what has happened to them. The therapist then starts to learn from the client. As they are not advised to engage in direct attempts to foster growth, they must be aware of the categories of PTG and listen for them in the client's sessions. If these arise, the therapist can then acknowledge them and discuss them in the clients own words. The therapist also must help the client to see that the growth is attributable to his or her own struggle and hard work and not as a result of events alone. This gives back power to the client and away from the trauma itself. Indeed, therapists need to be aware of the concept of the 'dark side', the difficulty clients can face when confronting the 'dark side' and yet the potential positive outcomes from doing so, such as the journey towards personal growth.

Although there are current debates within the academic field of PTG regarding methodology and assessment, Tedeschi and Calhoun purport that this line of argumentation may not be useful for the clinical setting where therapists work one to one; "we tend to simply accept as genuine the reports of growth that our clients make" (Calhoun & Tedeschi, 2013, p. 16). They argue that in their long history of research, they have not come across anyone whose narrative of growth was linked to 'self-enhancing distortions' (p. 16), and as such therapists are advised not to deny distress and go with the clients' understanding of what has happened to them. Overall, they argue that PTG should not be used solely as the sign of a good intervention as it is not a universal experience and therefore cannot be the benchmark for success (Tedeschi & Calhoun, 2008).

TRY ME

After learning about the 'expert companion', please think about a time when you may have acted as an 'expert companion' to a friend, fellow survivor or even client. How did you engage with them and this process? How might you engage with this experience in the future?

POSTTRAUMATIC GROWTH PROGRAMMES

The creation of posttraumatic growth programmes based on identified facilitators (e.g., social support, rumination and adaptive coping styles) has recently become a feasible endeavour, and there are currently several programmes under investigation (Joseph, 2012; Seligman & Mathews, 2011). PTG is a relatively malleable concept that has been shown to enhance after a relatively short amount of time and intervention (Wagner, Müller, & Maercker, 2011). These programmes can be thought of as interventions aimed at increasing the chance that engagement with the 'dark side' would be translated into personal growth instead of helplessness and depression.

At present, the most notable intervention is the singular module within the Comprehensive Soldier Family Fitness (CSFF) programme offered by the United States Army (Tedeschi & McNally, 2011). Informed by the original researchers of PTG, this module is one of many resilience-based online sessions that comprise the CSFF. During this module, participants are taught the biological (e.g., stress response) and psychological (e.g. shattered assumptions about the world, themselves and the future) responses to trauma. They are then taught techniques they can use to reduce their anxiety as well as manage their automatic and intrusive thoughts. Participants are also encouraged to engage in 'constructive self-disclosure', which is a key component to the Tedeschi and Calhoun model of PTG. Finally, the latter part of the module aims to help participants create a 'trauma narrative', identifying the trauma as a 'fork' in the road. Within this section, they are also asked to discuss the strengths they used to get through the trauma as well as identify instances where relationships improved; how their own spiritual life strengthened; how they appreciated life better; what new opportunities arose and what new philosophies they learned as a result of the struggle with their adversity (Seligman, 2011; Tedeschi & McNally, 2011). Although the full programme itself has been criticised (Eidelson et al., 2011), this module was the first of its kind and is arguably the largest-scale implementation of a PTG programme to date.

THRIVE (Joseph, 2013) is a self-help programme offered by the UK's leading PTG researcher and clinical practitioner, Professor Stephen Joseph (2012)[9]. Joseph offers six signposts that can help individuals reflect upon their experiences and potentially foster growth. Before this though, Joseph offers three main messages:

1   You are not alone in your experience.
2   Trauma is natural and a process.
3   Growth is a journey (pp. 185–186).

The first signpost is 'taking stock', where at a very basic level, individuals take stock of the resources they have and those that are missing. These basics include checking that the person is physically safe, obtaining the necessary medical and psychological attention and taking care of his or her body (eating, sleeping and being active). This signpost also encourages people to take care of themselves emotionally by engaging in relaxation and self-compassion techniques as well as engaging with their own emotions. The second signpost is 'harvesting hope', where survivors are encouraged to practice hope and look for examples within their frames of reference. 'Re-authoring', the third signpost, suggests the use of metaphors and expressive writing in re-authoring a person's mindset from victim to survivor and even thriver. 'Identifying change' asks the person to reflect upon the positive changes that have happened each day via a diary. 'Valuing change' encourages survivors to embrace what has gone well, what they value now and what they are grateful for. Finally, 'expressing change in action' encourages active engagement with the changes reported – essentially putting growth in action (Joseph, 2012, p. 220).

TRY ME

The main PTG programmes focus on re-writing the personal narrative. This is because after the shattering of previous assumptions, we need to 'rewrite' our previous goals, beliefs and so on in light of this new trauma information. Creating these new stories can help us make sense of and find meaning in experiences as well move forward and grow. One way we can do this is by writing about how you have grown as a person as a result of your struggles with your experience. You can draw upon the Values in Action (VIA) character strengths handouts (www.viacharacter.org) to reflect upon strengths that you have either used or developed. You also can reflect across the five domains of growth and how if at all these have changed. For example, how has this experience made you better able to meet future challenges? How have your relationships evolved? What new priorities do you have? What new goals would you like to achieve? How does your experience and confrontation with mortality change and enhance your day-to-day existence? Have you felt closer to humanity, the universe or nature? In what ways? This exercise asks you to reflect upon these questions over the next three days, taking approximately 20 minutes to work through these questions and possible new narratives.

Finally, group-based interventions have been found to help facilitate the PTG process (Cordova, 2008; Hefferon et al., 2008; Lechner, Stoelb, & Antoni, 2008). More specifically, physical activity group interventions as well as sport participation have garnered considerable attention recently as a potential facilitator of PTG (Hefferon et al. 2008; Kampman & Hefferon, 2014; Sabiston et al. 2007). These physical activity programmes take somewhat of an action-focused growth behaviour change approach to PTG (Hobfoll et al., 2007), which argue that perceptions of change and the experiential side of growth can be translated into actual behavioural change, thus cognition into action (Jayawickreme & Blackie, 2014). Using exploratory methods of inquiry, the engagement in group physical activity during traumatic experience (diagnosis and treatment of chemotherapy) has been found to be both a facilitator and an outcome of PTG. Cross-sectional research has found a positive association between reports of combined (strength and aerobic), recommended, cancer-specific exercise guidelines and PTG within gynecological (endometrial, ovarian and cervical) cancer survivors (moderated by marital status) (Crawford, et al., 2014). These findings show that further research into random-controlled trials (RCTs) and prospective research are needed to understand the relationships among physical activity, trauma and PTG. Furthermore, there may be a 'window of opportunity' (teachable moment) during the illness time line when interventions may be best placed to promote positive health behaviour changes (Hefferon, 2012; Hefferon et al., 2013; Mutrie et al., 2012).

In truth, the area of research that aims to understand transformation and growth following trauma is a fascinating field on the cusp of change itself. After establishing that the phenomenon exists, there is a call for several improved approaches to research inquiry including clarity of definitions and more sophisticated research designs. Research also would benefit from reflecting on different types of trauma and the unique ways in which they are experienced across a variety of populations to contextualise the process further (Hefferon, 2012; Shakespeare-Finch & Armstrong, 2010). Above all, we must be mindful of, and retreat from, the potential to engage in the 'tyranny of positive thinking' (Ehrenreich, 2010; Held, 2005) and emphasise that PTG is not necessarily universal – and that's OK.

CONCLUSION

In sum, the aim of this chapter was to reflect upon the possibility of positive outcomes (e.g., transformation and growth) when engaging with the 'dark side', conceptualised here as adversity and trauma. Whether challenging life experiences are presented early on during development or later on in life, in one-off events or prolonged occurrences, there is the possibility for learning and personal development from our struggle with the 'dark side'. We are now at an exciting phase in positive psychological research – a period to continue our understanding of how individuals are able to maintain equilibrium in the face of adversity, bounce back from difficult times and even report benefits and positive change from suffering. Indeed, we can and must push the boundaries of research design and sensitively test the applications of these findings for appropriate populations. The future is bright and rife with possibilities to challenge PP and embrace the 'dark side' of life.

SUMMARY – THIS CHAPTER HAS ACCOMPLISHED THE FOLLOWING

- Discussed the historical complexity of resilience research
- Considered varying definitions of resilience
- Reviewed how PP facilitates resilience in various settings
- Discussed links between resilience and PTG
- Critically discussed the research area of PTG
- Offered areas for application and future research

RESOURCES AND SUGGESTIONS

Websites

- This is the link to the posttraumatic growth research unit at UEL that aims to understand positive changes following trauma, specifically positive health behaviour changes (increased physical activity, body awareness, etc.): http://www.uel.ac.uk/psychology/research/ptg-unit/
- This is the link to the PTG research group at University of North Carolina. This is the group of the originators of PTG (Tedeschi and Calhoun): https://ptgi.uncc.edu

Books

- An excellent overview of the field can be found in Professor Stephen Joseph's book: Joseph, S. (2011). *What Doesn't Kill Us Makes Us Stronger: The New Psychology of Posttraumatic Growth*. Basic Books.
- This is a stunning account of human strength, perseverance and positive change: Frankl, V. (2004). *Man's Search for Meaning*. Random House Publishing.

NOTES

1   This was conceptualised in this case as those who went on to lead normal lives, for example, healthy (capacity for intimacy) relationships with spouse, children, family and friends; healthy personalities; and stable careers.
2   Some researchers would argue against these categorizations (e.g., Bonnano, 2004).
3   This is defined as '[a] theoretical concept or measurable construct that can be taught or practiced and was described or demonstrated to be associated with resilience and/or outcomes of resilience" (Meredith et al., 2011, p. 16).

4   'The factor has been studied, and there is clear and consistent evidence based on correlational or cross sectional observational analysis' (Meredith et al., 2011, p. 13).

5   'The factor has been studied, and there is clear and consistent evidence based on RCT or longitudinal analysis' (Meredith et al., 2011, p. 13).

6   This section will reflect upon sensitive topics. Please monitor your own emotions and feelings throughout.

7   Of these constructs, the most widely conflated concept is Benefit Finding (BF). BF is described as the 'process in which the patient re-assigns positive value to the illness based on the benefits he or she identifies. . . . BF usually starts immediately after trauma and is a subjective perception of positive changes (Jansen et al, 2011, p. 1158). PTG could be argued to be the ability to put 'cognitive BF processes into action' (Jayawickreme & Blackie, 2014).

8   These could and have be argued to be biased (Jayawickreme & Blackie, 2014).

9   THRIVE has not yet been tested as a full programme but, however, has been created based on empirical evidence.

BIBLIOGRAPHY

Antoni, M. H., Lehman, J. M., Kilbourn, K. M., Boyers, A. E., Yount, S. E., & Culver, J. L., et al. (2001). Cognitive-behavioral stress management intervention decreases the prevalence of depression and enhances the sense of benefit among women under treatment for early-stage breast cancer. *Health Psychology, 20,* 20–32.

Aspinwall, L.G., & Tedeschi, R.G. (2010). Of babies and bathwater: A reply to Coyne and Tennen's views on positive psychology and health. *Annals of Behavioral Medicine, 39*(1), 27–34.

Babyak, M., Blumenthal, J.A., Herman, S., Khatri, P., Doraiswamy, M., Moore, K., et al. (2000). Exercise treatment for major depression: Maintenance of therapeutic benefit at 10 months. *Psychosomatic Medicine, 62*(5): 633–638.

Beck, J.S. (2011). *Cognitive behavior therapy: Basics and beyond.* London: Guilford.

Beck, A.T., Rush, A.J., Shaw, B.F., & Emery, G. (1979). *Cognitive therapy of depression.* New York: Guilford.

Blumenthal et al. (1999). Effects of exercise training on older patients with major depression. *Archives of Internal Medicine, 159,* 2349–2356.

Blumenthal, J.A., Babyak, M.A., Doraiswamy, P.M., Watkins, L., Hoffman, B.M., Barbour, K. A. (2007). Exercise and pharmacotherapy in the treatment of major depressive disorder. *Psychosomatic Medicine, 69,* 587–596.

Bonanno, G.A., Wortman, C.B., Lehman, D.R., Tweed, R.G., Haring, M., Sonnega, J., & Nesse, R.M. (2002). Resilience to loss and chronic grief: a prospective study from preloss to 18-months postloss. *Journal of Personality and Social Psychology, 83*(5), 1150.

Bonanno, G. A. (2004). Loss, trauma, and human resilience: Have we underestimated the human capacity to thrive after extremely aversive events? *American Psychologist, 59*(1), 20–28.

Britt, T., Sinclair, R., & McFadden, A. (2013). Introduction: the meaning and importance of resilience. In R. Sinclair & T. Britt (Eds.), *Building psychological resilience in
military personnel*. Washington, DC: American Psychological Association.

Brunwasser, S.M., Gillham, J.E., & Kim, E.S. (2009). A meta-analytic review of the
Penn Resiliency Program's effect on depressive symptoms. *Journal of Consulting
and Clinical Psychology, 77*(6), 1042.

Calhoun, L.G., & Tedeschi, R.G. (2013). *Posttraumatic growth in clinical practice*. London: Routledge.

Calhoun, L., Tedeschi, R., Cann, A., & Hanks, A. (2010). Positive outcomes following
bereavement: Paths to posttraumatic growth. *Psychologica Belgica, 50*(1, 2), 125–143.

Cann, A., Calhoun, L.G., Tedeschi, R.G., Kilmer, R.P., Gil-Rivas, V., Vishnevsky, T., &
Danhauer, S.C. (2010). The Core Beliefs Inventory: A brief measure of disruption in
the assumptive world. *Anxiety, Stress & Coping, 23*(1), 19–34.

Connor, K. M., Davidson, J. R. T. (2003). Development of a new resilience scale: The
Connor–Davidson Resilience Scale (CD-RISC). *Depression and Anxiety, 18*, 76–82.

Cordova, M. (2008). Facilitating posttraumatic growth following cancer. In S. Joseph &
A. Linley (Eds.), *Trauma, recovery and growth* (pp. 185–206). New Jersey: John
Wiley & Sons.

Crawford, D. C., Crosslin, D. R., Tromp, G., Kullo, I. J., Kuivaniemi, H., & Hayes, M. G.,
et al. (2014). eMERGEing progressing enomics—the first seven years. *Front. Genet,
5*, 184.

Davidson, R. J. (2000). The functional neuroanatomy of affective style. In D. Lane
Richard & L. Nadel (Eds.), *Cognitive neuroscience of emotion* (pp. 371–388). New
York: Oxford University Press.

Demark-Wahnefried, W., Aziz, N.M., Rowland, J.H., & Pinto, B.M. (2005). Riding the
crest of the teachable moment: Promoting long-term health after the diagnosis of
cancer. *Journal of Clinical Oncology, 23*(24), 5814–5830.

Ehrenreich, B. (2010). *Smile or die: How positive thinking fooled America and the
world*. New York: Granta Books.

Eidelson, R., Pilisuk, M., & Soldz, S. (2011). The dark side of comprehensive soldier
fitness. *American Psychologist, 66*(1), 693.

Engelhard, I., Lommen, M., & Sijbrandij, M. (2014). Changing for better or worse?
Posttraumatic growth reported by soldiers deployed to Iraq. *Clinical Psychological
Science, 18*, 641–646.

Faulkner, G., Hefferon, K., & Mutrie, N. (2015). Positive psychology in motion. In S.
Joseph (Ed.), *Positive psychology in practice* (2nd ed.). New Jersey: John Wiley & Sons.

Frankl, V. (2004). *Man's Search for Meaning*. New York: Random House.

Frazier, P., Tennen, H., Gavian, M., Park, C., Tomich, P., & Tashiro, T. (2009). Does
self-reported posttraumatic growth reflect genuine positive change? *Psychological
Science, 20*(7), 912–919.

Fredrickson, B. (2001). The role of positive emotions in positive psychology – The
broaden-and-build theory of positive emotions. *American Psychologist, 56*(3),
218–226.

Fredrickson, B. L., Tugade, M. M., Waugh, C. E., & Larkin, G. R. (2003). What good are positive emotions in crisis? A prospective study of resilience and emotions following the terrorist attacks on the United States on September 11th, 2001. *Journal of Personality & Social Psychology, 84*, 365–376.

Friborg, O., Hjemdal, O., Rosinvenge, J. H., & Martinussen, M. (2003). A new rating scale for adult resilience: What are the central protective resources behind health adjustment? *International Journal of Methods in Psychiatric Research,12*, 65–76.

Gillham, J.E., Hamilton, J., Freres, D.R., Patton, K., & Gallop, R. (2006). Preventing depression among early adolescents in the primary care setting: A randomized controlled study of the Penn Resiliency Program. *Journal of Abnormal Child Psychology, 34*(2), 195–211.

Ginis, K., Bassett, R., &d Conlin, C. (2012). Body image and exercise. In E. Acevedo (Ed.), *The Oxford handbook of exercise psychology*. New York: Oxford University Press.

Groleau, J. M., Calhoun, L. G., Cann, A., & Tedeschi, R. G. (2013). The role of centrality of events in posttraumatic distress and posttraumatic growth. *Psychological Trauma: Theory, Research, Practice, and Policy, 5*(5), 477–483.

Harris, D. V. (1973). *Involvement in sport: A somatopsychic rationale*. Pennsylvania, PA: Lea & Febiger.

Hefferon, K. (2012). *Emotions in coaching and mentoring*. In J. Passmore (Ed.), *Handbook of coaching and mentoring*. London: Wiley.

Hefferon, K. (2013). *The body and positive psychology: The somatopsychic side to flourishing*. London: McGraw-Hill.

Hefferon, K., Grealy, M., & Mutrie, N. (2008). The perceived influence of an exercise class intervention on the process and outcomes of post-traumatic growth. *Journal of Mental Health and Physical Activity, 1*, 32–39.

Hefferon, K., Grealy, M., & Mutrie, N. (2009). Posttraumatic growth and life threatening physical illness: A systematic review of the qualitative literature. *British Journal of Health Psychology, 14*, 343–378.

Hefferon, K., Murphy, H., McLeod, J., Mutrie, N., & Campbell, A. (2013). Understanding barriers to exercise implementation 5-years post Breast Cancer diagnosis: a large-scale qualitative study. *Health Education Research, 28*(5), 843–856.

Held, K. (2003). Husserl's phenomenology of the life-world. In Donn Welton (Ed.), *The new Husseri. A critical reader*. Indiana: Indiana University Press.

Held, B. S. (2005). The "virtues" of positive psychology. *Journal of Theoretical and Philosophical Psychology, 25*, 1–34.

Helgeson, V.S., Reynolds, K.A., & Tomich, P.L. (2006). A meta-analytic review of benefit finding and growth. *Journal of Consulting and Clinical Psychology, 74*, 797–816.

Hobfoll, S.E., Hall, B.J., Canetti-Nisim, D., Galea, S., Johnson, R.J., & Palmieri, P.A. (2007). Refining our understanding of traumatic growth in the face of terrorism: Moving from meaning cognitions to doing what is meaningful. *Applied Psychology, 56*(3), 345–366.

Janoff-Bulman, R. (1989). Assumptive worlds and the stress of traumatic events: Applications of the schema construct. *Social Cognition, 7*, 113–136.

Janoff-Bulman, R. (1992). Happystance. A review of subjective well-being: An inter-disciplinary perspective. *Contemporary Psychology, 37*,162–163.

Janoff-Bulman, R. (2004). Posttraumatic growth: Three explanatory models. *Psychological Inquiry, 15*, 30–34.

Jansen, L., Hoffmeister, M., Chang-Claude, J., Brenner, H., & Arndt, V. (2011). Benefit finding and post-traumatic growth in long-term colorectal cancer survivors: prevalence, determinants, and associations with quality of life. *British Journal of Cancer, 105*(8), 1158–1165.

Jayawickreme, E., & Blackie, L. E. (2014). Post-traumatic growth as positive personality change: Evidence, controversies and future directions. *European Journal of Personality, 28*(4), 312–331.

Joseph, S. (2011). *What doesn't kill us makes us stronger: The new psychology of post-traumatic growth*. London: Basic Books.

Joseph, S. (2012). Trauma can be GOOD for you, says psychologist who helped survivors of the Zeebrugge disaster. *The Daily Mail*, January 30, p. 1.

Joseph, S. (2013). *What doesn't kill us: A guide to overcoming adversity and moving forward*. London: Piatkus.

Joseph, S., & Linley, P.A. (2005). Positive adjustment to threatening events: An organismic valuing theory of growth through adversity, *9*(3), *Review of General Psychology*, 262–280.

Joseph, S., & Linley, P. A. (Eds.). (2008). *Trauma, recovery, and growth. Positive psychological perspectives on posttraumatic stress*. New Jersey: Wiley.

Joseph, S., Linley, P. A., Andrews, L., Harris, G., Howle, B., Woodward, C., et al. (2005). Assessing positive and negative changes in the aftermath of adversity: Psychometric evaluation of the Changes in Outlook Questionnaire. *Psychological Assessment, 17*, 70–80.

Joseph, S., Maltby, J., Wood, A.M., Stockton, H., Hunt, N., & Regel, S. (2012). The Psychological Well-Being – Post-Traumatic Changes Questionnaire (PWB-PTCQ): Reliability and validity. *Psychological Trauma: Theory, Research, Practice, and Policy, 4*(4), 420.

Joseph, S., Williams, R., & Yule, W. (1993). Changes in outlook following disaster: The preliminary development of a measure to assess positive and negative responses. *Journal of Traumatic Stress, 6*, 271–279.

Kampman, H., & Hefferon, K. (2014). Find a sport and carry on: Posttraumatic growth and achievement in British Paralympic athletes. Poster presentation to the 7th European Positive Psychology Conference, Amsterdam, July 2014.

Lechner, S., Stoelb, B., & Antoni, M. (2008). Group based therapies for benefit finding in cancer. In S. Joseph, & A. Linley (Eds.), *Trauma, recovery and growth* (pp. 207–232). New Jersey: John Wiley & Sons.

Lepore, S., & Revenson, T. (2006). Resilience and posttraumatic growth: Recovery, resistance and reconfiguration. In R. G. Tedeschi & L. G. Calhoun (Eds.), *Handbook of posttraumatic growth* (pp. 24–46). Mahwah: NJ: Lawrence Erlbaum.

Linley, P.A., & Joseph, S. (2004). Positive change following trauma and adversity: A review. *Journal of Traumatic Stress, 17*, 11–21.

Lomas, T., Cartwright, T., Edginton, T., & Ridge, D. (2014). A religion of wellbeing? The appeal of Buddhism to men in London, United Kingdom. *Psychology of Religion and Spirituality, 6*(3), 198–207.

Manne, S., Ostroff, J., Winkel, G., Goldstein, L., Fox, K., & Grana, G. (2004). Posttraumatic growth after breast cancer: Patient, partner, and couple perspectives. *Psychosomatic Medicine, 66*(3), 442–454.

Masten, A. S., Cutuli, J. J., Herbers, J. E., & Reed, M.-G. J. (2009). Resilience in development. In C. R. Snyder & S. J. Lopez (Eds.), *Oxford handbook of positive psychology* (2nd ed., pp. 117–131). New York: Oxford University Press.

Masten, C. L., Eisenberger N. I., & Borofsky L. A. (2009). Neural correlates of social exclusion during adolescence: understanding the distress of peer rejection. *Social Cognitive Affective Neuroscience, 4,* 143–157.

Meredith, N. P., Horne, R.B., & Anderson, R. R. (2001). Substorm dependence of chorus amplitudes: Implications for the acceleration of electrons to relativistic energies. *Journal of Geophysical Research, 106,* 13,165–13, 178.

Meredith, L., Sherbourne, C., Gaillot, S., Hansell, L., Ritschard, H., Parker, A., & Wrenn, G. (2011). *Promoting psychological resilience in the U.S. military.* Santa Monica, CA: RAND.

Mutrie, N., Campbell, A., Barry, S., Hefferon, K., McConnachie, A., McLoed, J., Ritchie, D., & Tovey, S. (2012). Five year follow up of breast cancer survivors who had participated in an exercise intervention during adjuvant treatment. Are there lasting effects? *Journal of Cancer Survivorship, 6*(4), 420–430.

Pals, J. L., & McAdams, D. P. (2004). The transformed self: A narrative understanding of posttraumatic growth. *Psychological Inquiry, 15,* 65–69.

Park, C. L., & Lechner, S. (2006). Measurement issues in assessing growth following stressful life experiences. In L. G. Calhoun & R. G. Tedeschi (Eds.), *Handbook of posttraumatic growth* (pp. 47–67). New Jersey: Erlbaum.

Park, C. L., Cohen, L., & Murch, R. (1996). Assessment and prediction of stress-related growth. *Journal of Personality, 64,* 71–105.

Psychological Inquiry, 15, 65-69Peterson, C., Park, N., Pole, N., Dandrea, W., & Seligman, M. E.. (2008, April). Strengths of character and posttraumatic growth. *Journal of Traumatic Stress, 21*(2), 214–217.

Petruzzello, S. (2012). The ultimate tranquilizer? Exercise and its influence on anxiety. In E. Acevedo (Ed.), *The Oxford handbook of exercise psychology.* New York: Oxford University Press.

Rabe, S., Zoellner, T., Beauducel, A., Maercker, A., Karl, A. (2006). Neural correlates of post-traumatic growth after severe motor vehicle accidents. *Journal of Consulting and Clinical Psychology, 74,* 880–886.

Reed, J., & Buck, S. (2009). The effect of regular aerobic exercise on positive-activates affect: A meta analysis. *Psychology of Sport and Exercise, 10,* 581–594.

Reed, J., & Ones, D. (2006). The effect of acute aerobic exercise on positive activated affect: A meta-analysis. *Psychology of Sport and Exercise, 7,* 477–514.

Reivich, K., & Shatte, A. (2002). *The resilience factor: 7 keys to finding your inner strength and overcoming life's hurdles.* New York: Broadway Books.

Ryff, C.D. (1989). Happiness is everything, or is it? Explorations on the meaning of psychological well-being. *Journal of Personality and Social Psychology, 57*(6), 1069–1081.

Sabiston, C., McDonough, M., & Crocker, P. (2007). Psychosocial experiences of breast cancer survivors involved in a dragon boat program: Exploring links to positive psychological growth. *Journal of Sport & Exercise Psychology, 29*, 419–438.

Seligman, M. E. P. (2011). Helping American soldiers in time of war: Reply to comments on the Comprehensive Soldier Fitness [Special Issue]. *American Psychologist, 66*(7), 646–647.

Seligman, M. E. P., & Matthews, M. D. (Eds.). (2011). Comprehensive soldier fitness [Special issue]. *American Psychologist, 66*(1), 4–9.

Shakespeare-Finch, J., & Armstrong, D. (2010). Trauma type and posttrauma outcomes: Differences between survivors of motor vehicle accidents, sexual assault, and bereavement. *Journal of Loss and Trauma, 15*(2), 69–82.

Shakespeare-Finch, J., & Enders, T. (2008). Corroborating evidence of posttraumatic growth. *Journal of Traumatic Stress, 21*(4), 421–424.

Shakespeare-Finch, J., & Lurie-Beck, J. (2014). A meta-analytic clarification of the relationship between posttraumatic growth and symptoms of posttraumatic distress disorder. *Journal of Anxiety Disorders, 28*(2), 223–229.

Sinclair, R., Waitsman, M., Oliver, C. & Deese, M. (2013). Personality and psychological resilience in military personnel. In R. Sinclair & T. Britt (Eds.), *Building psychological resilience in military personnel*. Washington, DC: American Psychological Association.

Smith, B. W., Dalen, J., Wiggins, K., Tooley, E., Christopher, P., & Bernard, J. (2008). The Brief Resilience Scale: Assessing the ability to bounce back. *International Journal of Behavioral Medicine, 15*, 194–200.

Sodergren, S. C., & Hyland, M. E. (2000). What are the positive consequences of illness? *Psychology and Health, 15*, 85–97.

Stallard, P. (2003). *Think good-feel good: A cognitive behaviour therapy workbook for children and young people*. London: John Wiley & Sons.

Tedeschi, L. O., Cannas, A., & Fox D. G. (2010). A nutrition mathematical model to account for dietary supply and requirements of energy and other nutrients for domesticated small ruminants: The development and evaluation of the Small Ruminant Nutrition System. *Small Ruminant Research, 89*, 174–184.

Tedeschi, R.G., Addington, E., Cann, A., & Calhoun, L.G. (2014). Post-traumatic growth: Some needed corrections and reminders. *European Journal of Personality, 28*, 332–361.

Tedeschi, R. G., & Calhoun, L. G. (1995). *Trauma and transformation: Growing in the aftermath of suffering*. Thousand Oaks, CA: Sage.

Tedeschi, R. G., & Calhoun, L. G. (1998). The posttraumatic growth inventory: Measuring the positive legacy of trauma. *Journal of Traumatic Stress, 9*, 455–471.

Tedeschi, R. G., & Calhoun, L. G. (2006). T*he handbook of posttraumatic growth: Research and practice*. New York: Routledge.

Tedeschi, R., & Calhoun, L. (2008). Beyond the concept of recovery: Growth and the experience of loss. *Death Studies, 32*, 27–39.

Tedeschi, R. G., Park, C., & Calhoun, L. G. (1998). Posttraumatic growth: Conceptual issues. In R. G. Tedeschi, C. Park, & L. G. Calhoun (Eds.), *Posttraumatic growth* (pp. 1–22). Mahwah, NJ: Lawrence Erlbaum.

Tedeschi, R. G., & McNally, R. J. (2011). Can we facilitate posttraumatic growth in combat veterans? *American Psychologist, 66*(1), 19.

Vanderbilt-Adriance, E., & Shaw, D. S. (2008). Conceptualizing and re-evaluating resilience across levels of risk, time, and domains of competence. *Clinical Child and Family Psychology Review, 11*(1–2), 30–58.

Wagner, B., Müller, J., & Maercker, A. (2011). Death by request in Switzerland: PTSD and complicated grief after witnessing assisted suicide. *European Psychiatry, 27*, 542–546.

Weiss, T., & Berger, R. (2010). *Posttraumatic growth and culturally competent practice: Lessons learned from around the globe*. London: John Wiley & Sons.

Werner, E. E. (1993). Risk, resilience and recovery: Perspectives from the Kauai longitudinal study. *Development and Psychopathology, 5*(4), 503–515.

Werner, E. E. (1996). Vulnerable but invincible: High risk children from birth to adulthood. *European Child & Adolescent Psychiatry, 5*, 47–51.

Wilson, T. D., & Gilbert, D. T. (2005). Affective forecasting knowing what to want. *Current Directions in Psychological Science, 14*(3), 131–134.

Windle, G. (2010). What is resilience? A review and concept analysis. *Reviews in Clinical Gerontology, 21*(2), 152–169.

Windle, G. (2011). What is resilience? A review and concept analysis. *Reviews in Clinical Gerontology, 21*(2), 152–169.

Windle, G., Bennett, K. M., & Noyes, J. (2011). A methodological review of resilience measurement scales. *Health and Quality of Life Outcomes, 9*(8), 1–18.

5

Mortality and positive psychology

'Death is the key to the door of life'.

Kübler-Ross (1975)

Learning objectives – at the end of the chapter you will be able to do the following:
- Situate the role of mortality and death awareness within PP
- Consider the benefits of contemplating our mortality
- Offer philosophical perspectives on the importance of death contemplation for optimal functioning
- Appreciate the various models of mortality awareness (MA) and their links to wellbeing
- Compassionately discuss end-of-life death acceptance
- Introduce empirical measurement tools and interventions
- Offer areas for application and future research

List of topics:
- Reflections on death in society
- Existential perspectives on death
- MA
- Stage theory of death acceptance
- Terror management theory (TMT)
- Positive trajectories of terror management
- Meaning making theory
- Death reflection and salience interventions
- MA scales
- Death education
- Death doulas
- Death therapies

For some readers, the relationship between mortality and PP might not be immediately evident (Cozzolino, 2006). As humans, we tend to connect the word 'death' and its associations with taboo or 'negative' categories of conversation or thought, denying or suppressing its impending inevitability (Niemiec et al., 2010). However, what many fail to realise is that mortality awareness 'can provide sweetness to life – an added zest that makes living more meaningful' (Cozzolino, 2006, p. 278). Indeed, understanding how death can influence the good life has been proclaimed the 'new frontier' for PP (Wong, 2010). Following on from the previous chapter, this section will reflect upon the power of existential awareness, its potential to enhance our present circumstances, increase appreciation and give meaning to the every day. Thus, the 'dark side' is conceptualised here as mortality; death is indeed a challenging experience that evokes great discomfort in us. This discomfort is frequently avoided as it carries an engagement with fear, pain, distress and confusion. However, engaging with the challenge and discomfort of death has a great potential for growth, healing, insight and transformation. In other words, the 'dark side' contains the seed for a potential positive outcome, even when the path towards this outcome is testing.

This chapter will first explore the historical and social relationships with the concept of death before reviewing the current research and models on MA. From this latter approach, we will review how death can be a catalyst for personal growth and how it is being harnessed in some topic areas of PP to help understand the 'good life'. This chapter will also sensitively explore the area of terminal illness and the insights we can learn from individuals who are facing their own mortality. Measurement tools (e.g., Death Attitudes Profile – Revised) and interventions (e.g., obituary writing and death reflections) will also be offered alongside real-life case studies to highlight the genuine ways that contemplating or confronting death can potentially improve our current circumstances. Overall, this chapter aims to break down the barriers that place death as forbidden territory within PP research realms and urge the discipline area to embrace one of the most difficult human experiences to ensure we encompass the entirety of the human condition and its role in flourishing.

PRACTICE ESSAY QUESTIONS

- Critically argue the legitimacy of the statement: 'Death is the new frontier for the current positive psychology movement' (Wong, 2010, p. 75).

- Discuss the differences and similarities between Terror Management Theory and Positive Terror Management Theory.

CONTINUING A JOURNEY

It seems fitting that I begin to tackle this difficult subject on the approach to the 20th anniversary of my first real encounter with death. On the evening of 6 July 1994, my family and I were involved in a head-on motor vehicle collision that resulted in multiple casualties, which counted myself amongst the most critical. CT scans revealed a depressed skull fracture, a contusion of the right frontal lobe as well as a fracture through the right frontal sinus and right frontal bone. Added to the internal injuries were multiple skull, face and body lacerations. Following extensive reconstructive surgery, and indeed years of subsequent hospitalisations, scans and operations, my family and I survived. However, we were forever left with the daily physical and psychological reminders of the fragility of life.

There is no doubt this event inevitably shaped the way I look at death, not as a great mystery but as an assured reality – one that can (and will) happen at any given moment, no matter how young, old, rich, poor, good, bad or indifferent one is. Death is a tough subject, and I won't pretend that it is entirely comfortable for me to write about; however, from my own personal experiences and indeed the writings of philosophers, sociologists, anthropologists and psychologists, it is one that many believe we must include in our examinations of the 'good life' (Wong, 2013; Vail et al., 2012). To be sure, 'we can only truly live and enjoy and appreciate life if we realise at all times that we are finite' (Kübler-Ross, 1975, xxii). The good news is that we don't have to wait for death to come knocking at our door to utilise and befriend the messages it can give us: 'Begin to see death as an invisible, but friendly, companion on your life's journey – gently reminding you not to wait till tomorrow what you mean to do – then you can learn to live your life rather than simply passing through it' (Braga & Braga, 1975, p. 16).

As this chapter tackles a very uncomfortable topic, it is important for you to take responsibility for monitoring your own reactions and emotions to the sections presented. These feelings will be situated on how you think about your own death, the death of those you love and how you live your life at present (Braga & Braga, 1975). Despite this potential for discomfort, this engagement with the dark side, it is important to reflect upon this subject area as we can start to understand what makes life worth living only when it is studied within the context of death (Kübler-Ross, 1975; Wong, 2010).

REFLECTION

Have you experienced an event that has shaped or altered the way you look at your own mortality? What impact does it have on your day-to-day functioning and decision making?

DEATH DEFINED

What does the word 'death' mean to you? Death is ultimately the end of a person's life; however, when this happens is debated within medical fields (Dennis, 2008). Stages of death include clinical death (cessation of the heart); brain or cortical death (cessation of electrical activity in the brain) and cellular death (decomposition of the body cells). Further to these, the conceptualisation of death can be thought to be broken down into three further stages: 'i) Death as an event (the halting of life at a particular time point); ii) Death as a condition (a non-reversible condition that prevents life from occurring) and iii) Death as a state of non-existence (death is not thought of as an event or condition but about a state of existence after death)' (Dennis, 2008, p. 158). Death is defined within this chapter as 'the permanent loss of neural activity or brain functioning and the irreversible cessation of biological processes' (Spellman, 2014, p. 8).

Death is inevitable, indiscriminate and the one guarantee we have in this world. It is only fitting then that there is a whole area of study dedicated to understanding our relationship with death. Thanology, the academic discipline and research studies into death, started to take shape during the 1950s and gained momentum through the 1960s and 1970s. Thanology covers three mains streams of inquiry, including the contemplation and confronting of our own death (the fear of what comes next), the fear of the actual mechanisms of dying and the fear of our loved ones dying. Although extremely valuable avenues of research, for the purpose of this chapter, we will take a predominantly idiographic perspective, reflecting on the first field, our own confrontation and reflection of mortality, rather than the exact mechanisms to which we will demise or the repercussions of bereavement.

ENGAGING WITH DEATH ACROSS THE AGES

Across millennia, societies have approached and dealt with death in their own ways, according to the era and environmental circumstances they found themselves in. For example, in early human existence, nomadic group life perpetuated the likelihood of early death due to disease, illness, accident, natural means, lack of nutrition, predators and so on (Spellman, 2014). Violent deaths as a result of tribal fighting were also a main cause of death, especially for young males. Although a commonplace occurrence in early human development, the realisation of decay and personal death was not at the forefront of early human consciousness. As the species progressed, evidence of the recognition of this association was displayed via deliberately burying the dead with rites, rituals and/or possessions approximately 130,000 years ago. Other time points and cultures have been concerned with the posture and placement of the dead (Neolithic period) as well as the grounds upon where they are laid to rest (e.g., tombs, Mausoleums and vaults). The Egyptians were arguably the culture most known for its extravagant and intriguing burial practices and their presumed links between life and death. Through mummification, a process by which the internal organs were removed and the body wrapped and placed in a tomb, Egyptians believed that they were ensuring that their loved ones' 'essence' passed on with them to the afterlife (Spellman, 2014).

REFLECTION

Are humans the only creatures on Earth that can foresee their own demise? Some would argue not, highlighting the behaviours of select groups of animals (and early predecessors of humans) that act out behaviours that signify awareness of death (e.g. elephants and chimpanzees). What is arguably different is that our species is able to 'anticipate, reflect upon and ascribe some form of higher meaning to death' (Spellman, 2014, p. 22).

Greek and Buddhist philosophy ushered in an era of pondering the tensions between life and the imminence of death. Indeed, it can be argued that all philosophy focuses on death; its primary focus on life and the components of life that are worthwhile is inherently situated within the context of death: 'death is truly the inspiring genius of philosophy' (Schopenhauer, as cited in Kübler-Ross, 1975, p. 2). For example, eminent philosopher Epicurus argued that the fear of death and its constant reminders (conscious and unconscious) were the main reasons individuals could not fully embrace life (Yalom, 2008). Also, he deliberated that many citizens worried about the 'non-livingness' of life, the simple exclusion from future occasions, their own non-being. He continually disregarded this fear and denounced it as irrational, proffering several counter-arguments to this human-wide affliction. The first was that the soul was mortal and thus when consciousness ceased to exist, so therefore will the ability to recognise one's past, present and future. Secondly, he argued that following the death of the body and soul, perception ceased to exist, and therefore we cannot fear what we cannot perceive. Finally, Epicurus contended that we inevitably return to the state in which we existed before we were conceived, a state of 'non-existence' and non-beingness, and therefore as we have no recollection of this, there is nothing to fear.

Epicurus' teachings have heavily influenced existential philosophy (EP), an area inextricably linked to death studies. EP focuses on difficult and challenging subjects (e.g., loss and death) and argues that humans are perpetually seeking meaning whilst also balancing the experience of meaninglessness (Wong, 2009). An EP perspective embraces the 'dark side' and argues that these topics can shake and challenge who we are and thus, by doing so, we may go on to live more authentic lives (Thompson, 2014). Overall, the term really boils down to the concept of *existence* and that 'we humans are the only creatures for who our own existence is the problem' (Yalom, 2008, p. 200). There are several well-known existentialists (e.g., Sartre and Nietzsche), and they have all added their own takes on what existentialism means to them. Kierkegaard (1845), for example, was passionate about the importance of embracing life, with death being a constant reminder to live today as if it were our last. He contended that life was not to be wasted – people needed to stop 'sleepwalking' through life – and that reminders of death and the fragility of life could help us to become more fulfilled (Ferguson, 2013, p. 9).

RESEARCH AND PRACTICE CASE STUDIES

One of the most well-known contemporary pieces of existential literature is Albert Camus' (1942) novel, *L'etranger*. The book was originally written in French, however has been translated into several languages and remains Camus' most renowned example of his philosophical belief in the absurdity of life and meaninglessness of existence. Camus went on to write several other notable pieces and won the Nobel Prize for literature in 1957.

L'etranger is a very brief, but complex, novel which follows Meursault, a French Algerian, who has attended his mother's funeral and shown no sign of grief or sadness at her passing. This shortage of emotion becomes a hallmark and the downfall of Meursault as the reader watches him float through uncomfortable and immoral decisions with little empathy for the other characters in the book. After being tried and convicted for a motiveless murder, he again expresses no remorse. The book concludes with Meursault's reflections and resignations regarding the meaningless-ness of life and the utter indifference of the universe.

Reference

Camus, A. (1942). *L'etranger*. Collection Folio: Gallimard.

Buddhist philosophy also embraces the 'dark side' by focusing on the acceptance of the impermanence of life and that all things change and come to an end: 'objects decay, bodies age, people pass away' (Lomas, Hefferon, & Ivtzan, 2014, p. 138). We can thus alleviate our suffering (one of the four noble truths) by accepting this impermanence and detaching ourselves from our desires. Indeed, 'no human life can be filled with a sense of meaning and efficacious action unless it is lived in full acceptance of the fact of death' (Long, 1975, p. 65). A common practice within Buddhist meditation is the 'recollection of death', where practitioners are asked to engage with the topics of death and decay to highlight the importance of life and reduce the fear of death in general. These meditations can take two directions: The first is to contemplate the certainty of death – the uncertainty of when and the practicalities of what are important to us (e.g., mental and spiritual development vs. materials goods). The second approach is to actually visualise your own death, the cessation of mind and body, the physiology of death and the decay of flesh. One can do these by situating oneself in a mortality-salient environment (e.g., a cemetery), again highlighting the impermanence of life, the uncertainty of death and the importance of living a full life in the here and now (Long, 1975).

A DEATH-DENYING SOCIETY

If our own mortality has always been at the heart of philosophy and is a component that arguably affects all humans, their motivations, behaviours and ultimately, wellbeing, why do we still fear and deny death? Philosophers argue that we hold an innate biological tendency to suppress concerns and acknowledgements of death. However, this denial of our demise is ultimately doomed to fail (Wong & Tomer, 2011; Yalom, 2008). Death affects us all, even if we don't actually think it does (Wong & Tomer, 2011). These oppressed concerns and anxieties arguably manifest themselves into serious issues such as worry and depression (Yalom, 2008).

Different societies and cultures deal with death and the death process in their own ways, some remaining more open to the experiences and acceptance of death than others. These societies are called 'death-affirming' societies, where death is embraced and not hidden (e.g., aging is not seen as something to reverse; death is a journey and adventure to be celebrated) and therefore experience positive outcomes from this engagement with the 'dark side'. Western cultures, however, have traditionally been labelled 'death-denying' societies, sheltering citizens from the reality and process of passing on. This Westernised tendency to engage in death denial is arguably an injustice to ourselves as when we deny the 'dark side' (death), this can lead to lives that lack purpose or fulfilment. PP is arguably aligned to this former line of thinking, perpetuating transformation and growth. Thus, if our purpose in life is to grow, 'death is the final stage of growth in this life' (Kübler-Ross, 1975, p. 166).

There are three proposed reasons why Western societies have become death denying, and these are purported to feed the death-denying tendencies within Western cultures. The first is that individuals are sheltered from the concept of death; we remove children and family members from experiencing the death of others and are 'shielded' from the phenomenon (discussed further next). Secondly, we have become so far removed from the process of death to burial (e.g., preparation of the body) due to the vast majority of deaths now occurring in hospital settings and staff now occupying the roles that would have been the responsibility of the family many years ago (Nichols & Nichols, 1975). Some practitioners argue that including the family in the process from death to burial can help facilitate the grieving process and reconnect family and friends to practices conducted in earlier societies (Nichols & Nichols, 1975).

REFLECTION

Wakes were part of the death process in early society when individuals were more likely to die at home. This involved the body being laid out for visitors to observe in the home. Visitations can now occur in the funeral homes before the formalised service (Softka, 2014). What do you think of the concept of a wake or visitation?

The third potential element to the perpetuation of a death-denying society is argued to be the role of the hospital in the context of death and the changes to the hospital organisational context. Originally, the function of a hospital was where you took people who were ill and dying. Today, however, they are seen to be where one gets 'cured'. Mauksch (1975) argued that due to this shift in perceptions on the role and function of hospitals, when someone dies, this can act as a threat or even insult to the organisation, despite this being its original aim. The death of a patient can also challenge the competency of the staff and services within the hospital. Ultimately, death 'threatens the system' (p. 11).

Obviously, it is imperative to recognise the wonderful work that hospitals do to prolong life where many years ago they could not; however, this is more a reflection on their role in the death procedure in today's society. Again, the hospital setting perpetuates the separation of the family and the deceased from the pronouncement of death, whereas in previous centuries, the family would have had the responsibility of overseeing the transition from death to the final resting place (Nichols & Nichols, 1975). With almost 80 percent of deaths occurring now in a hospital or palliative care setting (Brennan, 2014), the role of the hospital is crucial in our understanding and placement of death in our society.

Psychologists argue that it is important we start to shift our societal tendencies from death denying to death acceptance. This denial of the 'dark side' can lead to anxiety and psychological discomfort and thwarts meaning. Death acceptance, on the other hand is the essence of PP as it can reduce this innate anxiety and increase meaning, purpose and growth. Indeed, the meanings that we associate with death have an impact on our behaviours, how we live and our overall wellbeing. As we move toward more death acceptance than death denying, this can create a 'fuller' life, not only for those passing away but also those left behind (Kübler-Ross, 1975). Authentic living arguably stems from the recognition of the finality of life and acceptance of death; by moving away from fear, we can move towards a more self-actualized existence (Wong, 2010): 'If we don't know death, how can we know life?' (Wong, 2010, p. 73).

Our attitudes towards death acceptance are arguably shaped by our environment and social situations (Wong, 2010). Wong has identified three different types of death acceptance in relation to wellbeing. 'Approach acceptance' is linked to religion, a belief in the afterlife and the concept of immortality. This sense of immortality can give comfort and hope to individuals and their loved ones. This type is consistently linked to death acceptance and lowered death anxiety (Wong, 2010). 'Escape acceptance' purports that death is a relief from the pains of living and is often expressed in the actions of suicide. In this case, the balance of fear of death shifts to fear of living. 'Neutral acceptance' is the recognition that death is inevitable and happens to everyone (Wong & Tomer, 2011). The next section will explicitly review the PP research that has shown positive links between death awareness and wellbeing, demonstrating instances when death is arguably 'good for life' (Vail et al., 2012, p. 1).

THE IMPORTANCE OF MORTALITY AWARENESS

As PP purports that we should aim to enhance the wellbeing of individuals and societies, including both their daily happiness (hedonic) but also personal growth (eudaimonic), embracing the 'dark side' and its inquiry appears appropriate and necessary to holistically understand flourishing. MA is defined as 'an awareness of death, of one's own inevitable demise, as an unavoidable outcome of life' (McDermott & Barik, 2014). We are arguably constantly negotiating our own and others' mortality on a day-to-day basis, and this can be triggered by major traumatic personal or cultural events or even the passing of peers. The majority of MA theories have taken a negative approach to inquiry (Levassuer, McDermott, & Hefferon, 2015), focusing predominantly on the anxiety and distress recognising our demise entails. This approach, however, is arguably short sighted, as death in inextricably linked with the concepts of meaning, purpose, gratitude, appreciation, authenticity and self-actualisation: 'the promise of death and the experience of dying, more than any other force in life, can move a human being to grow' (Kübler-Ross, 1975, p. 117).

At present, there are several theories on MA and its effects on our wellbeing. 'Terror management theory' (TMT) draws on the early work of Becker (1975) dictating that conscious and unconscious realisation of our own mortality causes paralysing fear. Following from copious experimental research into the effects of mortality on individual psychological functioning (Grabe et al., 2005), TMT argues that death awareness is a key motivator in human behaviours: 'when one is indirectly confronted their own mortality, the individual engages in defences to enhance their personal value and so to enhance their symbolic mortality' (Goldenberg et al., 2006, p. 155). Hundreds of cross-cultural studies conducted on TMT have found that when induced into a mortality salient (MS) environment ('an environment that consciously or subconsciously remind individuals of death'; Hefferon, 2013, p. 96), individuals tend to conform to their socially constructed beliefs and behaviors, draw self-esteem via adhering to cultural standards and can display evidence of increased materialism, greed, racial discrimination, prejudice and aggression (Grabe et al., 2005; Vail et al., 2012). These reactions arguably aid to manage the terror of our inevitable demise (see also Becker, 1962, 1975). Thus, MA has had a historical 'bad rap' for being a negative influence on our thoughts and behaviors, contributing to evaluative biases, defensive distortions and the aggressive protection of one's cultural beliefs and self-esteem (Harmon-Jones et al., 1997; Vail et al., 2012, p.3).

Although a well-established theory, there are several purported issues with TMT. The first is that the majority of research conducted has been at the unconscious level of awareness, inducing more subtle exposures to mortality. Though an important approach, it does not necessarily account for overt moments of MA, where individuals deliberately engage in death-related philosophical thought as well as the external exposure to trauma (e.g., illness or accidents). Secondly, the majority of tasks within TMT experiments are time limited, offering brief, manipulated exposure to MA. Lykins et al. (2007) argued that this brevity may induce defensiveness in participation; however, more longer-term mortality threats (e.g., philosophical reflections on mortality) may actually induce intrinsic goal shifts (e.g., PTG).

Cozzolino (2006) has also taken the concept of TMT and challenged the intricacies upon which is it founded. From his own research, he has found evidence that there are dual-existential systems at play when we are faced with death, and these try and explain why MA can impact our experience either by eliciting (a) *mortality-induced defensiveness* (as seen by TMT) or (b) *mortality-induced growth* (e.g., solidify personal relationships, increase positive health behaviours, choose intrinsic and growth-oriented goals, engage in community development, ascribe to positive social standards and engage in open-minded behaviours; Vail et al., 2012).

Cozzolino purports that mortality-induced defensiveness and mortality-induced growth are both 'two sides of the same existential coin' (2006, p. 278). Personalisation and specificity seem to be the two key components when predicting subsequent behaviour, thoughts and motivations following exposure to MA or MS environments. Cozzolino contends that when individuals are exposed to brief, abstract MS environments (that are usually outside of the person's consciousness), this will induce defence reactions. However, when experiments are delivered with specificity, with experiential reality (personalisation), people's reactions tend to be more intrinsic and growth orientated. Direct experience with death also has the potential to embed death and mortality into life and enhance intrinsic (versus extrinsic as dictated by TMT) life change, such as new appreciation for life, concern of others and meaning. This embedment was linked to enhanced vitality and 'zest' for life, and this differing trajectory following direct death confrontation was coined 'worldview capitulations' (Cozzolino, 2006, p. 279).

TRY ME

The following death reflections were created to induce MA in research participants. These are used regularly within TMT and other MA psychological experiments. The first is a more abstract reflection, whereas the second may be too explicit for some. You are invited to engage in these two activities; however, please remember to take care with your emotions and monitor how you are feeling during and after the intervention.

1. MS condition (Rosenblatt, Greenberg, Solomon, Pyszczynski, & Lyon, 1989)

This widely used intervention induces participants into an MS environment and asks them to think about their own death and the feelings, thoughts and so on that come from this. This is a more abstract death reflection scenario, and although this MS condition activity is well established and validated (as well as being found to enhance several beneficial states, e.g., intrinsic behaviours), it is arguably not as effective as the specific version that follows.

Instructions

'In as many words and in as much detail as possible, please describe the thoughts, feelings, and emotions you experience when thinking about your own death' (Frias et al., 2011, p. 157).

2. Death reflection scenario (Cozzolino et al., 2004)

This is a vivid and explicit scenario that asks individuals to reflect upon their own death and the feelings and thoughts they would experience.

Although graphic in nature, it is argued that its specificity can enhance impact (as seen within Frias et al., 2011). Please also note that distressing emotions (e.g., panic or fear) have been linked to engaging with this activity; however, this co-exists with growth-oriented experiences (Cozzolino, 2006).

Instructions

'Imagine that you are visiting a friend who lives on the 20th floor of an old, downtown apartment building. It's the middle of the night when you are suddenly awakened from a deep sleep by the sound of screams and the choking smell of smoke. You reach over to the nightstand and turn on the light. You are shocked to find the room filling fast with thick clouds of smoke. You run to the door and reach for the handle. You pull back in pain as the intense heat of the knob scalds you violently. Grabbing a blanket off the bed and using it as protection, you manage to turn the handle and open the door. Almost immediately, a huge wave of flame and smoke roars into the room, knocking you back and literally off your feet. There is no way to leave the room. It is getting very hard to breathe and the heat from the flames is almost unbearable. Panicked, you scramble to the only window in the room and try to open it. As you struggle, you realize the old window is virtually painted shut around all the edges. It doesn't budge. Your eyes are barely open now, filled with tears from the smoke. You try calling out for help but the air to form the words is not there. You drop to the floor hoping to escape the rising smoke, but it is too late. The room is filled top to bottom with thick fumes and nearly entirely in flames. With your heart pounding, it suddenly hits you, as time seems to stand still, that you are literally moments away from dying. The inevitable unknown that was always waiting for you has finally arrived. Out of breath and weak, you shut your eyes and wait for the end' (Cozzolino et al., 2004, p. 290).

1. Please describe in detail the thoughts and emotions you felt while imagining the scenario.

2. If you did experience this event, how do you think you would handle the final moments?

3. Again, imagining it did happen to you, describe the life you led up to that point.

4. How do you feel your family would react if it did happen to you?

(Cozzolino et al., 2004, p. 281)

Similar to Cozzolino (2006), Wong has proposed a divergence from TMT via his meaning management theory (MMT). MMT argues that all human behavior is motivated towards meaning making, and this protects us from the fear of death. MMT differs from TMT in that it claims that individuals first and foremost engage in a search for meaning, not the avoidance of death anxiety. MMT is a growth-oriented model (vs. a defense-oriented model) and posits that MS can create positive life orientations focused on transformation and growth unlike TMT, which predominantly focuses on the negative repercussions of MA.

POSITIVE TERROR MANAGEMENT THEORY (PTMT)

Despite this predominantly negative focus when researching MA and behaviour motivation, Vail et al. (2012) have reasoned that there are positive trajectories of terror management. Indeed, TMT research has actually linked unconscious death exposure (MA) to positive outcomes; however, the findings have been significantly overshadowed by negative findings (Vail et al., 2012).

'The awareness of mortality can motivate people to enhance their physical health and prioritise growth–oriented goals; live up to positive standards and beliefs; build supportive relationships and encourage the development of peaceful, charitable communities; and foster open-minded and growth oriented behaviours' (Vail et al., 2012, p. 1).

Their groundbreaking papers have provided theoretical and empirical evidence that the possibility of death can also foster creative and pro-social behavior. Proposing a rebalancing of the research into death and wellbeing, Vail et al. (2012) offer a new concept of 'positive terror management' (PTM) defined as 'existentially motivated attitudes or behaviors that minimize harm to oneself and others and promote wellbeing in physical, social and psychological domains' (p. 3). Differentiating between conscious and non-conscious death-related thoughts, Vail et al. (2012) have created a preliminary heuristic model of PTM that aims to understand constructive outcomes from MA.

For example, within the health domain, conscious reminders of death have found increased active health behaviors changes (e.g., exercise, smoking cessation, and sunscreen use) as well as the reduction of risky health behaviors following explicit exposure to mortality (e.g., cancer diagnosis; Hefferon et al., 2008, 2009). However, this is typically evident when there are levels of high health optimism; individuals perceived a sense of health efficacy, and there is the perception of available health-related coping options (Vail et al., 2012). Although unconscious, MS environments have been found to increase risk-taking (e.g., tanning or smoking) when the individuals derived self-esteem or self-worth from the activity (Goldenberg & Arnt &, 2008). Conversely, individuals who derived self-esteem from exercise participation actually increased exercise following death reminders. Vail et al. (2012) argue that health promotion can capitalize on this defense link and prime messages regarding health tests and practices to appeal to contingencies of self-worth (e.g., self-esteem or image contingencies of value).

Within eudaimonic wellbeing, the 'dark side' – defined here as conscious death thoughts – can cause individuals to re-prioritize their lives, goals and aspiration, moving from more extrinsically oriented goals to intrinsic and growth-oriented ones (Lykins et al., 2007). The first study aimed to reconcile the opposing theoretical positions of TMT and PTG (previous chapter) Lykins et al. (2007) and found that following exposure to MA (e.g., earthquake or 9/11), individuals altered their extrinsic goals orientations (e.g., materials or social popularity) to more intrinsic ones (e.g., close relationships with loved ones). Once again, duration was a key component in the processing of the events and subsequent goal shifts.

Conscious death reminders are also linked to increased appreciation and gratitude (Frias et al., 2011; Lykins et al., 2007). When students were induced into death reflection conditions, their levels of gratitude significantly increased in relation to control participants. They concluded that the death reflection exercise could be used as an intervention to enhance levels of gratitude and bring to the forefront the value and scarcity of life: '[w]hen death (or life's scarcity) is salient, life is, simply, better' (King et al., 2009, p. 1460). They also argue that further research is needed into longer-term variations of the study and explanations for the increase in appreciation and gratitude.

Although adherence to worldview can predict negative social outcomes (e.g., greed or prejudice), it can also lead to positive outcomes as well (Vail et al., 2012). For example, from a meta-perspective, connections to the environment and community can be increased via priming of death-related thoughts as individuals who derive self-esteem from being environmentally friendly have been found to increase their environmental concern (Vess & Arndt, 2008). Similarly, the strengthening of pro-social values can actually be used to help enhance tolerance, altruism, sense of compassion and empathy, forgiveness and kindness for the culture and society and social group one exists in (Vail et al., 2012). If cultural norms such as helping and kindness are endorsed, then this can be fostered via MA exposure. If one desires to keep to cultural norms and worldviews, then promoting pro-social values can perpetuate the likelihood of a person engaging in these after exposure to unconscious MS.

Finally, exposure to death has been found to enhance our own levels of creativity (Routledge & Juhl, 2010). Originally, a small subset of research argued that mortality reminders would restrict and stifle creativity as MS environments have been found to encourage 'cognitive and attitudinal rigidity' (p. 479). However, Routledge and Juhl (2010) found that creativity did actually increase in MS environments but only for those who scored low on personal need for structure (PNS; 'the extent to which one desires to perceive the world in a clear, certain and unambiguous terms', p. 479). Overall, they concluded that MS environments have the ability to open up creativity, novelty-seeking behaviors and thinking in people with low PNS and that MS research needs to start taking into account individual differences amongst participants when researching potential positive and negative effects of death.

PSYCHOMETRIC SCALES

There are several well-known (used) measurement tools that can be employed when undertaking research within mortality. Please see Table 5.1 for a brief overview of each as well as the full Death Attitudes Profile – Revised scale (Wong, Reker, & Gesser, 1994) for you to fill in and use yourself.

TABLE 5.1

Scale	Reference	Description
Death Attitude Profile – Revised	Wong, P. T. P., Reker, G.T., & Gesser, G. (1994). *Death Attitude Profile –Revised: A multidimensional measure of attitudes toward death.* In R. A. Neimeyer (Ed.), *Death anxiety handbook: Research, instrumentation, and application* (pp. 121–148). Washington, DC: Taylor & Francis.	- *Summation scale* - *32 items* - *5 dimensions (fear of death, death avoidance, neutral acceptance approach acceptance, escape acceptance)* - *1 to 7, strongly disagree (1) to strongly agree (7)*
Death Anxiety Scale	Templer, D. I. (1970). The construction and validation of a death anxiety scale. *The Journal of General Psychology, 82*(2), 165–177.	- *15 items* - *True or false forced answer* - *Two subscales: death anxiety and depression*
Death Depression – Revised Scale	Templer, D.I., Harville, M., Hutton, S., Underwood, R., Tomeo, M., Russell, M., . . . & Arikawa, H. (2001). Death depression scale-revised. *OMEGA—Journal of Death and Dying, 44*(2), 105–112.	- *21 items* - *1 to 5, strongly disagree (1) to strongly agree (5)*
Death Acceptance Scale	Klug, Sinha Klug, L., & Sinha, A. (1987). Death acceptance: A two-component formulation and scale. *OMEGA—Journal of Death and Dying, 18*(3), 229–235.	- *2 acceptance subscales*
Mortality Salience Attitude Survey	Rosenblatt, A., Greenberg, J, Solomon, S., Pyszczynski, T. & Lyon, D. (1989). Evidence for terror management theory I. The effects of mortality salience on reactions to those who violate or uphold cultural values. *Journal of Personality and Social Psychology, 57*(4), 681–690.	*2 open-ended questions* - *Aimed to prime MA*
Multidimensional Mortality Awareness Measure and Model (MMAMM)	Levasseur, O., McDermott, M.R., & Lafreniere, K. In press). The multidimensional mortality awareness measure and model (MMAMM): Development and validation of a new self-report questionnaire and psychological framework. *Omega: Journal of Death and Dying.*	- *36 items* - *5 sub-scales* - *Argued to be the architecture of MA*

DEATH ATTITUDE PROFILE – REVISED (DAP-R) WONG, REKER, & GESSER (1994)

This questionnaire contains a number of statements related to different attitudes towards death. Read each statement carefully and then decide the extent to which you agree or disagree. For example, an item might read: 'Death is a friend'. Indicate how well you agree or disagree by circling one of the following: SA = strongly agree; A = agree; MA = moderately agree; U = undecided; MD = moderately disagree; D = disagree; SD = strongly disagree. Note that the scales run both from strongly agree to strongly disagree and from strongly disagree to strongly agree. If you strongly agreed with the statement, you would circle SA. If you strongly disagreed, you would circle SD. If you are undecided, circle U. However, try to use the undecided category sparingly. It is important that you work through the statements and answer each one. Many of the statements will seem alike, but all are necessary to show slight differences in attitudes.

1	Death is no doubt a grim experience.	SD D MD U MA A SA
2	The prospects of my own death arouse anxiety in me.	SD D MD U MA A SA
3	I avoid death thoughts at all costs.	SD D MD U MA A SA
4	I believe that I will be in heaven after I die.	SD D MD U MA A SA
5	Death will bring an end to all my troubles.	SD D MD U MA A SA
6	Death should be viewed as a natural, undeniable and unavoidable event.	SD D MD U MA A SA
7	I am disturbed by the finality of death.	SD D MD U MA A SA
8	Death is an entrance to a place of ultimate satisfaction.	SD D MD U MA A SA
9	Death provides an escape from this terrible world.	SD D MD U MA A SA
10	Whenever the thought of death enters my mind, I try to push it away.	SD D MD U MA A SA
11	Death is deliverance from pain and suffering.	SD D MD U MA A SA

12	I always try not to think about death.	SD D MD U MA A SA
13	I believe that heaven will be a much better place than this world.	SD D MD U MA A SA
14	Death is a natural aspect of life.	SD D MD U MA A SA
15	Death is a union with God and eternal bliss.	SD D MD U MA A SA
16	Death brings a promise of a new and glorious life.	SD D MD U MA A SA
17	I would neither fear death nor welcome it.	SD D MD U MA A SA
18	I have an intense fear of death.	SD D MD U MA A SA
19	I avoid thinking about death altogether.	SD D MD U MA A SA
20	The subject of life after death troubles me greatly.	SD D MD U MA A SA
21	The fact that death will mean the end of everything as I know frightens me.	SD D MD U MA A SA
22	I look forward to a reunion with my loved ones after I die.	SD D MD U MA A SA
23	I view death as a relief from earthly suffering.	SD D MD U MA A SA
24	Death is simply a part of the process of life.	SD D MD U MA A SA
25	I see death as a passage to an eternal and blessed place.	SD D MD U MA A SA
26	I try to have nothing to do with the subject of death.	SD D MD U MA A SA
27	Death offers a wonderful release of the soul.	SD D MD U MA A SA
28	One thing that gives me comfort in facing death is my belief in the afterlife.	SD D MD U MA A SA
29	I see death as a relief from the burden of this life.	SD D MD U MA A SA

30	Death is neither good nor bad.	SD D MD U MA A SA
31	I look forward to life after death.	SD D MD U MA A SA
32	The uncertainty of not knowing what happens after death worries me.	SD D MD U MA A SA

Scoring: Dimension and Items

Fear of Death (7 items): 1, 2, 7, 18, 20, 21, 32

Death Avoidance (5 items): 3, 10, 12, 19, 26

Neutral Acceptance (5 items): 6, 14, 17, 24, 30

Approach Acceptance (10 items): 4, 8, 13, 15, 16, 22, 25, 27, 28, 31

Escape Acceptance (5 items): 5, 9, 11, 23, 29

Scores for all items are from 1 to 7 in the direction of strongly disagree (1) to strongly agree.

For each dimension, a mean scale score can be computed by dividing the total scale score by the number of items forming each scale.

DEATH ACCEPTANCE AND THE END OF LIFE

It would be remiss to write a chapter on mortality and not include the pioneer academic who arguably legitimized the discussion of death within scientific domains – Dr Elizabeth Kübler-Ross. Kübler-Ross' revolutionary text *On Death and Dying*, first published in 1970, changed the way in which the medical and helping professions viewed end-of-life experiences. The book was based upon the interactions Kübler-Ross, a medical doctor, had with her dying patients and the meanings surrounding the end of life. The main aim of the book was to give voice to those who had been overlooked, the dying, and offer insights into the emotional experiences of the patients themselves.

Since its publication, the book has heralded much intrigue, following and, indeed, criticism from researchers who argue against this one-size-fits-all, linear, stage-based model (Wong & Tomer, 2011). However, Kübler-Ross herself clearly stated that her book was neither a textbook, nor a how-to manual for doctors and nurses managing patients who were dying. She also declared that this work was not necessarily a research study (although the book explicitly states that 200 patients were interviewed without detailing the full procedures). Furthermore, Kübler-Ross noted that the proposed stages could actually overlap, co-occur or not occur in some individuals; stage theory was therefore a 'heuristic device' (Kellehear, 2009). Most importantly, Kübler–Ross' main aim of the book was to create dialogue with the dying and about dying itself, to break down barriers of power and status and start to provide better provisions for those who needed it most – the dying themselves. 'Death may get to be a routine to you, but it is new to me. You may not see me as unique, but I've never died before. To me, once is pretty unique!' (Anonymous, 1975). This next section will critically review the contributions of Kübler-Ross, including her later work, which proclaimed death as the *final stage* of personal growth (Kübler-Ross, 1975), an argument that fits well within the remit of this chapter.

STAGE THEORY OF DEATH

Kübler-Ross identified that there were several common defense and coping mechanisms that terminally ill patients used to deal with their own impending mortality. Upon the reception of a terminal diagnosis, many reacted with shock and then, subsequently, denial. Hence the first stage of this theory is 'denial and isolation'. Denial was perceived to be the rejection of the diagnosis (mix up of tests or names, incompetence of doctors), especially when individuals received the diagnosis from someone they did not know well and/or when delivered in prompt or un-compassionate ways. Kübler-Ross argued that denial and partial denial were most prominent in the first stages but could also be present later on during the illness journey, utilized as a 'healthy escape' mechanism to alleviate the burden of persistent thinking about impending demise. Once denial made its way to partial acceptance, the dawning of the actuality of the diagnosis caused intense feelings such as anger and rage. This second stage, 'anger', was quite difficult for the staff and family members of the diagnosed. The patients reported rational and irrational feelings of anger towards the doctors, the hospital, the tests and almost everything around them. Indeed, anger was projected towards any symbols of the life that was being taken away from them. One of the greatest causes of anger was the feeling of being devalued, ignored or disrespected by staff and others.

Following on from the attempts at denial and anger, Kübler-Ross (1975) identified that some individuals would enter into a third stage, 'bargaining'; '[i]f God has decided to take me from this earth and he did not respond to my angry pleas, he may be more favorable if I ask nicely' (p. 66). Bargaining was basically the perception of reward, or a prize, for good behavior and was a helpful technique, if conducted for short periods of time. The fourth stage observed was 'depression'. The progression of terminal illness, coupled with further surgeries and the decline in physical functioning can be akin to a profound sense of loss: 'loss of the past' (finances, occupation, identity and role and body parts) and 'impending loss' (of the self, family and life). This stage could be equated with the 'dark side', thus once embraced and dealt with can make way for final stage of 'acceptance'. By overcoming denial, anger and resentment towards life and the living, as well as experiencing the loss of past and future, individuals can come to a place where they are more accepting of their impeding death and foster *hope* – a very central component to the reaction of death and the process of death and dying.

RESEARCH AND PRACTICE CASE STUDIES

Sifting through the pages of the late Chris Peterson's last novel (Peterson, 2013), I was overjoyed when I came across the chapter dedicated to the 'positive psychology case study', Randy Pausch. For those who are not aware of the name, you may be more familiar with the medium in which he became a worldwide household name: *The Last Lecture*. Peterson highlighted Pausch's incredible story of strength and courage through terminal cancer diagnosis and stated that every student of PP should know this story. The following case study is therefore dedicated to Pausch's extraordinary example of transformation and growth during end of life.

Randy Pausch was a computer science professor at Carnegie Mellon University. At the age of 47, he was diagnosed with terminal pancreatic cancer and given three to six months to live. During this time, Pausch made major changes to his living conditions, moving to be closer to family as well as campaigning for more awareness and funding for pancreatic cancer. Unaware of his condition, his university approached Pausch to deliver a 'last lecture', part of a network of talks where lecturers are asked to consider their 'last lecture', to think about their own demise and impart knowledge that they felt mattered most to them.

During his 'last lecture', titled 'Really Achieving Your Childhood Dreams' (Pausch & Zaslow, 2010), Randy decided to dedicate the presentation to departing his wisdom and legacy to his children. The main themes he touched upon focused on (a) how to live with joy and happiness, (b) his appreciation for life and (c) the values he held dear (honesty, integrity and gratitude).

His book has sold millions of copies, and the lecture has nearly 17 million hits on YouTube. His inspirational message of living life, right now, continues to touch millions after his death. In keeping with this, you may want to engage with his main message to us:

'What wisdom would we impart to the world if we knew it was our last chance? If we had to vanish tomorrow, what would we want as our legacy?'.

Reference:

Pausch, R. & Zaslow, J. (2010). *The last lecture*. London: Hachette.

DYING AND REGRETS

In her best-selling book, *The Top 5 Regrets of the Dying*, Ware (2011) reflects upon the top five regrets that she came across during her career as a carer to those who were terminally ill. Although not a research project, pieces of work such as this can help us refocus and learn wisdom of how to live from the words of those who are facing death. The top five regrets included:

1   I wish I'd had the courage to live a life true to myself, not the life others expected of me.
2   I wish I hadn't worked so hard.
3   I wish I'd had the courage to express my feelings.
4   I wish I had stayed in touch with my friends.
5   I wish I had let myself be happier.

Regrets are closely linked to the 'dark side' of fear of death and dying, and many of us will experience these within our lifetime (Compton & Hoffman, 2012). These regrets can be for actions we may have taken, causing us to feel anger upon reflection or regret for our own inaction, which can then lead to feelings of despair (Compton & Hoffman, 2012). Research has shown that it is typically regret for our own inaction that is the most prevalent form of regret. Regrets can be a huge burden on the person involved and have a detrimental impact on their own physical and psychological health. Regrets, however have been given 'a bad name' (Yalom, 2008, p. 145) and, when looked at from an alternative perspective, can actually be catalysts for possibility, maturation and growth (King & Hicks, 2007). The discomfort of contemplating these types of regrets needn't necessarily be a negative experience – they can actually become a positive motivation to change things today and remove the possibility for future regrets to occur (Yalom, 2008). Ultimately, Nietzsche begged for humankind to not live the 'unlived life'. He proclaimed that only by living our lives fully and in accordance to who we truly are would we die without regret.

REFLECTION . . .

If you were approaching your imminent demise, what would your top five regrets be?

AGING AND THE 'GOOD DEATH'

Every night we go to sleep and wake up, a small death has occurred, a decaying bringing us closer to our inevitable end. Every change we experience in life can also be a small death (Imara, 1975) and therefore by default, the older we get, the more of these 'mini' deaths we accrue. We also encounter 'milestones' across the lifespan that can 'awaken' us to our own mortality (Yalom, 2008). These can be major or relatively minor occasions or decisions which can bring to the foreground of our consciousness that time is passing. These 'awakening experiences' (e.g., birthdays, anniversaries, making a will, attending reunions, etc.) can all magnify the finality of time and enhance our experience of life (Yalom, 2008).

For those who will be fortunate to live a long life, aging brings with it a lot of loss, such as loss of our loved ones and the loss of our own physical selves (e.g., 'youth, health, vitality, resources and life'; Snyder et al., 2011, p. 308). There are, however, some wisdoms we can garner from the implicit connections between older age and death (Snyder et al., 2011), including meta-perspectives on life achievements, accepting and basking in the love and care from family members and a return to simple pleasures that can be experienced every day.

Linked to aging is the concept of the 'good death'. The good death is indeed a subjective one, involving several characteristics depending on where in the circle of death you may be (the dying, the loved one left behind, the carer, etc.; O'Neil, 1983). Each person may have an idea of what their own good death might be; however researchers have found shared commonalities across reports of what defines a 'good death'. These include the following:

> [b]eing in control, being comfortable, having a sense of closure, affirmation or recognition of the value of the dying person, having trust in healthcare providers, have one's beliefs and values honoured, minimizing burden to the family, optimising relationships, appropriateness of death (timing), leaving a legacy and family care (for those left behind and also in the process of death and after care of the dead). (Kehl, 2014, p. 229–231)

The repercussions of a good death are that those left behind may feel closure and peace with the process.

BECOMING A DEATH-AFFIRMING SOCIETY

Reflecting on the ways in which death has the potential to help us live the 'good life', what can we do about it now? How can we become a more death affirming society – one that transforms from the denial of the 'dark side', into one that engages in a healthy and flourishing relationship with our own demise. The next section will review three ways in which we can harness the wisdom reflected upon in this chapter: role models, death education and death therapies.

ROLE MODELS

Kübler-Ross (1975) dictated that it is important to deal with the 'dark side' of death and accept mortality before you come to the real thing as this will make the experience more meaningful and growth oriented. When we have been exposed to and had direct contact with someone who has dealt with their own death positively, this can have a positive impact on our own acceptance of and approach to death (Vail et al., 2012). Previous contact with someone who has accepted death and adjusted to the process of dying with acceptance has been linked to increased emotional adjustment facing one's own demise (Carey, 1975). When one has witnessed the death of another, who truly recognised its meaning, they are able to grow and become more 'fully human' (Kübler-Ross, 1975, p. 117). Indeed, Kübler-Ross argues that one can become more at peace and accepting of death, and their own death, if he or she has exposure to positive and coping experiences with others. This is ultimately about experiencing versus shielding of death.

Death doulas are also a form of role modelling. Death doulas (as opposed to birth doulas) are individuals who support the preparation, process and experience of death. After specialised training, the doula becomes a mentor and companion for both the person dying and his or her family, providing education, knowledge and companionship. Overall, the doula's aim is to help to maintain quality of life and wellbeing within the context of dying (http://livingwelldyingwell.net). Death doulas provide a bridge between the professional care that one receives and the family support provided.

RESEARCH AND PRACTICE CASE STUDIES

An excellent example of a positive role model in death is the story of the last few months of Morrie Schwartz. Immortalised within *Tuesdays With Morrie*, Schwartz enters our world through the eyes of his prodigal student, Mitch Albom. Morrie, a former sociology professor at Brandeis University, Massachusetts, is dying of amyotrophic lateral sclerosis (ALS). The disease is slowly taking away the activities and freedoms Schwartz loved dearly (e.g., dancing wildly to music for hours on end). It is at this point Morrie asks himself: 'Do I wither up and disappear or do I make the best of my time left?' (Albom, 1997, p.10). Death became his 'final project' and becomes the focal point of his teaching for his last semester. His unique project was also aired on the renowned TV show Nightline, which sparked national interest in this man and his journey. Indeed, it was this airing that brought back Morrie to the awareness of his previous, beloved student, Mitch Albom. They rekindled their student–teacher dynamic 16 years later, Morrie taking on the moniker 'Coach'.

For 14 Tuesdays, Morrie and Mitch met after breakfast to discuss important topics such as how to really live, how to love, the meaning of life and so on. Throughout the book, we see Morrie impart his knowledge and wisdom, including the attendance at his own 'living funeral', believing that funerals for the dead were a waste as the deceased never got to hear any of the wonderful things that were said. The readers watch as Mitch realises the cocooned extrinsically focused life he has led for the previous 16 years and learns difficult lessons on the importance of life and simplicity of what makes life worth living.

Reference:

Albom, M. (1997). *Tuesdays with Morrie: An old man, a young man, and life's greatest lesson*. London: Hachette.

DEATH EDUCATION

To overcome anxieties and fears of death, Wong (2010) purports that it is the duty of psychologists and educators to help foster death acceptance via education on death: 'we need to talk about death in a way that is liberating, humanizing and life enhancing' (p.75). However, there is a real social taboo behind discussions around mortality (Taylor, 2012). 'Death education' is defined as 'a developmental process in which death-related knowledge and the implications resulting from that knowledge are transmitted' (Leviton, 1977, as cited in Dennis, 2008, p. 197). Death education can take place on a formal and information level: Informally, parents and adults can take the time to acknowledge conversations around death, for example, a dead plant or insect (Balk, 2014). On a more formal level, death education aims to help prepare individuals for their own demise as well as break down taboos about dying and create a more comfortable atmosphere with regard to death, dying and bereavement.

The inclusion of death education within schools has been a hotly debated topic. Although some argue that death education in schools may contradict home beliefs and interfere with familial concepts of death and the afterlife, teachers and parents have been found to be quite supportive of including death education in the curricula due to its natural and inevitable part of life. As such, death education has been included across all school years, including primary, secondary and higher-level learning. Outcomes from these programmes include: more realistic understanding and acceptance of death; importance of forgiveness; acknowledgement of own death; accepting regrets and highlighting the importance of living a fulfilled life now (Denis, 2008). Furthermore, the success of the programme has been linked to the teacher's own comfort with the topic area. Additional criticism of death education is that it has been found to increase anxiety surrounding death relative to others who have not been exposed to such curricula (Dennis, 2008). However, as we saw in the previous sections, this anxiety and discomfort that stem from confronting the 'dark side' can give rise to positive change.

DEATH THERAPIES

There are several forms of therapy that address the anxieties and potential for growth via the contemplation and confrontation of death. 'Existential psychotherapy' focuses on our own dealings with existence and concentrates on four *ultimate concerns*: '[d]eath, isolation, meaning in life and freedom' (Yalom, 2008, p. 201). Yalom's take on existential therapy ascertains that death anxiety is the foremost issue and spends time working on this whilst also addressing the other three areas of concern when the client is ready. 'Meaning therapy' is a person-centred approach and focuses on the will to meaning. 'Logotherapy' originated with Viktor Frankl. Through his horrific experiences during the Holocaust, Victor Frankl (existentialist, psychiatrist and psychologist) focused his life work on the human, innate need to search for meaning and to understand our own reasons for existing as opposed to sex or power, as his contemporaries proposed (Längle, 2009). This approach has continued with the works of Paul Wong, who purports that meaning therapy is inextricably linked with death acceptance and wellbeing and is argued to be a form of PP. (See exercises in the following sections.)

Not only is death discussed in professional therapies, but there are now more tested interventions that can be used at home, without a therapist, to help us reflect on our own mortality. Mindfulness is one such exercise. Individuals who score low on trait mindfulness have been found to display higher defense responses to MS manipulations as well as higher self-esteem striving, as per TMT (Niemiec et al., 2010). Individuals with high trait mindfulness, however, were found to spend longer amounts of time contemplating their own death and engage in fewer death suppression thoughts than those with low trait mindfulness (Niemiec et al., 2010). Thus, in addition to all its additional physical and psychological benefits (see Lomas et al., 2014), trait mindfulness may also protect the negative repercussions of MS environments (Niemiec et al., 2010).

TRY ME

1. My most feared obituary (Frisch, 2005)

This activity is a staple of the popular quality of life therapy (Frisch, 2005). Frisch argues that by reflecting on a more gloomy account of the self and your current life status, this may encourage reflection and momentum for change.

Instructions

'Pretend that you have failed to change unhealthy and unhappy patterns that you have now and project how these problems will get worse as you get older and die. The Most Feared Obituary is based on living a long life without any positive changes in your current standards, priorities and goals. In fact, problems can be expected to get much worse over the many years that you "let yourself go," deteriorate, and do nothing to make your life happier or healthier in any way. Next, pretend that you

have agreed to write your own obituary just before you die. This is a very personal and detailed obituary for all of your friends and family to see (Frisch, 2005, p. 38)'.

2. Legacy (Seligman, Rashid, & Parks, 2006)

This activity comes from one of the six-week exercises completed within PP and asks individuals to reflect on what they want their legacy to be (Seligman, Rashid, & Parks, 2006). This intervention exists in many PP programmes; however, specific testing of the intervention on its own has yet to be conducted.

Instructions

'Imagine that you had passed away after living a fruitful and satisfying life. What would you want your obituary to say? Please write a 1–2 page essay summarising what you would like to be remembered for the most (Seligman, Rashid, & Parks, 2006, p. 6)'.

POSITIVE PSYCHOLOGY AND THANOLOGY: A FRUITFUL FUTURE

'The dance with death can be a delicate but potentially elegant stride towards living the good life'.
— (Vail et al., 2012, p. 18)

In addition to the areas discussed throughout the chapter, PP has a real chance to close the gaps and explore unchartered territories with regard to death and wellbeing. For example, this chapter has purposely predominantly given an idiographic account of how we deal with our own thoughts on mortality and how it affects us as people. There are of course copious amounts of research on bereavement and the potential for growth following the tragic loss of another (Calhoun, Tedeschi, Cann, & Hanks, 2010). We could also look deeper at the aging process and how this inherent proximity to death affects our MA and wellbeing. Interventions that have been linked to reduced defensive responses (e.g., mindfulness; Niemiec et al., 2010) can also be further tested. Moreover, although outside the merit of this chapter, there are several other branches of death research that have not been included but are worthy pursuits of exploration. These include, but are not limited to, the role of religion and afterlife beliefs, levels of spirituality (discussed in depth in Chapter 7), near death experiences, euthanasia and right-to-die debates.

Coming full circle, this chapter has been another branch of my continuing journey with my relationship with death. Despite my expectations from writing this chapter, I must admit that I feel no more enlightened than whence I started. Perhaps, I am simply vindicated on what I believed I already knew – that *'[d]eath does not need to be a catastrophic, destructive thing; indeed, it can be viewed as one of the most constructive, positive and creative elements of culture and life'* (Kübler-Ross, 1975, p. 2). This may be due to my early death exposure experiences or my not entirely serendipitous career as a researcher in understanding the effects of mortality on wellbeing. What this chapter has done, however, is remind me of these precious insights and recall the importance of reflecting on our own mortality for the 'good life'. As discussed in Chapter 1 on the dialectic of emotions, perhaps the word 'death' need not strike terror into the hearts of those who read it but appreciation for the here and now. Perhaps we can move forward and diverge from pigeonholing words and areas of research as 'negative' and view them from a more dialectic perspective. We alone have the power to move ourselves away from a state of death denying to death affirming (Imara, 1975); acceptance of this is the first stage to growth.

SUMMARY – THIS CHAPTER HAS ACCOMPLISHED THE FOLLOWING

- Situated the role of mortality and death awareness within PP
- Consider the benefits of contemplating our mortality
- Offered philosophical perspectives on the importance of death contemplation for optimal functioning
- Appreciated the various models of MA and their links to wellbeing
- Compassionately discussed end-of-life death acceptance
- Introduced empirical measurement tools and interventions
- Offered areas for application and future research

RESOURCES AND SUGGESTIONS

Websites

- Living well Dying well is a UK-based charity that provides information and support in the preparation of death: http://livingwelldyingwell.net
- The 'Last Lecture' by Randy Pausch can be observed via this link: http://www.youtube.com/watch?v=ji5_MqicxSo
- You can learn more about the book and play *Tuesdays with Morrie* via this link: http://www.tuesdayswithmorrie.com/

Books

- One of the greatest books written on dealing with death anxiety:
  Yalom, I. (2008). *Staring at the sun: Overcoming the terror of death*. London: Piatkus Books.
- A key read for anyone interested in the links between death and growth:
  Kübler-Ross, E. (1975). *Death: The final stage of growth*. New York: Simon & Schuster.

BIBLIOGRAPHY

Albom, M. (1997). *Tuesdays with Morrie: An old man, a young man, and life's greatest lesson*. London: Hachette.

Anonymous. (1975). Death in the first person. In E. Kübler-Ross (Ed.), *Death: The final stage of growth*. New York: Simon & Schuster.

Aspinwall, L. G., & Tedeschi, R. G. (2010). The value of positive psychology for health psychology: Progress and pitfalls in examining the relation of positive phenomena to health. *Annals of Behavioral Medicine*, *39*(1), 4–15.

Balk, D. (2014). Death education. In M. Brenna (Ed.), *An A–Z of death and dying*. Santa Barbara, CA: Greenwood.

Becker, E. (1962). *The birth and death of meaning*. New York: Free Press.

Becker, E. (1975). *Escape from evil*. New York: Academic Press.

Blackie, L. E., & Cozzolino, P. J. (2011). Of blood and death: A test of dual-existential systems in the context of prosocial intentions. *Psychological Science*, *22*(8), 998–1000.

Braga, M. N., & Braga, P. I. S. (1975). Aspectos ecologicos da vegetacao na campina da reserve biologoca INPA-SUFRAMA (Manaus-Caracarai, km 62). *Acta Amazonica*, *5*, 247–260.

Brennan, M. (2014). *An A–Z of death and dying*. Santa Barbara, CA: Greenwood.

Burkeman, O. (2012). *The antidote: Happiness for people who can't stand positive thinking*. London: Cannongate.

Burns, D. J., Hart, J., & Kramer, M. E. (2014). Dying scenarios improve recall as much as survival scenarios. *Memory*, *22*(1), 51–64.

Calhoun, L. G., Tedeschi, R. G., Cann, A., & Hanks, E. A. (2010). Positive outcomes following bereavement: Paths to posttraumatic growth. *Psychologica Belgica*, *50*(1), 125–143.

Camus, A. (1942). *L'etranger*. Gallimard Collection Folio.

Carey, J. W. (1975). A cultural approach to communication. *Communication, 2*, 1–22.

Compton, W. C., Hoffman, E. (2012). *Positive psychology: The science of happiness and flourishing* (2nd ed.). California: Wadsworth.

Cozzolino, P. J. (2006). Death contemplation, growth, and defense: converging evidence of dual-existential systems? *Psychological Inquiry*, *17*(4), 278–287.

Cozzolino, P. J., Staples, A. D., Meyers, L. S., & Samboceti, J. (2004). Greed, death, and values: From terror management to transcendence management theory. *Personality and Social Psychology Bulletin*, *30*(3), 278–292.

Dennis, D. (2008). *Living, dying, grieving*. Sudbury, MA: Jones and Bartlett.

Ferguson, R. (2013). *Life lessons from Kierkegaard*. London: Macmillan.

Frias, A., Watkins, P. C., Webber, A. C., & Froh, J. J. (2011). Death and gratitude: Death reflection enhances gratitude. *The Journal of Positive Psychology, 6*, 154–162.

Frisch, M. B. (2005). *Quality of life therapy: Applying a life satisfaction approach to positive psychology and cognitive therapy*. London: John Wiley & Sons.

Goldenberg, J. L. (2006). The body stripped down: An existential account of ambivalence toward the physical body. *Current Directions in Psychological Science, 14*, 224–228.

Goldenberg, J. L., & Arndt J. (2008). The implications of death for health: A terror management health model for behavioral health promotion. *Psychology Review*, 115(4):1032–1053.

Goldenberg, J. L., Hart, J., Pyszczynski, T., Warnica, G. M., Landau, M. J., & Thomas, L. (2006). Terror of the body: Death, neuroticism, and the flight from physical sensation. *Personality and Social Psychology Bulletin, 32*, 1264–1277.

Goldenberg, J. L., Pyszczynski, T., Greenberg, J., Solomon, S., Kluck, B., & Cornwell, R. (2001). I am not an animal: Mortality salience, disgust, and the denial of human creatureliness. *Journal of Experimental Psychology, 130*, 427–435.

Goldenberg, J., & Shackelford, T. (2005). Is it me or is it mine? Body self integration as a function of self esteem, body esteem and mortality salience. *Self and Identity, 4*, 227–241.

Grabe, S., Cook, A., Routledge, C., Anderson, C., & Arndt, J. (2005). In defense of the body: The effect of mortality salience on female body objectification. *Psychology of Women Quarterly, 29*, 33–37.

Harmon-Jones, E., Simon, L., Greenberg, J., Pyszczynski, T., Solomon, S., & McGregor, H. (1997). Terror management theory and self-esteem: Evidence that increased self-esteem reduces mortality salience effects. *Journal of Personality and Social Psychology, 72*, 24–36.

Hefferon, K. (2013). *Positive psychology and the body: The somatopsychic side to flourishing*. London: McGraw-Hill International.

Hefferon, K., Grealy, M., & Mutrie, N. (2008). The perceived influence of an exercise class intervention on the process and outcomes of post-traumatic growth. *Journal of Mental Health and Physical Activity, 1*, 32–39.

Hefferon, K., Grealy, M., & Mutrie, N. (2009). Posttraumatic growth and life threatening physical illness: A systematic review of the qualitative literature. *British Journal of Health Psychology, 14*(2), 343–378.

Hefferon, K., Grealy, M., & Mutrie, N. (2010). Transforming from cocoon to butterfly: The potential role of the body in the process of posttraumatic growth. *Journal of Humanistic Psychology, 50*(2), 224–247.

Imara, M. (1975). Dying as the last stage of growth. In E. Kübler-Ross (Ed.), *Death: The final stage of growth*. New York: Simon & Schuster.

Kashdan, T. B., Nathan DeWall, C., Schurtz, D. R., Deckman, T., Lykins, E. L., Evans, D. R., . . . & Brown, K. W. (2014). More than words: Contemplating death enhances positive emotional word use. *Personality and Individual Differences, 71*, 171–175.

Kehl, K. (2014). Good death. In M. Brenna (Ed.), *An A–Z of death and dying*. Santa Barbara, CA: Greenwood.

Kellehear, A. (2009). Introduction. In E. Kübler-Ross (Ed.), *On death and dying*. New York: Routeldge.

Kierkegaard, S. (1845). *Thoughts on crucial situations in human life*. (D. F. Swenson, Trans., L. M. Swenson Ed.). Canada: Augsburg Publishing House (now Augsburg Fortress Publishers), 1941.

King, L.A., & Hicks, J.A. (2007). Whatever happened to "What might have been"? Regrets, happiness, and maturity. *American Psychologist, 62*(7), 625–636.

King, L. A., Hicks, J. A., & Abdelkhalik, J. (2009). Death, life, scarcity and value: An alternative perspective on the meaning of death. *Psychological Science, 20,* 1459–1462.

Klug, Sinha Klug, L., & Sinha, A. (1987). Death acceptance: A two-component formulation and scale. *OMEGA—Journal of Death and Dying, 18*(3), 229–235.

Kübler-Ross, E. (1975). *Death: The final stage of growth.* New York: Simon & Schuster.

Kübler-Ross, E. (1997). *On death and dying.* New York: Simon and Schuster.

Längle, A. (2009). Viktor Frankl. In S. J. Lopez (Ed.), Encyclopedia of positive psychology, Vol 1 (pp. 412–413).Malden, MA: Wiley.

Levasseur, O., McDermott, M. R., & Lafreniere, K. (2015). The multidimensional mortality awareness measure and model (MMAMM): Development and validation of a new self report questionnaire and psychological framework. *Omega: Journal of Death and Dying, 70*(3), 317–341.

Levasseur, O., McDermott, M. R., & Hefferon, K. (2015). The multidimensional mortality awareness measure and model (MMAMM): Development and validation of a new self report questionnaire and psychological framework. *Omega: Journal of Death and Dying, 70*(3), 317–341.

Leviton, D. (1977). The scope of death education. *Death Education, 1*(1), 41–56.

Lomas, T., Cartwright, T., Edginton, T., & Ridge, D. (2014). A religion of wellbeing? The appeal of Buddhism to men in London, United Kingdom. *Psychology of Religion and Spirituality, 6*(3), 198–207.

Lomas, T., Hefferon, K., & Ivtzan, I. (2014). *Applied positive psychology: Integrated positive practice.* Thousand Oaks, CA: Sage.

Long, J. B. (1975). The death that ends death in Hinduism and Buddhism. In E Kübler-Ross (Ed.), *Death: The final stage of growth.* New York: Touchstone.

Lykins, E. L. B., Segerstrom, S. C., Averill, A. J., Evans, D. R., & Kemeny, M. E. (2007). Goal shifts following reminders of mortality: Reconciling posttraumatic growth and terror management theory. *Personality and Social Psychology Bulletin, 33*(8), 1088–1099.

Mauksch, H. (1975). *The organizational context of dying.* In E. Kübler-Ross (Ed.), *Death: The final stage of growth.* New York: Simon & Schuster.

McDermott, M. R., & Barik, N. B. (2014). Developmental antecedents of proactive and reactive rebelliousness: the role of parenting style, childhood adversity, and attachment. Journal of Motivation, Emotion, and Personality, 2(1), 22–31.

Nichols, R., & Nichols, J. (1975). *Funerals: A time for grief and growth.* In E. Kübler-Ross (Ed.), *Death: The final stage of growth.* New York: Simon & Schuster.

Niemiec, C. P., Brown, K. W., Kashdan, T. B., Cozzolino, P. J., Breen, W. E., Levesque-Bristol, C., & Ryan, R. M. (2010). Being present in the face of existential threat: The role of trait mindfulness in reducing defensive responses to mortality salience. *Journal of Personality and Social Psychology, 99*(2), 344.

O'Neil, R. (1983). Defining "a good death," *International Journal of Applied Philosophy, 1*(4), 9–17.

Park, C. L. (2010). Making sense of the meaning literature: An integrative review of meaning making and its effects on adjustment to stressful life events. *Psychological Bulletin, 136*(2), 257.

Pausch, R., & Zaslow, J. (2010). *The last lecture*. London: Hachette.

Peterson, C. (2013). *Pursuing the good life*. New York: Oxford University Press.

Rosenblatt, A., Greenberg, J., Solomon, S., Pyszczynski, T., & Lyon, D. (1989). Evidence for terror management theory I: The effects of mortality salience on reactions to those who violate or uphold cultural values. *Journal of Personality and Social Psychology, 57*, 681–690.

Routledge, C., & Juhl, J. (2010). When death thoughts lead to death fears: Mortality salience increases death anxiety for individuals who lack meaning in life. *Cognition and Emotion, 24*(5), 848–854.

Routledge, C., & Juhl, J. (2012). The creative spark of death: The effects of mortality salience and personal need for structure on creativity. *Motivation and Emotion, 36*(4), 478–482.

Routledge, C., Ostafin, B., Juhl, J., Sedikides, C., Cathey, C., & Liao, J. (2010). Adjusting to death: The effects of mortality salience and self-esteem on psychological well-being, growth motivation, and maladaptive behavior. *Journal of Personality and Social Psychology, 99*(6), 897.

Seligman, M. E., Rashid, T., & Parks, A. C. (2006). Positive psychotherapy. *American Psychologist, 61*(8), 774.

Snyder, C. R., Lopez, S. J., & Pedrotti, J. T. (2011). Positive psychology: *The scientific and practical exploration of human strengths*. Thousand Oaks, CA: Sage.

Softka, C. (2014). Wakes and visitations. In M. Brenna (Ed.), *An A–Z of death and dying*. Santa Barbara, CA: Greenwood.

Spellman, W. M. (2014). *A brief history of death*. London: Reaktion Books.

Taylor, D. (2012). Battling illness and health illiteracy. *Philadelphia Inquirer*, February 8.

Templer, D. I. (1970). The construction and validation of a death anxiety scale. *The Journal of General Psychology, 82*(2), 165–177.

Templer, D. I., Harville, M., Hutton, S., Underwood, R., Tomeo, M., Russell, M., . . . & Arikawa, H. (2001). Death depression scale-revised. *OMEGA—Journal of Death and Dying, 44*(2), 105–112.

Thompson, N. (2014). Existentialism. In M. Brenna (Ed.), *An A–Z of death and dying*. Santa Barbara, CA: Greenwood.

Vail, K. E., Juhl, J., Arndt, J., Vess, M., Routledge, C., & Rutjens, B. T. (2012). When death is good for life considering the positive trajectories of terror management. *Personality and Social Psychology Review, 16*(4), 303–329.

Vess, M., Arndt, J., Routledge, C., Sedikides, C., & Wildschut, T. (2008). *Nostalgia as self-esteem resource*. Columbia: University of Missouri Press.

Ware, B. (2011). The top five regrets of the dying. Carlsbad, CA: Hay House.

Wong, P. (2009) Existential psychology. In S. Lopez (Ed.), *The encyclopedia of positive psychology* (pp. 361–368). Chichester, UK: Blackwell.

Wong, P. T. P. (2010). Meaning therapy: An integrative and positive existential psycho-therapy. *Journal of Contemporary Psychotherapy, 40*(2), 85–93.

Wong, P. (2011). Positive psychology 2.0: Towards a balanced interactive model of the good life. *Canadian Psychology, 52*(2), 69–81.

Wong, P. T. P. (2013). Meaning, self-transcendence, and well-being. A keynote address at the Conference on Life and Death Education, National Taipei University of Nursing & Health Science, Taipei, Taiwan.

Wong, P. T. P., Reker, G. T., & Gesser, G. (1994). Death Attitude Profile – Revised: A multidimensional measure of attitudes toward death. In R. A. Neimeyer (Ed.), *Death anxiety handbook: Research, instrumentation, and application* (pp. 121–148). Washington, DC: Taylor & Francis.

Wong, P. T., & Tomer, A. (2011). Beyond terror and denial: The positive psychology of death acceptance. *Death Studies, 35*(2), 99–106.

Yalom, I. (2008). *Staring at the sun: Overcoming the terror of death*. London: Piatkus Books.

6

Wellbeings: Suffering, compassion and interconnectedness

'All the suffering in this world arises from wishing ourselves to be happy; all the happiness there is in this world arises from wishing others to be happy'.

Shantideva

Learning objectives – at the end of the chapter you will be able to do the following:
- Articulate the differences among compassion, empathy and sympathy
- See that compassion inherently involves embracing the 'dark side' of life (i.e., suffering)
- Consider the value placed on compassion by traditions like Christianity and Buddhism
- Appreciate a range of 'other-regarding' qualities in addition to compassion, including loving kindness, generosity and sympathetic joy
- Differentiate various models of selfhood, including individualism and intersubjectivism
- Generate compassion through meditative practices
- Understand how cultivating compassion can engender self-transcendence
- Appreciate self-transcendence as a key component of psychospiritual development

List of topics:
- Definitions and models of compassion
- Universal egoism versus empathy–altruism
- Collectivism versus intersubjectivism
- I–it versus I–thou
- Religious teachings on compassion

- Buddhist theories of the self
- Tonglen meditation
- Self-transcendence
- Psychospiritual development
- Union with the sacred

As one begins to contemplate the concept of compassion, almost at once one is beguiled by its mysterious qualities. On one hand, one might not hesitate to place it in a typology of 'positive' qualities. For instance, in Compton's (2005, p. 4) *Introduction to Positive Psychology*, compassion nestles in nicely alongside authentic happiness, creativity and savouring in an 'A–Z' of topics. However, the moment one reflects upon the meaning of the word, the picture darkens somewhat. Its etymology is revealing, deriving from the Latin terms *com* (with) and *pati* (to suffer). Thus, at an instance, we can see that valorising compassion within PP immediately places us in second wave territory. Yes, we value this quality;

however, its dynamics are too nuanced and dialectical to depict it simply as a 'positive' emotion; it inherently and necessarily involves opening ourselves up to the 'dark side' of life, to feelings of sadness and distress. As Schulz et al. (2007, p. 6) put it, compassion involves 'a sense of shared suffering, combined with a desire to alleviate or reduce such suffering'. And yet, in cultivating compassion, even as this means opening ourselves up to the 'dark side' of life, coming face-to-face with suffering, one may also experience profoundly meaningful states of fulfilment and connection.

This apparent paradox is a perfect example of the definition of the 'dark side' outlined in the introduction. Recall that the 'dark side' refers to challenging experiences and mental states which trigger discomfort in us and which we therefore tend to avoid (as it means engaging with fear, pain, distress or confusion). However, engaging with the challenge and discomfort has a great potential for growth, healing, insight and transformation; thus the 'dark side' contains the seed for a potential positive outcome, even when the path towards this outcome is testing. How can we explain this seeming paradox? We will attempt to do so here over three parts. We shall begin in part one by considering how compassion has been understood within academia. In part two, we then start to explain our paradox by introducing various models of selfhood and suggest that in contrast to the 'individualistic' sense of self that many people commonly experience, compassion allows us to enter into a more 'intersubjective' identity. Finally, we explore how such intersubjectivity may be beneficial to wellbeing, with potentially profound consequences in terms of psychospiritual development. As such, this chapter illustrates the potentially transformative effects of allowing ourselves to engage with the darker aspects of life – in this case, being touched and moved by the suffering of others – and then allowing ourselves to be deeply changed by this process.

PRACTICE ESSAY QUESTIONS

- What significance does compassion hold for the way in which we conceptualise the self in PP?

- Critically evaluate the concept of psychospiritual development and the role that compassion might play in this process.

COMPASSION

We begin by clarifying what we mean by compassion. Theoretical models view this as being multifaceted (Ozawa-de Silva et al., 2012), involving various components – cognitive (the ability to empathically recognise emotions in others), emotional (experiencing sympathetic distress), motivational (the will to reduce the other's suffering) and behavioural (a resulting action). As such, compassion involves not only empathy (the ability to understand and share the emotional experience of another person) and sympathy (consequent feelings of sorrow or concern for the other as a result of appraising distress) but goes further in that it also includes motivation and behaviour (Eisenberg, 2002). Thus, in compassion, one 'suffers with' the other and acts to relieve the suffering as if it were one's own (which, in a sense, it is, as one is sharing in the suffering). That said, some perspectives hold that compassion need not necessarily involve experiences of sympathetic distress; for example, in Buddhism, compassion is regarded as a state 'beyond sadness' (Houshman et al., 2002, p. 15): while sympathetic distress may act as a catalyst for compassion, it is not an essential component of it; one may experience compassion with equanimity instead of distress. Indeed, Buddhists regard such equanimous responding as the 'highest' level of compassionate activity (we shall return to Buddhist perspectives on compassion later). Nevertheless, generally speaking, compassion involves opening ourselves up to the suffering of another and seeking to relieve this out of care and concern.

REFLECTION

When was the last time you felt a strong sense of compassion for another person? Try to recall this experience in as much detail as possible. To what extent were these four components (cognitive, emotional, motivational, and behavioural) present? How would you characterise this state overall – positive, negative, or something beyond both of these? What did it *mean* to you?

For many scientists and philosophers, compassion is a conundrum, a fly in the ointment of their particular view of human nature as being fundamentally selfish and self-serving, a perspective known as 'universal egoism' (Batson, 1991). Some such people are well versed in evolutionary theory, where living beings are seen as driven by the reproductive prerogatives of their 'selfish' genes (Dawkins, 1976) and where life is a dog-eat-dog 'survival of the fittest'. In this view, caring for others (who do not share our genes) is almost regarded as an aberration of nature and is certainly a difficult phenomenon to account for. Others are persuaded by the overlapping notion of 'rational choice' theory, which holds that human behaviour is ultimately motivated by self-interest (Ostrom, 1998). While still buying into the competitive discourses of evolutionary biology, this latter perspective does allow room for compassion; however, it regards it cynically as ultimately self-serving, a form of 'enlightened self-interest'. Some advocates of this view contend that people act compassionately primarily to reduce their own feelings of distress (evoked by the other's pain) (Cialdini et al., 1987). Similarly, others argue that compassion can be self-serving in terms of helping people to prosper through mechanisms such as conforming to social norms, developing a good reputation, and/or increasing the likelihood that they will themselves be reciprocally rewarded in future (Trivers, 1971).

However, these types of cynical explanations are somewhat undermined by the very *existence* of the compassionate impulse; even if we may be motivated to help others to reduce our own distress, this does not really explain why we feel distress in response to their suffering in the first place. Thus, as theorists such as Batson (1991) have recognised, first and foremost, people are genuinely moved by the plight of another, even if other motives then contribute to their decision to respond. The existence of such intuitive empathy is powerfully demonstrated by the existence of mirror neurons (Gallese, 2001), where studies have found that brain regions that are activated when an individual experiences emotions are likewise activated when the same emotions are observed in other people (Preston & De Waal, 2002). As such, Batson's 'empathy–altruism' hypothesis holds that, contrary to the universal egoism model, people can and do genuinely care for other people, regardless of whether it benefits them personally. This benign view of human nature is echoed by philosophies such as Buddhism, which views people as being fundamentally compassionate, even if this core nature does unfortunately often get obscured all too easily. As expressed by His Holiness the Dalai Lama (2002, p. 70), people have a 'natural ability to connect spontaneously and deeply with the suffering of others'. Or, in the language of this book, people do not necessarily shut out the 'dark side' of life (e.g., the distress of other people) but can be acutely attuned to it and willing to engage with it (e.g., trying to help alleviate this distress).

However, even if compassion were shown to be 'natural' – an inherent feature of our common humanity – this in itself would not be sufficient to recommend it to people, to argue that one should ideally be compassionate. For a start, many generally undesirable traits, from anger to anxiety, are likewise 'natural'; this is not evidence in their favour. Moreover, there are those who warn of potential dangers of compassion. Most forcefully and provocatively, there is an 'anti-compassion' tradition in philosophy, associated most prominently with the polemical work of Nietzsche (1887/1969), who argued that compassion is ultimately detrimental to both the giver and the recipient (because it hinders the latter from developing self-sufficiency). From a different angle, based on her studies of the American and French revolutions, Arendt (1963) worried that compassion (e.g., for society's downtrodden victims) could all too easily morph into violence (against their oppressors). On a less dramatic note, but still a cause for concern, many scholars have highlighted the potential burden that compassion – and continual engagement with the 'dark side' of life – may impose upon the giver, so-called compassion fatigue. Here the literature is replete with warnings of the potential emotional strain faced by people who are in long-term caring roles, whether looking after family members (Figley, 1997) or in the helping professions (Schulz et al., 2007). While such analyses do not undermine the value of compassion – rather, they highlight the need for carers to receive compassion and support themselves – they again give us pause for thought in terms of arguing that one ideally should be compassionate.

Given these concerns, why would one advocate compassion, advocate opening oneself up to this aspect of the 'dark side' of life (to the suffering of others)? Answers to this are naturally less forthcoming within scientific literature because science generally endeavours to be 'value neutral' (analysing phenomena dispassionately rather than arguing for particular outcomes). However, we can find myriad supportive voices from the fields of moral philosophy and religion. Within Western philosophy, perhaps the most prominent articulation of the value of compassion was provided by Schopenhauer (1840/1995), who regarded it as the solution to the 'great mystery of ethics'. He saw compassion as the only possible foundation for any moral framework: morality is not upheld through people rationally assenting to a system of laws – the position taken by Kant (1785/2002), with his notion of the categorical imperative (i.e., act in ways that you would will to become a general law) – but rather because people care in a deep and mysterious way about the suffering of others. On this view, compassion is the cornerstone of morality and thus of any genuine social cohesion and solidarity. The importance of compassion is likewise asserted in the great religious traditions. For instance, in his epistle to the Corinthians, St. Paul preached that of the three great theological virtues in Christianity – faith, hope and charity – 'the greatest of these is charity'. ('Charity' was selected by the translators of the King James Bible as an equivalent of the Greek *agape*; however, as Hitchens (2011) argues, *agape* is arguably better rendered as selfless or compassionate love.) Likewise, His Holiness the Dalai Lama (1997) calls compassion the 'essence' of Buddhism, which indeed has been called a 'religion of compassion' (Price, 2010).

ART LINKS

One of Vincent van Gogh's most famous paintings was of an old weather-beaten pair of worker's boots. According to Wilber (2001), a profound personal experience of compassion lay at the heart of this artwork. When asked by his friend, the painter Gauguin, about its meaning, van Gogh reported that as a young man, he had wanted to follow his father and become a religious pastor. One day, while pursuing this vocation, there was an awful fire in the local mine. One of the miners was horribly burned, to the extent that he had been given up for dead. Consumed by a fevered sense of mission, van Gogh spent one whole month nursing this pour soul back from the brink of death. These shoes, which van Gogh had worn at the time, came to symbolise the near-divine sense of purpose and meaning he had felt during this numinous time. According to Gauguin, as he was recounting the story, van Gogh took on an almost Christ-like sense of being imbued with sacrality, crying, 'I am the holy spirit, I am whole in spirit' (in Wilber, 2001, pp. 114).

However, when we consider the centrality placed on compassion by religions like Christianity and Buddhism, the stirring thought occurs: is compassion simply valued as a basis of morality, as a foundation for social cohesion, or is something deeper, more radical, being alluded to? Yes of course, compassion is a wonderful gift for the recipients, helping them to feel loved, cared for and supported. But what if compassion also has the potential to transform the *giver* in profound, unanticipated ways, as reflected in the example of van Gogh? In Christianity, Jesus preached the radical message that we should be compassionate to all people, including those who may have harmed us: 'Love your enemies, and pray for those that persecute you, so that you may be children of your father in heaven' (Matthew 5:44). The last phrase, 'so that you may be children of your father', seems very telling: it seems to suggest that, by being compassionate and loving, a person might be changed somehow, as if ushered into a new way of being, or even sharing in the divinity of God, as a believer might put it (Smith, 2011). Now, to our 21st-century ears, these phrases and notions may sound odd and out of place. Nevertheless, when we contemplate the nature of compassion, it becomes apparent that something potentially quite remarkable may possibly occur to the giver. In the language of contemporary psychology, we might interpret this prospect in terms of theories of identity, raising the tantalising possibility that, through cultivating compassion, a person may experience significant changes in his or her sense of self, as the next section explores.

IDENTITY AND INTERCONNECTEDNESS

What can it mean to say that, by being compassionate – by opening oneself up to the 'dark side' of life and allowing oneself to be moved by the suffering of another person – one might experience changes in one's sense of self? To answer this question, we need to begin by recognising that there are different ways of conceptualising 'the self'. Indeed, this is a vast understatement: the concept of the self – and related terms like 'identity', 'ego', and 'subjectivity' – is one of the most perplexing, contested and complex constructs in the history of thought. Thus, we cannot hope to give a comprehensive account here of all the myriad ways in which identity and selfhood have been appraised even within psychology, let alone by thinkers throughout the ages. On a positive note, this acknowledgment opens the door to the liberating idea that our taken-for-granted notions of the self are a product of our particular historico-cultural context and are neither inevitable nor unalterable. However, this still leaves the issue of how we get to grips here with the shape-shifting concept of the self because, in an academic context, we must at least try to define our terms for the discussion to proceed at all. So, at the risk of greatly oversimplifying a vast field of enquiry, we might note that the various perspectives on selfhood fall roughly into two broad categories: individualism and intersubjectivism[1]. We'll begin here by exploring individualism, which as we will see, is regarded as the predominant conception of selfhood in the West, before going on to introduce the notion of intersubjectivism.

It is often asserted that there is, in the West, an ideology of individualism (Becker & Marecek, 2008). What can this mean; surely all human beings are 'individuals'? Well, yes they are, but the concept of individualism captures a particular view of the self that is thought to have emerged over the course of the last few centuries in Western societies: the idea that the self exists as an autonomous entity, a discrete unit, complete unto itself. As Geertz (1983, p. 59) put it, the self is regarded in the West as 'a bounded, unique, more or less integrated motivational and cognitive universe'. Similarly, Taylor (1995, p. 60) suggested that individualism conceptualises the self as 'a centre of monological consciousness': this means that the person is constituted by a private, 'inner space', in which they alone exist, over which they alone have control, and through which they alone act. Other people of course exist but only either as objects 'out there' or as mental representations 'in here'. This is the view of selfhood that underpins contemporary psychology and indeed PP; it is reflected in the myriad constructs prefixed by the term 'self', from self-determination to self-esteem, and in all the related discourses of self, from authenticity to autonomy (Ryan & Deci, 2006). With individualism, it is not just that the main object of concern is the individual; people are fundamentally seen as existing as separate individuals – unique, autonomous and self-contained. The social, to the extent that it is recognised at all, is simply an aggregation of individuals.

This may seem like the unproblematic, common-sense way of looking at the self; however, its 'naturalness' is undermined when we consider that this may be a rather specific construction particular to our current age and cultural context. It is suggested that this vision of the self was forged in the heat of the extraordinary period of cultural ferment and development in the West that we now refer to as the Renaissance and the Enlightenment (Taylor, 1995). In contrast to the largely diminished view of humankind that had dominated the West through the Middle Ages – where humans were regarded as the sinful, errant children of a displeased God – the Renaissance gave (re)birth to a confident, elevated picture of the strength, intelligence, dignity and autonomy of humankind (Tarnas, 1991). Although many thinkers contributed to this new, emerging view of selfhood, one philosopher above all proved to be particularly influential: Rene Descartes (1641). In his quest to establish a secure basis for knowledge, Descartes found that *everything* was subject to doubt, *except* . . . the fact that he was doubting, leading to the immortal statement *cogito ergo sum* (I think therefore I am). Thus, even if nothing else is real, the 'monological consciousness' exists. Such was the power of Descartes' articulation of this vision – this 'reification of the disengaged first-person-singular self' (Taylor, 1995, p. 59) – that it came to dominate Western thinking over subsequent centuries to the extent that the individualised sense of selfhood is frequently referred to as the 'Cartesian I'.

However, even if we are so accustomed to viewing the self in this way that individualism has become 'naturalised', it is not the only way of appraising the self. The first counterargument to individualism derives from other cultures. Throughout the 20th century, anthropologists have sought to highlight variation in views of selfhood among the different world cultures, both historical and current. Some such analyses are very specific, focusing on one particular locale. For instance, in Vietnam, Marr (2000) suggests that people have historically been viewed primarily in terms of their location within, and contribution to, the suprapersonal social order. Marr contends that the concept of the 'individual' only entered into the Vietnamese lexicon in the 20th century and even then only in a pejorative sense, whereby a person acting in his or her own interests could be accused of perpetrating the antisocial misdeed of 'individualism'. This notion of a more group-oriented view of selfhood in Vietnam fits in with perhaps the most widely researched and discussed cross-cultural generalisation within psychology: the idea that Western societies are 'individualist', whereas Eastern cultures are 'collectivist' (Hofstede, 1980). Developed by Markus and Kitayama (1991, p. 224), this theory holds that contrary to Western individualism, Asian societies have 'distinct conceptions of individuality that insist on the fundamental relatedness of individuals', where the 'emphasis is on attending to others, fitting in, and harmonious interdependence with them'.

However, as enduring as this individualist–collectivist distinction has proved – analysed and to an extent corroborated across hundreds of empirical studies (Taras et al., 2010) – it still serves to reinforce the notion of individualism but simply limits it to 'Western' cultures. The picture may be far more nuanced though. For a start, notions of 'West' versus 'East' are themselves cultural constructions, homogenising and obscuring myriad differences at regional and local levels (Said, 1995). The idea that 'the East' lacks its own strains of individualism, and likewise that 'the West' does not possess its own collectivist traditions and voices, is a fallacy that does disservice to the rich heterogeneity of both arenas (Spiro, 1993). Moreover, a binary 'East–West' distinction constructs these hemispheres as if discretely bounded and hermetically sealed, overlooking the complex inter-transmission of people and ideas across boundaries. The last 100 years in particular have witnessed an incredible cross-fertilisation of cultures, with supposedly Western ideologies such as consumer capitalism finding fertile ground in countries like China and 'Eastern' practices such as meditation finding hugely receptive audiences in the West (King, 1999). Thus, the notion of ubiquitous individualism in the West has been challenged, with it being recognised that 'intersubjective[2]' experiences of self are perhaps more universal than the individualist–collectivist dichotomy appears to suggest (Larsen, 1990). Consequently, various contemporary theories of identity have emerged capturing this sense of 'intersubjectivity'.

In their various ways, these theories argue that people can come to transcend a narrow view of selfhood – the autonomous, bounded individual 'I' depicted – and learn to identify with other people (using identity here in a strong sense to mean that the person experiences his or her life as 'bound together' in some way). This intersubjective sense of self goes by various names, including the 'dialogical self' (Hermans et al., 1992), the 'permeable self' (Larsen, 1990) and 'identity fusion' (Swann et al., 2012). We are entering into tricky conceptual territory here, so we must be careful with our elucidation of this intersubjective self, especially as psychopathologies such as schizophrenia are often explained in terms of the disruption of self–other distinctions and the 'dissolution of the self' (Parnas, 2000, p. 117). Without denying the possibility that there can be dysfunctional intersubjective experiences of self, what we are really talking about here is the *transcendence* of a narrow self-identity rather than an obliteration of it. Now, what do we mean by transcendence? A useful approach to this much-contested concept is provided by Wilber (1995). Wilber draws on the philosophy of Hegel (1807/1973, pp. 163–164), who argued that to transcend means 'at once to negate and preserve'. In self-transcendence, what is negated is an exclusive identification with a particular view of self; however, this does not mean that the old view of self is completely lost – it is preserved but simply set in a larger context that means it is 'seen through'.

All this is sounding rather esoteric, so let us explain it with a very common, yet no less powerful, example. Imagine a mother (or a father) with a newborn baby. Before the birth, let us suppose that the mother had a somewhat individualistic sense of selfhood; she may well have loved and cared for others, but her selfhood was entirely bounded to herself – she was, in Watts' (1961, p. 18) neat phrase, a 'skin-encapsulated ego'. However, with the birth all this has changed. Our idealised mother literally experiences the baby as a 'part' or 'extension' of herself – granted, they no longer share the same 'skin-encapsulated' physical body, but cognitively, emotionally and motivationally, they remain essentially one: the baby's pain is her pain; its smile is her joy; her 'sphere of concern' encompasses her baby totally. Thus, we might say that the mother has transcended her previous individualistic identity to take on a larger sense of selfhood that includes her new progeny. Here we can really appreciate the meaning of transcendence: this is not a 'dissolution' of the self: rationally, the mother can still recognise and identify herself as a separate being. (Note: this is in contrast to the newborn, who *does* experience this dyadic relationship in an 'undifferentiated' way, who has yet to develop any self–other distinction (Mahler et al., 2000).) Thus, the mother has transcended her previous sense of selfhood: it has been preserved (she can still recognise herself as a separate being) and yet negated (her identity has been enlarged to also encompass the little being who has emerged into the world).

Now, returning to the overall theme of the chapter, we can interpret the mother's (or father's) identification with and concern for the newborn as the very epitome of compassion and not only compassion – consideration and care generally. The Jewish philosopher Martin Buber (1958) made a beautiful distinction between 'I–it' and 'I–thou' relationships. In the former, the other person is regarded as an object to be valued only to the extent that he or she helps one fulfil one's own needs. With I–thou relationships, the person meets the other with unconditional regard, as equally worthy of love, care and respect as oneself. Parental love for an infant is perhaps the zenith of I–thou regard. In this there is not only compassion but care for the other generally. For instance, in Buddhism, it is recognised that when one cares for another in this I–thou kind of way, one does not only react with compassion when in distress but responds with love to all joys, sorrows and needs (Eisenberg, 2002). Thus, in addition to exuding *karuna* (compassion), the person embodies qualities such as *metta* (loving kindness: treating the other with love generally), *mudita* (sympathetic joy: rejoicing in another's happiness and successes), and *dana* (giving benevolently and unreservedly: responding to needs as they arise). One could see how our hypothetical parent would evince these wonderful pro-social qualities with regard to his or her beloved child. This parent would thus be utterly open and receptive to both the light and dark aspects of the child's life, reacting with joy to the light (e.g., the child's happiness) and responding with care to the dark (e.g., the child's distress).

We can recognise that this is a somewhat idealised example. Not all mothers may feel this kind of identification, and even with those that do, it is unlikely to be constant; there will be moments of selfishness amidst the care. In an odd way, though, this gives us hope. It suggests that this kind of concern is not a trait-like all-or-nothing affair (you either have it or you don't) but rather an intersubjective mode that we can, at our best, enter into. Granted, it would be almost impossible to generalise the kind of concern a parent shows towards a baby to everyone we encounter. This does not mean though that we cannot have our moments of compassion and grace, instances when we do step outside of our individualistic self-regard and act purely out of concern for the other, as illustrated in the following box. So, let us imagine a continuum between total selfishness (the kind of absolute, solipsistic disregard for others found in psychopathy) and total selflessness (the kind of absolute compassion manifested by a Buddha). We might imagine that everyone is located, by temperament and development, *somewhere* along this line. Let us add further nuance here: the person's various relationships may each be situated differentially along this continuum, some being characterised by greater degrees of selflessness than others. Furthermore, the location of each of these relationships may shift depending on certain factors (e.g., if the person is feeling happy, there may be movement in the direction of selflessness). As such, arguably nearly all people will act with some degree of selflessness, at least in some of their relationships some of the time.

RESEARCH AND PRACTICE CASE STUDIES

Extraordinary situations can bring out extraordinary qualities in people, even to the extent that they will selflessly sacrifice their lives for people to whom they may not even be related by blood. A moving example of this can be found in Sebastian Junger's (2010) powerful account of American personnel serving in Afghanistan, in which a soldier is reported as saying, 'I'd actually throw myself on the hand grenade for them . . . because I actually love my brothers' (p. 246).

Finally, the key point here is that wherever a person is situated on this continuum, and however their various relationships are configured along it, they can endeavour to *move along* this spectrum in the direction of greater selflessness. People can practice and cultivate a greater sense of compassion by opening their hearts to the suffering of others, by allowing themselves to be touched and moved by this dimension of the 'dark side' of life. Indeed, people can work on the whole constellation of other-regarding qualities, including loving kindness, sympathetic joy and benevolent giving. The idea that these qualities can be developed is the premise behind specific psychological practices, such as loving kindness meditation (LKM; Salzberg, 1995), and indeed is a key teaching in philosophies and religions such as Buddhism and Christianity, as already noted. However, what we have not yet addressed is *why* such religions lay such a strong emphasis on the importance and value of compassion. Yes, of course it is beneficial to the recipient and serves to uphold a moral vision articulated by these religions. And yet we've raised the possibility that compassionate acts – and the self-transcendence that such acts facilitate – may also potentially have a profound impact on the actor themselves, as our final section explores.

Self-transcendence through compassion

As Western psychology begins to awaken to the value of compassion, we are beginning to see the diverse ways in which this quality contributes to wellbeing. Understandably, much of this research has focused on the positive social impact of compassion and on how it benefits its recipients and the collective commons generally. For example, following Schopenhauer (1840/1995), Ozawa-de Silva et al. (2012, p. 145) identified compassion as 'the most stable foundation for a secular ethics' because it is based on the 'fundamental human aspiration' towards happiness, and thus 'transcends religious, cultural, and philosophical divides'. Moreover, Ozawa-de Silva et al. have developed a practical form of 'cognitively based compassion training' to help engender exactly this kind of ethical sensibility. Interestingly, a large segment of the pro-social research on compassion has been in terms of its positive *environmental* impact. One of the outcomes of self-transcendence, as we shall explore, is enhanced feelings of 'interconnected-ness' – not only with other people but with the world around (Hungelmann et al., 1996). Just as such interconnectedness can lead one to treat people more compas-sionately, recent work – both theoretical (Daniels, 2010) and empirical (Davis et al., 2009) – has shown that this care can extend to nature, leading to more environmen-tally friendly behaviour.

However, as valuable as such research is, it somewhat fails to capture the profound impact that compassion may potentially have on the actors themselves. That is not to say that this has been entirely overlooked in PP; a number of studies have suggested that compassion is linked to wellbeing, particularly eudaimonic flourishing. For exam-ple, introducing the notion of 'positive social work', Radey and Figley (2007) argue that, if the right factors are in place (e.g., adequate work resources), social workers can attain fulfilment through engaging compassionately with clients. Likewise, Seligman et al. (2006, p. 777) argue that serving and belonging to 'something that one believes is bigger than the self' is central to finding meaning in life; clearly, caring for others would fall within such a description. Arguably though, the true import of compassion has not yet been quite articulated within PP perhaps because the field, like psychology generally, is still largely rooted in the individualistic view of selfhood (Becker & Marecek, 2008). As Harrington (2002) argued, because compassion is fundamentally an inter-subjective phenomenon that happens 'in between' individual selves, it has remained a lacuna within Western science. This conventional psychological perspective – centred as it is on discrete, bounded, atomistic individuals – struggles to accommodate the type of ontological shift implied by the concept of self-transcendence and as such fails to appre-ciate the significance of compassion (which helps engender this shift). So, to appreciate why self-transcendence may be valuable for wellbeing, we end this chapter by briefly considering another school of thought which has given much attention to these issues, namely Buddhism.

Buddhism comprises such a vast body of knowledge, accumulated over 2,500 years, that even a lifetime would be insufficient for fully appreciating the depth of the wisdom contained within. It goes without saying then that this chapter can but scratch the surface of these teachings, hoping merely to draw upon certain glimmers of insight that can illuminate some of the ideas already discussed. And here we find that Buddhism has a very helpful perspective on the value of allowing oneself to engage with the 'dark side' of life – being open to and moved the suffering of others – especially in terms of the way such engagement facilities self-transcendence. In particular, compassion and subsequent self-transcendence are valued because Buddhism attributes much of the unhappiness and suffering in this world to one specific cause: the *self*. Now, as we would expect with a tradition as rich as Buddhism, with its various schools of thought that have emerged over the centuries, it does not feature just one single perspective on the self. However, without getting lost here in esoteric philosophising around subtle doctrinal differences, Buddhism generally upholds a teaching of *anātman* (a Sanskrit term meaning no-self or soul). That is, Buddhism regards the self, *as conventionally understood*, to be an unhelpful construct or, phrased more powerfully, a destructive 'illusion' (Epstein, 1988). The individualistic model of self-hood (the idea that we exist as separate, fixed, bounded entities) is not only regarded as an incorrect fiction but a fiction that underlies many of the problems in the world.

To put this view of selfhood into context, Buddhism proposes that existence is charac-terised by three key qualities: *anātman* (no self or insubstantiality), *anitya* (impermanence) and *duhkha* (frustration or suffering) (Sangharakshita & Subhuti, 2013). All phenomena, including humans, are ultimately seen as insubstantial (they are not self-existing entities; their existence depends on a network of supporting conditions) and impermanent (they change as their supporting conditions change). A useful metaphor is that of a whirlpool in a river: the configuration of the natural environment is such that a repeating pattern of water is created; however, the whirlpool does not exist as a separate object apart from these conditions. (You could not send a person down to the river with a bucket and ask them to bring back the whirlpool for you!) In Buddhism, the self is regarded in much the same way; out of the ongoing flux of subjective experience (the thoughts, feelings and sensations flowing through our streams of consciousness), processes such as memory and language provide the illusion of the self as a fixed entity, when really there is nothing actually 'there'. However, Buddhism further argues that people tend to deny these two fundamental aspects of reality (*anātman* and *anitya*) and instead regard phenomena, includ-ing their own self, as being stable and permanent. Crucially, it is this misperception that is seen as the cause of the third aspect of existence, *duhkha*. This is partly because people become attached to phenomena that are inherently subject to change; people then suffer when this change does in fact occur. It is also because, in the case of the self, attaching to the idea that one exists as a separate individual is the premise and foundation for a con-stellation of destructive behaviours, whether pertaining to the drive to aggrandise the self (e.g., egotism, pride and jealousy) or the urge to defend and protect it (e.g., hatred and aggression towards anything which threatens it).

Given these key teachings, given the idea that clinging to the notion of a separate self is the root cause of much unhappiness, Buddhism holds that the way to overcome suffering is by transcending the self (Ho, 1995). To return to our definition of self-transcendence, this does not mean the kind of dissolution of self–other boundaries that may occur in psychopathology but rather appreciating one's narrow view of selfhood as an unhelpful construct and 'seeing through' it. (After all, Buddhist adepts are certainly still capable of clothing and feeding their 'fictional' selves; yet in a deeper sense they have come to regard it as ultimately illusory.) This is the point of many meditative practices in Bud-dhism: to understand, on a deep experiential level, that the self is 'not real', to transcend this narrow sense of selfhood and to create a more expansive identity, one encompassing other people. We saw this kind of 'intersubjective' selfhood perhaps emerging naturally in the case of parents caring for their baby. Even if we did acknowledge this as an idealised example, Buddhist practices endeavour to at least move people *towards* this I–thou regard for the other, along the continuum towards the ideal of selflessness. This is the point of practices like LKM, in which one is encouraged to generate feelings of love and care for other people. And, as this section is attempting to argue, empirical studies indicate that such practices are associated with increases in wellbeing, partly because people feel greater connectedness with others (Fredrickson et al., 2008). A less-well known practice is *Tonglen* meditation, which prompts people to reflect on the darker aspects of existence – the distress of other people – thus evoking feelings of compassion and care, which in turn may facilitate self-transcendence (as well as actual efforts to reach out and help those suffering). This practice, a perfect illustration of engaging in a positive way with the 'dark side' of life, is introduced in the following box:

TRY ME

In Buddhism, a beautiful practice for evoking *karuna* (compassion) is Tonglen meditation, a cyclical visualisation process in which the practitioner imagines 'taking in' another person's suffering, and 'giving' them happiness in return (Lomas, 2014). If you would like to try this, please sit in a quiet, comfortable place, and follow these instructions:

- Close your eyes, and take a few moments to feel your breath slowing down.

- Bring to mind a person to whom you are close who has recently suffered hardship.

- Spend a few moments reflecting on his or her suffering and how you would like to relieve him or her of this if possible.

- Visualise the suffering as a cloud of noxious, black smoke, enveloping him or her.

- Breathing in, imagine that you are drawing in this smoke through your nostrils.

- As you do, softly say, 'May I take away your troubles'.

- At the still point at the end of the in breath, imagine this black smoke being dissolved in your heart by the force of your affection for this person.

- Visualise this affection as a clear, white light.

- Breathing out, imagine that you are emanating this white light, which bathes the person in a radiant cloud of your affection.

- As you do, softly say, 'May I give you happiness'.

- Repeat this process, 'taking in' suffering on each in breath and 'giving out' happiness on each out breath.

- Continue for as long as you feel comfortable, ideally for no less than five minutes.

It is not only that cultivating compassion, and thereby transcending the self, can help alleviate one's suffering (as well as the suffering of others); more radically, some scholars view this process of self-transcendence as the very definition of psychospiritual growth (Wilber, 1995). There are of course many different ways of conceptualising such development; even in canonical Buddhist teachings, there are at least six different stage-wise conceptions of the spiritual path (Bucknell, 1984). However, scholars such as Wilber have sought to identify commonalities across all these different conceptualisations, with one conclusion being that psychospiritual development can be defined, at least in part, by an expansion of one's moral concern. Transcending one's individualistic view of selfhood and developing a deep sense of care for another – whether a parent's devotion to his or her child or any other dyad suffused with love – is a beautiful start. However, this is perhaps just the beginning of a much longer spiritual journey in which we can attempt to expand our vision of selfhood in an ongoing process of transcendence. Wilber argues that we can continue to extend our circle of compassionate concern, not stopping at the inclusion of one other beloved person but including all those we come into contact with and even beyond, up to and including all sentient beings. Indeed, this expansion of care is cultivated in Buddhist practices like LKM – which expand 'outwards' in just such a way – and is central to Buddhist moral philosophy, which argues that we have a duty to protect all beings in the universe (Lecso, 1988).

And finally, without straying too much into esoteric mystical territory, we might ask, what is the omega point, the goal of this journey of psychospiritual development? Where does this process of self-transcendence – of expanding one's circle of compassionate care, of entering into an ever-wider intersubjective experience of selfhood – lead to? Many religious traditions suggest that the ultimate endpoint of this development is an experiential union with some kind of numinous power, whatever name we give to this. Monotheistic religions might describe this as sharing in the divinity of God; as the 13th-century Christian mystic Meister Eckhart (1980, p. 217) phrased it, 'I discover that I and God are one'. Likewise, Buber (1958) felt that the particular power of I–thou relationships was that they constituted a spiritual relationship in which both partners entered into the 'eternal thou', a suprapersonal union suffused with the grace of God. Alternatively, non-theistic religions such as Buddhism might conceptualise this as union with the *bhavanga*, with the 'ground of being' (Wallace, 2001). And what do people experience in such a union? In the end, most reports characterise this ultimate intersubjective selfhood as being suffused with an overwhelming sense of love. As Wallace (2001, pp. 4–5) puts it, 'Buddhist contemplatives have . . . concluded that the nature of this ground of being is loving-kindness'. Although such ideas may currently sound rather radical from the perspective of conventional psychology, these kinds of reports do suggest that the cultivation of compassion may have great, even profound consequences. Thus, opening up to the 'dark side' of life, in this case by becoming attuned to the suffering and distress of those around, may potentially be the first step on a life-transforming journey of transcending one's narrow self-identity and entering into a far greater sense of being.

SUMMARY – THIS CHAPTER HAS ACCOMPLISHED THE FOLLOWING

- Summarised different conceptualisations of compassion within psychology
- Positioned compassion as one of a number of 'other-regarding' qualities
- Shown that compassion involves opening up to the 'dark side' (other people's suffering)
- Explored the pro-social impact of compassion, including as a foundation for morality
- Examined how other-regarding qualities might also be highly beneficial to the actor
- Suggested that compassion is connected to self-transcendence
- Linked self-transcendence to psychospiritual development

RESOURCES AND SUGGESTIONS

- A wonderful resource on compassion is the 'Charter for Compassion', for which Karen Armstrong was awarded the TED prize in 2008. It aims to help people take action to create a peaceful global community: http://www.charterforcompassion.org/
- In terms of activities and interventions to cultivate compassion, for more information on cognitively based compassion training: http://www.tibet.emory.edu/cbct/

NOTES

1   Intersubjectivism is perhaps more commonly referred to as 'collectivism' (Hofstede, 1980). However, as explained later in this chapter, 'intersubjectivity', associated with the phenomenological philosophy of Husserl (1931/1999), is arguably a more useful term here.

2   As indicated above, this label is preferred here to the term 'collectivist'. For a start, the word 'collectivist' has been tainted by association with the horrors of totalitarian communist regimes like Stalinist Russia (Conquest, 1987). This usage is connected to the idea that collectivist models of selfhood often deny the right of people to exist as autonomous individuals per se rather viewing them as fungible parts of a larger collective social entity. In contrast, intersubjectivity does not dismiss people's claims to individuality and agency; it simply recognises that their being is also formed through their interconnections with other people (Husserl, 1931/1999).

BIBLIOGRAPHY

Arendt, H. (1963). *On revolution*. London: Penguin Books.

Batson, C.D. (1991). *The altruism question: Toward a social-psychological answer*. Hillsdale, NJ: Erlbaum.

Becker, D., & Marecek, J. (2008). Dreaming the American dream: Individualism and positive psychology. *Social and Personality Psychology Compass, 2*(5), 1767–1780.

Buber, M. (1958). *I and thou*. New York: Scrivener.

Bucknell, R.S. (1984). The Buddhist path to liberation: An analysis of the listing of stages. *Journal of the International Association of Buddhist Studies, 7*(2), 7–40.

Cialdini, R.B., Schaller, M., Houlihan, D., Arps, K., Fultz, J., & Beaman, A.L. (1987). Empathy-based helping: Is it selflessly or selfishly motivated? *Journal of Personality and Social Psychology, 52*(4), 749–758.

Compton, W.C. (2005). *Introduction to positive psychology*. Sydney, Australia: Thomson/Wadsworth.

Conquest, R. (1987). *The harvest of sorrow: Soviet collectivization and the terror-famine*. Oxford, UK: Oxford University Press.

Daniels, P.L. (2010). Climate change, economics and Buddhism—Part I: An integrated environmental analysis framework. *Ecological Economics, 69*(5), 952–961.

Davis, J.L., Green, J.D., & Reed, A. (2009). Interdependence with the environment: Commitment, interconnectedness, and environmental behavior. *Journal of Environmental Psychology, 29*(2), 173–180.

Dawkins, R. (1976). *The selfish gene*. Oxford, UK: Oxford University Press.

Descartes, R. (1641/2008). *Meditations on first philosophy: With selections from the objections and replies* (M. Moriarty, Trans.). Oxford, UK: Oxford University Press.

Eckhart, M. (1980). *Breakthrough: Meister Eckhart's creation spirituality* (M. Fox, Trans.). London: Doubleday Books.

Eisenberg, N. (2002). Empathy-related emotional responses, altruism, and their social-isation. In R.J. Davidson & A. Harrington (Eds.), *Visions of compassion: Western scientists and Tibetan Buddhists examine human nature* (pp. 131–164). Oxford, UK: Oxford University Press.

Epstein, M. (1988). The deconstruction of the self: Ego and 'egolessness' in Buddhist insight meditation. *The Journal of Transpersonal Psychology, 20*(1), 61–69.

Figley, C.R. (Ed.). (1997). *Burnout in families: The systemic costs of caring*. Miami FL: CRC Press.

Fredrickson, B.L., Cohn, M.A., Coffey, K.A., Pek, J., & Finkel, S.M. (2008). Open hearts build lives: Positive emotions, induced through loving-kindness meditation, build consequential personal resources. *Journal of Personality and Social Psychology, 95*(5), 1045–1062.

Gallese, V. (2001). The 'shared manifold' hypothesis: From mirror neurons to empathy. *Journal of Consciousness Studies, 8*(5–7), 33–50.

Geertz, C. (1983). *Local knowledge*. London: Fontana Press.

Harrington, A. (2002). A science of compassion or a compassionate science: What do we expect from a cross-cultural dialogue with Buddhism. In R.J. Davidson & A. Harrington (Eds.), *Visions of compassion: Western scientists and Tibetan Buddhists examine human nature* (pp. 18–30). Oxford, UK: Oxford University Press.

Hegel, G.W.F. (1807/1973). *Phenomenology of Mind*. Frankfurt, Germany: Verlag Ullstein.

Hermans, H.J., Kempen, H.J., & Van Loon, R.J. (1992). The dialogical self: Beyond individualism and rationalism. *American Psychologist, 47*(1), 23–33.

His Holiness the Dalai Lama. (1997). *The heart of compassion*. Twin Lakes, WI: Lotus Press.

His Holiness the Dalai Lama. (2002). Understanding our fundamental nature. In R.J. Davidson & A. Harrington (Eds.), *Visions of compassion: Western scientists and Tibetan Buddhists examine human nature* (pp. 66–80). Oxford, UK: Oxford University Press.

Hitchens, C. (2011). *Arguably: Selected prose*. London: Atlantic Books.

Ho, D.Y. (1995). Selfhood and identity in Confucianism, Taoism, Buddhism, and Hinduism: Contrasts with the West. *Journal for the Theory of Social Behaviour, 25*(2), 115–139.

Hofstede, G. (1980). *Culture's consequences: Comparing values, behaviors, institutions and organizations across nations*. Beverly Hills, CA: Sage.

Houshman, S., Harrington, A., Saron, C.D., & Davidson, R.J. (2002). Training the mind: First steps in a cross-cultural research collaboration in neuroscientific research. In R.J. Davidson & A. Harrington (Eds.), *Visions of compassion: Western scientists and Tibetan Buddhists examine human nature* (pp. 3–17). Oxford, UK: Oxford University Press.

Hungelmann, J., Kenkel-Rossi, E., Klassen, L., & Stollenwerk, R. (1996). Focus on spiritual well-being: Harmonious interconnectedness of mind-body-spirit—use of the JAREL Spiritual Well-Being Scale: Assessment of spiritual well-being is essential to the health of individuals. *Geriatric Nursing, 17*(6), 262–266.

Husserl, E. (1931/1999). *Cartesian meditations: An introduction to phenomenology* (D. Cairns, Trans.). London: Kluwer Academic.

Junger, S. (2010). *War*. London: Fourth Estate.

Kant, I. (1785/2002). *Groundwork for the metaphysics of morals* (A.W. Wood, Trans., A.W. Wood, Ed.). New York: Yale University Press.

King, R. (1999). *Orientalism and religion: Post-colonial theory, India and "the mystic East."* London: Routledge.

Larsen, S. (1990). Our inner cast of characters. *The Humanistic Psychologist, 18*(2), 176–187.

Lecso, P.A. (1988). To do no harm: A Buddhist view on animal use in research. *Journal of religion and health, 27*(4), 307–312.

Lomas, T. (2014). *Masculinity, meditation, and mental health*. London: Palgrave MacMillan.

Mahler, M.S., Pine, F., & Bergman, A. (2000). *The Psychological birth of the human infant symbiosis and individuation*. New York: Basic Books.

Markus, H.R., & Kitayama, S. (1991). Culture and the self: Implications for cognition, emotion, and motivation. *Psychological Review, 98*(2), 224–253.

Marr, D. (2000). Concepts of 'individual'and 'self'in twentieth-century Vietnam. *Modern Asian Studies, 34*(04), 769–796.

Nietzsche, F. (1887/1969). *On the genealogy of morals* (W. Kaufmann, Trans.). New York: Vintage Books.

Ostrom, E. (1998). A behavioral approach to the rational choice theory of collective action: Presidential address, American Political Science Association, 1997. *American Political Science Review, 91*(1), 1–22.

Ozawa-de Silva, B.R., Dodson-Lavelle, B., Raison, C.L., Negi, L.T., Silva, B., & Phil, D. (2012). Compassion and ethics: Scientific and practical approaches to the cultivation of compassion as a foundation for ethical subjectivity and well-being. *Journal of Healthcare, Science and the Humanities, 2*, 145–161.

Parnas, J. (2000). The self and intentionality in the pre-psychotic stages of schizophrenia. In D. Zahavi (Ed.), *Exploring the self: Philosophical and psychopathological perspectives on self-experience* (pp. 115–147). Amsterdam, The Netherlands: John Benjamins.

Preston, S.D., & De Waal, F. (2002). Empathy: Its ultimate and proximate bases. *Behavioral and Brain Sciences, 25*(01), 1–20.

Price, J. (2010). *Sacred scriptures of the world religions: An introduction*. New York: Continuum Books.

Radey, M., & Figley, C. (2007). The social psychology of compassion. *Clinical Social Work Journal, 35*(3), 207–214.

Ryan, R.M., & Deci, E.L. (2006). Self-regulation and the problem of human autonomy: Does psychology need choice, self-determination, and will? *Journal of Personality, 74*(6), 1557–1586.

Said, E.W. (1995). *Orientalism: Western conceptions of the Orient*. London: Penguin.

Salzberg, S. (1995). *Loving-kindness: The revolutionary art of happiness*. Boston: Shambala.

Sangharakshita, U., & Subhuti, D. (2013). *Seven papers* (2nd ed.). Triratna Buddhist Community.

Schopenhauer, A. (1840/1995). *On the basis of morality* (E. F. J. Payne, Trans.). New York: Berghahn Books.

Schulz, R., Hebert, R. S., Dew, M. A., Brown, S. L., Scheier, M. F., Beach, S. R., et al. (2007). Patient suffering and caregiver compassion: New opportunities for research, practice, and policy. *The Gerontologist, 47*(1), 4–13.

Seligman, M. E. P., Rashid, T., & Parks, A. C. (2006). Positive psychotherapy. *American Psychologist, 61*(8), 774–788.

Smith, P. R. (2011). *Integral Christianity: The spirit's call to evolve*. Colorado: Paragon House.

Spiro, M. E. (1993). Is the Western conception of the self "peculiar" within the context of the world cultures? *Ethos, 21*(2), 107–153.

Swann Jr, W. B., Jetten, J., Gómez, A., Whitehouse, H., & Bastian, B. (2012). When group membership gets personal: A theory of identity fusion. *Psychological Review, 119*(3), 441.

Taras, V., Kirkman, B. L., & Steel, P. (2010). Examining the impact of culture's consequences: A three-decade, multilevel, meta-analytic review of Hofstede's cultural value dimensions. *Journal of Applied Psychology, 95*(3), 405–439.

Tarnas, R. (1991). *The passion of the Western mind*. London: Random House.

Taylor, C. (1995). The dialogical self. In R. F. Goodman & W. R. Fisher (Eds.), *Rethinking knowledge: Reflections across the disciplines* (pp. 57–66). New York: SUNY.

Trivers, R. L. (1971). The evolution of reciprocal altruism. *Quarterly Review of Biology, 46*(1), 35–57.

Wallace, B. A. (2001). Intersubjectivity in Indo-Tibetan Buddhism. *Journal of Consciousness Studies, 8*(5–7), 209–230.

Watts, A. W. (1961). *Psychotherapy East and West*. Harmondsworth: Penguin.

Wilber, K. (1995). *Sex, ecology, spirituality: The spirit of evolution*. Boston: Shambhala.

Wilber, K. (2001). *The eye of spirit: An integral vision for a world gone slightly mad*. Boston: Shambhala.

7

Spirituality – transcending the self

Spirituality does not resolve difficulties. Frequently, the spiritual journey will take you even deeper into feelings of discomfort. This is the meaning of being human. On your path towards enlightenment, you will have to engage with such experiences.

Learning objectives – at the end of the chapter you will be able to do the following:

- Define and elaborate on the concept of spirituality
- Understand the relationship between spirituality and wellbeing
- Understand self-transcendence theory and research
- Grasp the relationships amongst self-transcendence, PP, and wellbeing
- Explore the relationship between psychology and spirituality in connection with self-awareness
- Explore the 'dark side' of self-awareness
- Realise the transformative power of self-awareness while experiencing it
- Discuss the role of self-acceptance and self-compassion in this transformative process.

List of topics:

- Spirituality
- Psychological wellbeing
- Self-transcendence
- Self-awareness
- Self-acceptance
- Self-transcendence scale

- Self-compassion
- Rumination
- Self-transcendence and PP
- The 'dark side' of self-awareness
- 'Exploring sensations in the body' meditation

THE ESSENCE OF SPIRITUALITY

What does being spiritual mean? How does being spiritual influence the way we experience life? And finally, how does it challenge us? This chapter attempts to answer these questions, linking spirituality with the place the 'dark side' of life occupies in PP. As discussed in the introduction to this book, the 'dark side' could lead to great discomfort. In this chapter the 'dark side' is engagement with yourself. That moment of observing and seeing yourself without masks or avoidances could be a difficult one. However, engaging with that difficult observation, and the negative emotions it might trigger, could lead to wonderful growth and positive change. The 'dark side' of spirituality, true engagement with yourself, carries the seed for important transformation.

In the world we live in, spirituality plays a major role in the lives of many individuals. The recent American Religious Identification Survey (ARIS), by Kosmin and Keysar (2013), showed that 32 percent of the surveyed population had a religious worldview, 32 percent defined themselves as spiritual, and only 28 percent stated they were non-religious. In a survey of 1,509 adults in the United States, 69 percent of the participants expressed a pressing need and a strong urge to experience spiritual growth in their lives (Gallup & Johnson, 2003). In a survey of 729 adults in the United States, 47 percent of the participants strongly agreed that the definition 'a person who is spiritually committed' suited them (Winseman, 2002). Spirituality seems to be fundamental to human beings and is deeply linked with PP via concepts such as wellbeing, relationships, meaning, self-awareness and self-growth.

A substantial body of research supports the existence of a positive correlation between the level of spirituality and the psychological wellbeing of individuals (Pargament & Mahoney, 2009). A comprehensive survey determined that individuals who were more developed spiritually also showed higher levels of optimism, happiness and self-esteem (Ellison & Fan, 2008). At the heart of the link between spirituality and wellbeing lies the concept of meaning in life. Spirituality creates in us a deeper sense of meaning and purpose, which has a powerful positive impact on our psychological wellbeing (Ivtzan et al., 2011). Emmons (2005) argued that meaningful spiritual goals often predict wellbeing. Meaning and purpose that are based on spiritual principles such as commitment to the sacred and pursuit of the divine in everyday life, are linked with better mental health. A study by Kass et al. (1991) showed that in adult psychiatric patients, their level of spirituality correlated positively with their level of meaning in life at the end of their treatment. There are different ways to find meaning in life, and yet spirituality offers an opportunity to commit ourselves to transcending our own self (Peterson & Seligman, 2004). To better understand this expanded spiritual perspective that transcends the self, we must fully comprehend the meaning of spirituality and thereby the concept of transcendence.

Although the scientific study of spirituality has become popular, the classifications and definitions proposed for spirituality continue to be confusing and far from universal (Hill & Pargament, 2003). Spirituality has been commonly used to describe the inner, subjective pursuit of the sacred (Ellens, 2008). According to Tart (1975), spirituality is a deep human aptitude for transcending the self and engaging with the ultimate purpose – the sacred in our lives, higher entities, God, love, compassion, and meaning. According to Vaughan (1991), spirituality essentially stands for our inner motivation to gain experience and knowledge of the sacred, of life or of God. We engage in spirituality in search for the sacred, for deep meaning, and it ultimately signifies the pursuit of purpose in life. PP has been comprehensively engaged with the classification and definition of spirituality as part of the Values in Action (VIA) character strengths (Peterson & Seligman, 2004). Adopting the notion of transcendence, the VIA handbook (Peterson & Seligman, 2004, p. 600) stated that spirituality refers to 'beliefs and practices that are grounded in the conviction that there is a transcendent (nonphysical) dimension of life'. Furthermore, the 24 character strengths are divided into six groups of distinct virtues; transcendence is the sixth virtue and has been found to be so central that it incorporates several strengths. The virtue of transcendence, which is part of spirituality, focuses on strengths that enable deepening one's connection with the universe. Spirituality has been chosen as a VIA strength because it is universal; although the content of spiritual beliefs may change, each and every culture includes an understanding of the divine, the sacred and the transcendent (Peterson & Seligman, 2004). Evidently, the one common thread that runs through most definitions and perspectives of spirituality is the concept of self-transcendence. To understand the meaning of the spiritual experience, we must first be acquainted with the way self-transcendence is theorised, researched and applied.

SELF-TRANSCENDENCE

Transcendence is at the heart of the spiritual experience as it allows engaging with the sacred. When we ponder over the question of how to apply the sacred to our lives, the spiritual answer calls for transcendence. What is it that we transcend? We transcend the constructs of our own self to engage in the divine, the sacred, which is deeply meaningful. It allows us to identify and connect with something that is 'bigger than the self' (Seligman et al., 2006, p. 777). Self-transcendence allows expanding self-boundaries and becoming more aware of life dimensions that exceed the self (Upchurch, 1999). Reed (1991a) suggested that self-boundaries may expand in different ways. We already encountered the concept of transcendence in Chapter 6, where Dr Lomas discussed the way cultivating compassion for others might lead one to transcend narrow self-identity and experience interconnectedness with others. As such, that chapter focused on a very specific type of transcendence, namely, experiencing an intersubjective union with other people. In contrast, this current chapter considers transcendence in a much wider and deeper sense, focusing particularly on the way it can allow people to connect with the sacred. According to Reed (1991a), self-boundaries could expand inward (by experiencing greater self-acceptance), outward (as we reach out to others or connect with nature, as explored in Chapter 6), upward (as we reach out to a higher entity or greater purpose) and temporally (integrating the past and the future with the present).

It is therefore possible to convert self-transcendence from a theoretical concept into practical interventions. Individuals may be involved in activities such as volunteer or altruistic work, lifelong learning or group therapy, artistic or creative performances, sharing wisdom with others and reflecting on their spirituality (for practical applications see: Coward, 2005; Coward & Reed, 1996; Reed, 2008; and Young & Reed, 1995). Another area where self-transcendence has been increasingly developing is gerontology: the study of the psychological, social and biological aspects of aging (Hooyman & Kiyak, 2008). Tornstam (1996, p. 38) defined gerotranscendence as 'a shift in metaperspective, from a midlife materialistic and rational vision to a more cosmic and transcendent one, accompanied by an increase in life satisfaction'. Piedmont (1999) established further the relevance of self-transcendence for human development by adding spiritual-transcendence as a sixth factor to the five factors of human personality defined by Costa and McCrae (1992): openness, conscientiousness, extraversion, agreeableness and neuroticism. According to Piedmont (1999, p. 988) spiritual transcendence is 'the capacity of individuals to stand outside their immediate sense of time and place to view life from a larger, more objective perspective'. Self-transcendence has gradually become a central theme in a number of disciplines such as personality theory and psychiatric genetics (Cloninger, Svrakic, & Przybeck, 1993), transpersonal development (Levenson et al., 2005; Wade, 1996; Wilber, 2000), gerontology (Braam et al., 2006) and nursing theory (Coward, 1996; Reed, 1991b; Runquist & Reed, 2007). In this context, the concept of self-transcendence should be demystified. The term 'self-transcendence' often invokes a mystical experience that is impossible to observe or fully understand. In fact, this concept is being researched (Stinson & Kirk, 2006), theorised (Reed, 1996) and measured (Reed, 2009) scientifically. We are gradually advancing our understanding of self-transcendence and its benefits.

PSYCHOMETRIC SCALES

In an attempt to examine and measure self-transcendence, a number of assessment scales have been devised; these include Reed's (1991a) self-transcendence scale, Piedmont's (1999) spiritual transcendence scale, the adult self-transcendence inventory by Levenson et al. (2005) and the self-transcendence subscale created by Cloninger et al. (1993) within the Temperament and Character Inventory (TCI). In the self-transcendence scale, Reed attempted to decode self-transcendence and break it into clear, measurable and applicable dimensions of life. This is an important step towards demystifying the concept of self-transcendence, as discussed. Test yourself and observe your own levels of self-transcendence according to this scale. Does it correspond to your intuitive understanding of your own self-transcendence experiences?

Instructions

Please indicate the extent to which each item below describes you. It is important for you to realise that there are no 'right' or 'wrong' answers to these questions. Please respond according to the way you see yourself at this time in your life. Follow this four-point scale, and choose the appropriate answer for each statement:

1. Not at all

2. Very little

3. Somewhat

4. Very much

At this time of my life, I see myself as:

_____ 1. Having hobbies or interests I can enjoy

_____ 2. Accepting myself as I grow older

_____ 3. Being involved with other people or my community when possible

_____ 4. Adjusting well to my present life situation

_____ 5. Adjusting to changes in my physical abilities

_____ 6. Sharing my wisdom or experience with others

_____ 7. Finding meaning in my past experiences

_____ 8. Helping others in some way

_____ 9. Having an ongoing interest in learning

_____ 10. Able to move beyond some things that once seemed so important

_____ 11. Accepting death as a part of life

_____ 12. Finding meaning in my spiritual beliefs

_____ 13. Letting others help me when I may need it

_____ 14. Enjoying my pace of life

_____ 15. Letting go of my past losses

- Scoring: Final scores are obtained by summing up the scores of all 15 items. Higher scores stand for higher experience of self-transcendence.

RESEARCH AND PRACTICE CASE STUDIES

In a fascinating publication titled 'The Spiritual Brain: Selective Cortical Lesions Modulate Human Self-Transcendence', Urgesi, Aglioti, Skrap, & Fabbro (2010) investigated the roles specific areas in the brain play in the experience of self-transcendence. Self-awareness, as part of spirituality, has been shown to alter the experience of self, causing a weaker self–other boundary and feelings of strong connection of self to the universe (Cahn & Polich, 2006; Lutz, Slagter, Dunne, & Davidson, 2008). Electrophysiological and neuroimaging studies with religious or spiritual participants, such as Catholic nuns or Buddhist monks, revealed that these introspective changes are accompanied by neural changes in a cortical network that includes, for example, the prefrontal and cingulate cortex (Azari et al., 2001; Beauregard & Paquette, 2006; Brefczynski-Lewis, Lutz, Schaefer, Levinson, & Davidson, 2007).

For this reason, Urgesi et al. (2010) anticipated that the levels of self-transcendence would significantly change in patients undergoing surgery to remove a brain glioma (a type of cancer that affects neural brain tissues). They predicted that the posterior parietal areas play a causative role in the experience of self-transcendence because lower activity in that area allows for extended self-referential awareness (awareness aware of itself), which characterises individuals with high self-transcendence. They expected selective damage caused in the operation to the posterior parietal areas to increase the levels of self-transcendence. To measure the levels of self-transcendence before and after the operation, they used the TCI, with its self-transcendence sub-scale (Cloninger et al., 1993). The results confirmed their predictions, showing that in patients who had brain tissue removed from the posterior parietal areas, the level of self-transcendence after the operation was significantly higher than the pre-operation levels. Urgesi et al. (2010, p. 316) concluded by saying, 'Our symptom-lesion mapping study demonstrates a causative link between brain functioning and self-transcendence. In particular, the study shows that damage to posterior parietal areas may induce unusually fast changes of a stable personality dimension related to transcendental self-referential awareness. Thus, dysfunctional parietal neural activity may underpin altered spiritual and religious attitudes and behaviours'. Their final point is thought-provoking; they suggest that under certain circumstances, where brain damage is involved, changes in neural activity may result in an increased spiritual and self-transcendent experience. We have a long road to walk before we fully understand the neuropsychological dimensions of spirituality and self-transcendence; however, studies such as this one make a significant contribution to our body of knowledge in this area.

SELF-TRANSCENDENCE IN POSITIVE PSYCHOLOGY

The concept of self-transcendence fits perfectly into several PP theories. One example is Wong's (2009, 2011) theory of chaironic happiness, which necessitates experiencing self-transcendence. The term 'chaironic' is derived from the Greek root *chairo*, meaning 'blessing, joy or the gift of happiness'. It describes the kind of happiness and joy one feels standing on a mountaintop and watching the sun set. Suddenly everything falls into place, and the person is flooded with an overwhelming surge of love, joy and acceptance that flow from the heart. A similar feeling may emerge during deep meditation. Wong (2009) describes the calm joy of Zen monks and the ecstasy of Christian mystics as examples of chaironic happiness. Chaironic happiness offers a spiritual path to happiness. It is a path in which the self is transcended and one experiences a relationship with something greater than oneself – whether it is called life, God, humanity, or unity consciousness. However, as described later in this chapter, self-transcendence requires self-awareness, which in turn requires an engagement with the 'dark side'. Self-awareness might trigger the challenge of seeing yourself, fully, as you are, which could be a difficult experience for most of us.

Another PP theory where self-transcendence is prominent is flow (Csikszentmihalyi, 1975). A state of flow incorporates a number of different conditions and characteristics; one of them is the loss of a sense of self. In a state of flow the concept of self slips below the threshold of awareness; the information gathered to tell ourselves who we are is discarded for the duration of the flow experience. The interesting point is that this loss of self-concept does not weaken the experience; on the contrary, it intensifies it and allows us to become completely absorbed in the state of flow. A deeper, more enjoyable and productive relationship with the moment is experienced, displaying the power of self-transcendence. A study by Teng (2011) investigated the question of who is more likely to experience flow. The experiment evaluated the impact of temperament and character on the likelihood that an individual would experience flow. This is an important question as it is now clear that flow is beneficial for wellbeing; its benefits include better academic and behavioural outcomes for students (Shernoff & Csikszentmihalyi, 2009), greater wellbeing at work (Bryce & Haworth, 2002), optimal performances in sports (Hanin, 2003) and higher purpose and meaning in life (Adlai-Gail, 1994; Hektner, 1996). Csikszentmihalyi (1997) and Seligman (2002) showed that the ability to experience flow goes hand in hand with an individual's level of happiness. This apparent positive correlation between flow and wellbeing adds importance to gathering knowledge about the way personality influences flow. The findings of Teng (2011) indicate that there is a positive correlation between the likelihood of experiencing flow and self-transcendence. Self-transcendence was found to be one of the most important character features that increases the propensity for experiencing flow. In other words, as flow is so clearly related to wellbeing, and self-transcendence allows for flow, self-transcendence is an important agent of our experience of wellbeing.

Self-transcendence is strongly linked with enhanced wellbeing. Self-transcendence has been found to be associated with or to predict resilience and purpose in life (Nygren et al., 2005), alleviate depression (Klaas 1998; Stinson & Kirk, 2006) and improve the quality of life and emotional wellbeing in homeless people (Runquist & Reed, 2007) and in seriously ill patients (Neill, 2002). It was also found to be negatively correlated with neuroticism and positively correlated with meditation practice (Levenson et al., 2005), quality of life, and mindfulness (Zappala, 2007).

A study (Coward, 1996) of 152 healthy adults found a significant correlation between self-transcendence and hope, purpose in life, and cognitive and emotional wellbeing. It is clear, then, that self-transcendence enhances wellbeing; however, to experience self-transcendence, certain requirements involving self-awareness have to be met. These requirements involve the' dark side' and the specific manner in which we engage with knowledge acquired via self-awareness. To understand these requirements and their relation to self-awareness, we must clarify the interaction between psychology and spirituality.

PSYCHOLOGY AND SPIRITUALITY

Because psychology addresses the mind and its processing, it has an important role in our journey towards self-awareness. Psychology is the means to explore your mind, map it out and understand its hidden motivations. The mind stores fragmentary information that ultimately defines who you are. This information shapes and structures your self (Rosenberg, 1986). Psychology helps you get in touch with this information and gain insights into who you are and how you define yourself and enhances self-awareness (Duval & Wicklund, 1972). Spirituality, on the other hand, aims to transcend this rational processing and definition of self. That is the core of self-transcendence discussed earlier (Reed, 1991a). The ability to transcend *that which has been acknowledged* is the point where psychology and spirituality meet. To transcend something, one must be aware that it actually exists. In other words, 'self-awareness' is the key word. To experience self-transcendence you must first recognise those aspects of the self that are going to be transcended. Since the self-concept is based upon mind constructs, the awareness gained through psychological processing is necessary for spiritual transcendence (Ivtzan, 2015). By exploring your own psychological processes, you get acquainted with your mind's definitions and constructs of yourself which, consequently, allows you to transcend them. Psychology is therefore crucial for the spiritual journey of transcendence. This creates a strong bond between psychology and spirituality: psychology is the means by which you develop self-awareness and get to know your mind, whereas spirituality enables you to transcend your mind. They are essential for one another. This meeting point, where we come in touch with deeper and greater self-awareness, is where the 'dark side' could emerge.

THE DARK SIDE OF SELF-AWARENESS

Self-awareness theory is concerned with the self-reflective quality of consciousness (Silvia & Duval, 2001). Just as we are aware of external or environmental stimuli, we can be aware of our own existence: 'When attention is directed inward and the individual's consciousness is focused on himself, he is the object of his own consciousness' (Duval & Wicklund, 1972, p. 2). In other words, the concept of self-awareness refers to our engagement with our own internal experience. The question, in this case, is 'what is our relationship with the content of our self-awareness'? The answer to this question is crucial as it shapes our engagement with the 'dark side' in our lives. Our relationship with our self-concept is frequently complex and filled with doubts, difficulties and discomfort (Higgins et al., 1985; Lee-Flynn et al., 2011). We frequently push away, reject and deny certain aspects of our self that we feel less comfortable with; these aspects are our 'psychological shadow' (Schimel et al., 2000). Self-awareness, and the process of self-observation as part of it, confronts us with a truly difficult task: engaging with various aspects of our self that we normally tend to avoid because of the potential discomfort they involve. Many individuals find self-awareness burdensome and aversive (Goverover & Chiaravalloti, 2014; Wicklund, 1975) due to the internal mechanism of reaction to the observed material. This reaction is frequently characterized by self-judgement, including negative cognitive and emotional processing of the content of self-awareness, which results in deep uneasiness. Baumeister (1990) described the stages of this process:

1   An experience where outcomes fall below the standards and expectation one has set for oneself. This has nothing to do with any 'objective' measurement; it is the person's own subjective judgement that determines the internal reaction here.
2   The individual sees the outcomes as his or her own failure; blame and judgement are triggered.
3   At this stage an aversive state of self-awareness is experienced. The content of self-awareness triggers discomfort, accompanied by the feeling that one is incompetent, unattractive, inadequate or guilty.
4   Finally, negative emotions arise as a result of the reactions to this content of self-awareness.

This is the 'dark side' of self-awareness. Our judgmental engagement with the content of our self-awareness leads to such intense discomfort that we frequently choose easier options: avoid, reject and escape. The common strategy to deal with this difficulty is to divert attention and focus it on safer issues. By this, we keep self-awareness at a relatively low level and reduce this way the potential discomfort it may create (Baumeister, 1990). In other words, avoidance is used as a defence mechanism: as long as I avert self-awareness, I don't have to cope with the content it brings out, and therefore I can evade the tension and distress it involves. The cost of this strategy is, obviously, that an abundance of important material we could be engaging with to self-transcend is ignored. As already mentioned, it is impossible to self-transcend what we don't know. We will not be able to recognize the true content of our self as long as we avoid self-awareness. And we avoid self-awareness because of the discomfort it causes. We seem to be trapped in a vicious circle, ignoring our self and failing to achieve self-transcendence. However, a solution does exist: changing our *relationship* with the content of self-awareness.

REFLECTION

We all have certain areas in our lives that are frequently subject to self-judgement and self-criticism. This naturally provokes the 'dark side' of self-awareness by impacting our relationship with the content of our awareness. It might be interesting for you to reflect on different areas of your life and find which of them prompts self-judgement most often. In what circumstances are you harshest with yourself? What expectations that you have of yourself or of others lead to this reaction? Bringing your awareness to these questions may make it easier to detect moments in which you experience the 'dark side' of self-awareness and transform them into self-acceptance and self-compassion, as discussed further following.

SELF-ACCEPTANCE AND SELF-COMPASSION: TRANSFORMING SELF-AWARENESS

While investigating earlier perspectives on the core dimensions of psychological wellbeing, Ryff (1989, p. 1071) said:

> The most recurrent criterion of wellbeing evident in the previous perspectives is the individual's sense of self-acceptance. This is defined as a central feature of mental health, as well as a characteristic of self-actualisation, optimal functioning, and maturity. Life span theories also emphasise acceptance of self and of one's past life. Thus, holding positive attitudes toward oneself emerges as a central characteristic of positive psychological functioning.

Of Ryff's (1989) popular six dimensions for measuring psychological wellbeing, the first is self-acceptance. High self-acceptance is operationalised as acknowledging and accepting multiple aspects of one's self. Notice how the concept includes both self-awareness (acknowledging) and a healthy attitude towards the content of awareness (accepting). Self-acceptance leads to higher levels of wellbeing: Within a Swedish population sample, self-acceptance was found to be strongly related to greater satisfaction in life and higher levels of positive affect (Garcia, 2011, 2012). Self-acceptance is crucial for the psychological wellbeing of patients suffering from chronic illness (Gregg, 2013) and has been linked with happiness (Szentagotai & David, 2013) and unconditional positive regard (Patterson & Joseph, 2013). Finally, Wood and Joseph (2010) found that individuals with lower levels of self-acceptance risked higher levels of depression.

These findings seem to correspond to Reed's (1991a) theory of self-transcendence. The first dimension within which self-boundaries expand is the inward dimension; it might refer to a certain personality characteristic you perceive in yourself – jealousy, for example. The first stage would be recognising and acknowledging it. This cannot happen unless your attitude is open and accepting; as discussed earlier, a judgmental reaction would lead to decreased self-awareness to reduce the level of discomfort. This is a reaction to the 'dark side' that we frequently employ to avoid the psychological distress that has been triggered. Alternatively, when you deal with the jealousy you harbor within you in a self-accepting manner, it becomes easier to recognise, be aware of, embrace and self-transcend. When the conflict and tension cease, self-expansion is possible. The same is true of the other dimensions proposed by Reed (1991a). As part of the second dimension, the outward one, you also could self-transcend ideas relating to your relationship with others (as explored by Dr Lomas in Chapter 6). These relationships may be inhibited by a certain idea that you have, perhaps the concept that other people are not very important in your life or that they might hurt you. Engaging with such concepts in a stance of self-acceptance would allow you to become aware of them and gradually transcend those aspects of the self, making possible deeper connections with others. The third dimension, the upward one, includes our self-concepts, which separate and disconnect us from a higher entity or greater purpose. Engaging with these self-concepts in a stance of self-acceptance would allow a similar process of transformation, leading to self-expansion and connection in an upward direction. Finally, the fourth dimension, the temporal one, allows your present to come to terms with past events and future vision in a way that replaces potential struggles with the past or the future with peace. Self-transcending these struggles would result in a coherent life narrative that is filled with acceptance.

PRACTICE ESSAY QUESTIONS

Evaluate the self-transcendence theory critically: Is it well rooted both in psychology and spirituality? If so, in what ways?

How might we utilise our knowledge of self-awareness in PP research and in enhancing wellbeing?

RESEARCH AND PRACTICE CASE STUDIES

In an interesting study by Garcia, Nima, and Kjell (2014), self-acceptance was found to predict a sense of harmony in life. Their study measured the relationship between psychological wellbeing as defined by Ryff (1989) (where self-acceptance is one of the dimensions) and a harmonious life that stands for our ability to adapt to a changing environment and live in harmony with our surroundings. The affective profiles of all the participants were evaluated; the profiles were based on four descriptive categories: self-fulfilling (high positive affect, low negative affect), high affective (high positive affect, high negative affect), low affective (low positive affect, low negative affect) and self-destructive (low positive affect, high negative affect). The results of their study illustrate the remarkable importance of self-acceptance as a predictor of harmony in life across the four affective profiles. As part of their conclusions, the researchers stated that self-acceptance could serve as a tool to transform one's affective profile from self-destructive to self-fulfilling while also increasing the levels of harmony in life.

Similarly to self-acceptance, the concept of self-compassion stands for a healthy relationship with the content of self-awareness. Self compassion refers to 'an emotionally positive self-attitude that should protect against the negative consequences of self-judgement, isolation, and rumination' (Neff, 2003a, p. 85). It is a state of mind filled with kindness, acceptance, and understanding towards oneself, especially under difficult circumstances (when the mind is prone to producing an avalanche of self-judgment and criticism. Self-compassion involves opening oneself to one's pain without avoiding it or disconnecting from it (Wispe, 1991)). Under these circumstances the relationship with the pain and its potential causes is non-judgmental, kind and accepting. Research has shown that self-compassionate people appraise themselves with significantly less self-enhancement or self-deprecation than those with lower levels of self-compassion (Leary et al., 2006). This indicates an open attitude towards one's self, an attitude where judgement is significantly reduced. This is an invitation relating to your relationship with the 'dark side': when you engage with aspects of yourself which would normally make you turn away and avoid, could you apply self-compassion? Such a kind interaction with the content of your self-awareness would enhance wellbeing and lead to positive transformation in your relationship with yourself.

On the face of it, self-compassion could lead to passivity or inaction as it tolerates with kindness any perceived weakness that might have spurred one to change. The case, however, is quite the opposite. When the content of self-awareness is approached with harsh judgement due to the failings of the self, the ego would continue blocking inadequacies from one's self-awareness. This would be a protective measure to ensure that self-esteem is not threatened (Horney, 1950; Neff, 2003a). In other words, when your ego recognises that your approach is unforgiving and judgmental, it does its best to make sure you do not injure your self-esteem; it does that by not letting certain materials into your self-awareness to circumvent self-criticism. This is a classic example of the 'dark side' of self-awareness discussed in this chapter. A process that has the potential to bring about awareness, acceptance and self-transcendence turns into an experience that is so painful that your defence mechanisms enter into action to preserve your psychological wellbeing. And in the absence of self-awareness, this content will remain unchallenged, unobserved and not open to transcendence. On the other hand, a compassionate relationship with the content of self-awareness offers us an internal safe space, where we are able to observe the self without fear of judgement and thereby without negative consequences (Brown, 1999). Research has shown that self-compassion is an excellent predictor of wellbeing, resilience and mental health. Neff (2003b) found that self-compassion is positively associated with social ties and life satisfaction and negatively associated with variables such as rumination, anxiety, neurotic perfectionism, depression and self-criticism. Shapiro et al. (2005) found that self-compassion was an important factor in stress reduction, and Gilbert & Proctor (2006) established that self-compassion predicted enhanced psychological health.

TRY ME

An important question arising from this text is *how* to transform our relationship with self-awareness from a reactive and judgmental one to an accepting and compassionate one? The answer focuses on the art of mindfulness. To start a process of engaging with the content of your self-awareness in an accepting manner, you could practice the meditation described here. This meditation, in which you explore the sensations in your body, invites you to visualise a situation that your mind perceives as difficult and then bring your awareness inside your body, where the judgments and reactions may be felt, and adopt a compassionate relationship with whatever you find. The following point is important: choose a mild difficulty, one that would trigger some internal challenge but would not be too demanding. Remember, you are aiming for self-compassion. This means that you want to engage with an issue you are able to deal with and not with one that overwhelms your consciousness and is impossible to observe with kind acceptance. To practice the meditation, find a quiet room, sit comfortably and take a few deep breaths. When you feel that you are ready, follow these instructions:

Deliberately bring to mind a mild difficulty that you are facing at the moment – something you don't mind thinking about for a few minutes. It does not have to be very important, but it does have to be *unresolved*.

- Allow the troubling thought or situation to stay in your mind. Allow your awareness to experience the story for a minute. Allow the uncomfortable thoughts to remain in your mind.

- Shift your attention into your body so that you become aware of the physical sensations that accompany the thought and the emotions it evokes.

- Bring your full attention to the area in the body where the sensation is strongest. You can use your breath as a vehicle to go there.

- You are not trying to change the sensation. Simply tell yourself: 'It is here now. It is OK to feel this. It is already here; let me open up to it'.

- Breathe into your heart, find the feeling and quality of kindness and compassion within you, and approach the sensation with these feelings.

- Soften and open up to the sensations, letting go of any tensing and bracing.

- When you feel that you are ready, allow your awareness to gradually shift from these sensations and reconnect to your whole body and to the room around you before you slowly open your eyes.

REFLECTION VERSUS RUMINATION

In discussing the importance of self-awareness, a distinction must be made between reflection and rumination (Silvia, Eichstaedt, & Phillips, 2005). Reflection and rumination both stem from intense attention to one's self, but the motivation for this attention is fundamentally different in each. Trapnell and Campbell (1999, p. 297) defined rumination as 'self-attentiveness motivated by perceived threats, losses, or injustices to the self', and reflection as 'self-attentiveness motivated by curiosity or epistemic interest in the self'. Rumination relates to psychological distress, whereas reflection relates to openness to experience. Let us examine these two concepts to identify the circumstances under which investigation of the self is productive and beneficial (reflection) and those that turn out to produce a harmful psychological state of mind (rumination). To differentiate between the two, all one needs is to ask: 'Why am I attending to myself right now?' If the answer has anything to do with past frustrations, anger, dissatisfaction or disappointment, then you are ruminating. If, on the other hand, you realise that the answer to this question turns around the excitement of curiosity, the fascination of noticing and understanding new aspects of yourself, then you are reflecting.

PSYCHOMETRIC SCALES

Are you inclined by nature to reflect or ruminate? To test yourself, complete the following Rumination–Reflection Questionnaire (Trapnell & Campbell, 1999).

Instructions

For each of the following statements, rate your level of agreement using the following scale: Strongly disagree (1), Disagree (2), Neutral (3), Agree (4), Strongly agree (5).

Rumination

1   My attention is often focused on aspects of myself I wish I'd stop thinking about.

2   I always seem to be rehashing in my mind recent things I've said or done.

3   Sometimes it is hard for me to shut off thoughts about myself.

4   Long after an argument or disagreement is over with, my thoughts keep going back to what happened.

5   I tend to 'ruminate' or dwell over things that happen to me for a really long time afterward.

6   I don't waste time rethinking things that are over and done with.

7   Often I'm playing back over in my mind how I acted in a past situation.

8   I often find myself reevaluating something I've done.

9   I never ruminate or dwell on myself for very long.

10   It is easy for me to put unwanted thoughts out of my mind.

11   I often reflect on episodes in my life that I should no longer concern myself with.

12   I spend a great deal of time thinking back over my embarrassing or disappointing moments.

Reflection

13   Philosophical or abstract thinking doesn't appeal to me that much.

14   I'm not really a meditative type of person.

15   I love exploring my 'inner' self.

16   My attitudes and feelings about things fascinate me.

17   I don't really care for introspective or self-reflective thinking.

18   I love analyzing why I do things.

19   People often say I'm a 'deep', introspective type of person.

20   I don't care much for self-analysis.

21   I'm very self-inquisitive by nature.

22   I love to meditate on the nature and meaning of things.

23   I often love to look at my life in philosophical ways.

24   Contemplating myself isn't my idea of fun.

Scoring: Scale scores are obtained by reversing the scores (1 = 5, 2 = 4 and 3 = 3) on items 6, 9, 10, 13, 14, 17, 20 and 24 and then summing up all the results. Higher scores stand for a higher tendency to ruminate or reflect.

By definition, self-compassion invites us to transform our relationship with the content of self-awareness from a judgmental interaction with the 'dark side' into an embracing relationship with it, accepting whatever is being observed. As we engage with the 'dark side' in this manner, it gradually transforms into positive change. This transformative experience is healing as struggle and inner conflict cease to exist.

In this ocean of peaceful acceptance, one may find it easy to become fully aware of that which had been rejected in the past: all the things that were previously perceived as failures, shortcomings, inadequacies and negative emotions are suddenly embraced instead of being pushed away. Observing this content without conflict promotes potential self-transcendence. This is the heart of spirituality, and an engagement with the 'dark side' of self-awareness which transforms into self-transcendent experiences demonstrates it beautifully.

SUMMARY – THIS CHAPTER HAS ACCOMPLISHED THE FOLLOWING

- Described the concept of spirituality and its role in our lives
- Investigated self-transcendence theory, research and practical influence
- Discussed the role of self-awareness, its relationship with the 'dark side' and its contribution to self-transcendence
- Invited us to connect with the 'dark side' of self-awareness
- Explained the potential transformation promised by self-acceptance and self-compassion
- Offered a practical meditative exercise to connect with the transformative power of self-awareness

RESOURCES AND SUGGESTIONS

- To expand your experience of self-compassion, we recommend practicing the LKM. You can use a search engine to find a variety of websites offering instructions; for example: https://thebuddhistcentre.com/text/loving-kindness-meditation.
- The leading researcher of compassion is Kristin Neff; we recommend reading more about her research in her writings; her website is: http://www.self-compassion.org/
- To further investigate the relationship between psychology and spirituality, we recommend reading *Awareness Is Freedom: The Adventure of Psychology and Spirituality* by Dr Itai Ivtzan.
- Chaironic happiness is a fascinating example of the meeting point between positive psychology and self-transcendence. To better understand it, we recommend reading Wong's works, primarily:
- Wong, P. T. P. (2009). Positive existential psychology. In *Encyclopedia of positive psychology*. Oxford: Blackwell.
- Wong, P. T. P. (2011). Positive psychology 2.0: Towards a balanced interactive model of the good life. *Canadian Psychology, 52 (2)*, 69–81.

BIBLIOGRAPHY

Adlai-Gail, W. S. (1994). Exploring autotelic personality. PhD diss., University of Chicago. Cited in M. Csikszentmihalyi & B. Schneider. (Eds.), *Becoming adult: How teenagers prepare for the world of work*. New York: Basic Books.

Archer, T., Adrianson, L., Plancak, A., & Karlsson, E. (2007). Influence of affective personality on cognitive-mediated emotional processing: Need for empowerment. *European Journal of Psychiatry, 21*, 21–44.

Azari, N. P., Nickel, J., Wunderlich, G., Niedeggen, M., Hefter, H., Tellmann, L., Herzog, H., et al. (2001). Neural correlates of religious experience. *European Journal of Neuroscience, 13*, 1649–1652.

Baumeister, R. F. (1990). Suicide as escape from self. *Psychological Review, 97*, 90–113.

Beauregard, M., & Paquette, V. (2006). Neural correlates of a mystical experience in Carmelite nuns. *Neuroscience Letters, 405*, 186–190.

Braam, A. W., Bramsen, I., Van Tilburg, T. G., Van der Ploeg, H. M., & Deeg, D. J. (2006). Cosmic transcendence and framework of meaning in life: Patterns among older adults in the Netherlands. *Journal of Gerontology, 61*(3), 121–128.

Brefczynski-Lewis, J. A., Lutz, A., Schaefer, H. S., Levinson, D. B., & Davidson, R. J. (2007). Neural correlates of attentional expertise in long-term meditation practitioners. *Proceedings of the National Academy of Sciences USA, 104*, 11483–11488.

Brown, B. (1999). *Soul without shame: A guide to liberating yourself from the judge within*. Boston: Shambala.

Bryce, J., & Haworth, J. (2002). Wellbeing and flow in sample of male and female office workers. *Leisure Studies, 21*, 249–263.

Cahn, B. R., & Polich, J. (2006). Meditation states and traits: EEG, ERP, and neuroimaging studies. *Psychological Bulletin, 132*, 180–211.

Cloninger, C. R., Svrakic, D. M., & Przybeck, T. R. (1993). A psychobiological model of temperament and character. *Archives of General Psychiatry, 50*(12), 975–990.

Costa, P. T., & McCrae, R. R. (1992). Normal personality assessment in clinical practice: The NEO personality inventory. *Psychological Assessments, 4*, 5–13.

Coward, D. D. (1996). Self-transcendence and correlates in a healthy population. *Nursing Research, 45*, 116–121.

Coward, D. (2005). Reed's self-transcendence theory. In A. M. Tomey & M. R. Alligood (Eds.), *Nursing theorists and their work* (6th ed., pp. 643–662). St. Louis, MO: Mosby.

Coward, D., & Reed, P. G. (1996). Self-transcendence: A resource for healing at the end of life. *Issues in Mental Health Nursing, 17*(3), 275–288.

Csikszentmihalyi, M. (1975). *Beyond boredom and anxiety: Experiencing flow in work and play*. San Francisco: Jossey-Bass.

Csikszentmihalyi, M. (1997). *Finding flow: The psychology of engagement with everyday life*. New York: Basic Books.

Duval, S., & Wicklund, R. A. (1972). *A theory of objective self awareness*. New York: Academic Press.

Ellens, J. H. (2008). *Understanding religious experiences: What the Bible says about Spirituality*. Westport, CT: Praeger.

Ellison, C. G., & Fan, D. (2008). Daily spiritual experiences and psychological well-being among US adults. *Social Indicators Research, 88*, 247–271.

Emmons, R. A. (2005). Striving for the sacred: Personal goals, life meaning, and religion. *Journal of Social Issues, 61*, 731–745.

Gallup, G., & Johnson, B. R. (2003). New index tracks "spiritual state of the union." Gallup Poll News Service. Retrieved from http://www.gallup.com/poll/7657/New-Index-Tracks-Spiritual-State-Union.aspx

Garcia, D. (2011). *Adolescents' happiness: The role of the affective temperament model on memory and apprehension of events, subjective well-being, and psychological well-being*. PhD diss., University of Gothenburg, Gothenburg.

Garcia, D. (2012). The affective temperaments: differences between adolescents in the big five model and Cloninger's psychobiological model of personality. *Journal of Happiness Studies, 13*, 999–1017.

Garcia, D., Nima, A. A., & Kjell, O. N. E. (2014). The affective profiles, psychological well-being, and harmony: environmental mastery and self-acceptance predict the sense of a harmonious life. *PeerJ, 13*(2), e259.

Gilbert, P., & Procter, S. (2006). Compassionate mind training for people with high shame and self-criticism: Overview and pilot study of a group therapy approach. *Clinical Psychology and Psychotherapy, 13*, 353–379.

Goverover, Y., & Chiaravalloti, N. (2014). The impact of self-awareness and depression on subjective reports of memory, quality-of-life and satisfaction with life following TBI. *Brain Injury, 28*(2), 174–180.

Gregg, J. A. (2013). Self-acceptance and chronic illness. In Bernard, M. E. (Ed.), *The strength of self-acceptance* (pp. 247–262). New York: Springer.

Hanin, Y. L. (2003). Performance related emotional states in sport: A qualitative analysis. *Forum Qualitative Sozialforschung/Forum: Qualitative Social Research [On-line Journal], 4*(1). Retrieved from http://www.qualitative-research.net/index.php/fqs/article/view/747/1619

Hektner, J. M. (1996). Exploring optimal personality development: A longitudinal study of adolescents. PhD diss., University of Chicago. In M. Csikszentmihalyi & B. Schneider (Eds.), *Becoming adult: How teenagers prepare for the world of work*. New York: Basic Books.

Higgins, E. T., Klein, R., & Strauman, T. (1985). Self-concept discrepancy theory: A psychological model for distinguishing among different aspects of depression and anxiety. *Social Cognition, 3*, 51–76.

Hill, P. C., & Pargament, K. I. (2003). Advances in the conceptualization and measurement of religion and spirituality: Implications for physical and mental health research. *American Psychologist, 58*, 64–74.

Hooyman, N. R., & Kiyak, H. A. (2008). *Social gerontology: A multidisciplinary perspective*. Boston: Pearson/Allyn & Bacon.

Horney, K. (1950). *Neurosis and human growth: The struggle toward self-realization*. New York: Norton.

Ivtzan, I. (2015). *Awareness is freedom: The adventure of psychology and spirituality*. London: John Hunt.

Ivtzan, I., Chan, C. P. L., Gardner, H. E., & Prashar, K. (2011). Linking religion and spirituality with psychological wellbeing: Examining self-actualisation, meaning in life, and personal growth initiative. *Journal of Religion and Health, 51*, 13–30.

Kass, J. D., Friedman, R., Lescrman, J., Zuttermeister, P. C., & Benson, H. (1991). Health outcomes and a new index of spiritual experience. *Journal for Scientific Study of Religion, 30*, 203–211.

Klaas, D. (1998). Testing two elements of spirituality in depressed and non-depressed elders. *International Journal of Psychiatric Nursing Research, 4*(2), 452–462.

Kosmin, B. A., & Keysar, A. (2013). *American Religious Identification Survey (ARIS 2012)*. Hartford, CT: ISSSC, Trinity College.

Leary, M. R., Tate, E. B., Adams, C. E., & Allen, A. B. (2006). Self-compassion and reactions to unpleasant self relevant events: The implications of treating oneself kindly. Unpublished manuscript.

Lee-Flynn, S. C., Pomaki, G., DeLongis, A., Biesanz, J. C., & Puterman, E. (2011). Daily cognitive appraisals, daily affect, and long-term depressive symptoms: The role of self-esteem and self-concept clarity in the stress process. *Personality & Social Psychology Bulletin, 37*, 255–268.

Levenson, M. R., Jennings, P. A., Aldwin, C. M., & Shiraishi, R. W. (2005). Self transcendence: Conceptualization and measurement. *International Journal of Aging and Human Development, 60*(2), 127–143.

Lutz, A., Slagter, H. A., Dunne, J. D., & Davidson, R. J. (2008). Attention regulation and monitoring in meditation. *Trends in Cognitive Sciences, 12*, 163–169.

Miller, W. R., & Thoresen, C. E. (2003). Spirituality, religion, and health: An emerging research field. *American Psychologist, 58*, 24–35.

Neill, J. (2002). Transcendence and transformation in the life patterns of women living with rheumatoid arthritis. *Advances in Nursing Science, 24*, 27–47.

Neff, K. D. (2003a). Self-compassion: An alternative conceptualization of a healthy attitude toward oneself. *Self and Identity, 2*, 85–102.

Neff, K. D. (2003b). The development and validation of a scale to measure self-compassion. *Self and Identity, 2*, 223–250.

Norlander, T., Johansson, Å., & Bood, S. Å. (2005). The affective personality: Its relation to quality of sleep, well-being and stress. *Social Behavior and Personality, 33*, 709–722.

Nygren, B., Aléx, L., Jonsén, E., Gustafson, Y., Norberg, A., & Lundman, B. (2005). Resilience, sense of coherence, purpose in life and self-transcendence in relation to perceived physical and mental health among the oldest old. *Aging & Mental Health, 9*(4), 354– 362.

Pargament, K. I., & Mahoney, A. (2009). Spirituality: The search for the sacred. In S. J. Lopez & C. R. Snyder (Eds.), *Handbook of positive psychology* (pp. 611–619). New York: Oxford University Press.

Patterson, G. T., & Joseph, S. (2013). Unconditional positive regard. In Bernard, M. E. (Ed.), *The strength of self-acceptance* (p. 93–106). New York: Springer.

Peterson, C., & Seligman, M. E. P. (2004). *Character strengths and virtues: A handbook and classification.* Washington, DC: Oxford University Press.

Piedmont, R. L. (1999). Does spirituality represent the sixth factor of personality?: Spiritual transcendence and the five-factor model. *Journal of Personality, 67*(6), 985–1013.

Reed, P. G. (1991a). Self-transcendence and mental health in oldest-old adults. *Nursing Research, 40*(1), 5–11.

Reed, P. G. (1991b). Toward a nursing theory of self-transcendence: Deductive reformulation using developmental theories. *Advances in Nursing Science, 13*(4), 64–77.

Reed, P. G. (1996). Transcendence: Formulating nursing perspectives. *Nursing Science Quarterly, 9*(1), 2–3.

Reed, P. G. (2008). The theory of self-transcendence. In M. J. Smith & P. Liehr (Eds.), *Middle range theory for nursing* (2nd ed., pp. 105–130). New York: Springer.

Reed, P. G. (2009). Demystifying self-transcendence for mental health nursing practice and research. *Archives of Psychiatric Nursing, 23*(5), 397–400.

Rosenberg, M. (1986). *Conceiving the self* (Reprint ed.). Melbourne, FL: Krieger.

Runquist, J. J., & Reed, P. G. (2007). Self-transcendence and well-being in homeless adults. *Journal of Holistic Nursing, 25*(1), 5–13.

Ryff, C. D. (1989). Happiness is everything, or is it? Explorations on the meaning of psychological well-being. *Journal of Personality and Social Psychology, 57*(6), 1069–1081.

Schimel, J., Pyszczynski, T., Greenberg, J., O'Mahen, H., & Arndt, J. (2000). Running from the shadow: Psychological distancing from others to deny characteristics people fear in themselves. *Journal of Personality and Social Psychology, 78*, 446.

Seligman, E. P. (2002*). Authentic happiness*. New York: Free Press.

Seligman, M. E. P., Rashid, T., & Parks, A. C. (2006). Positive psychotherapy. *American Psychologist, 61*(8), 774–788.

Shapiro, S. L., Astin, J. A., Bishop, S. R., & Cordova, M. (2005). Mindfulness-based stress reduction for health care professionals: Results from a randomized trial. *International Journal of Stress Management, 12*, 164–176.

Shernoff, D. J., & Csikszentmihalyi, M. (2009). Flow in schools: Cultivating engaged learners and optimal learning environments. In R. Gilman, E. S. Huebner, & M. Furlong (Eds.), *Handbook of positive psychology in schools* (pp. 131–145). New York: Routledge.

Silvia, P. J., & Duval, T. S. (2001). Objective self-awareness theory: Recent progress and enduring problems. *Personality and Social Psychology Review, 5*, 230–241.

Silvia, P. J., Eichstaedt, J., & Phillips, G. (2005). Are rumination and reflection types of self-focused attention? *Personality and Individual Differences, 38*, 871–881.

Stinson, C. K., & Kirk, E. (2006). Structured reminiscence: An intervention to decrease depression and increase self transcendence in older women. *Journal of Clinical Nursing, 15*(2), 208–218.

Szentagotai, A., & David, D. (2013). Self-acceptance and happiness. In M. E. Bernard (Ed.), *The strength of self-acceptance* (pp. 121–137). New York: Springer.

Tart, C. T. (1975). Introduction. In C. T. Tart (Ed.), *Transpersonal psychologies* (pp. 3–7). New York: Harper and Row.

Teng, C. (2011). Who are likely to experience flow? Impact of temperament and character on flow. *Personality and Individual Differences, 50*(6), 863–868.

Tornstam, L. (1996). Gerotranscendence: A theory about maturing into old age. *Journal of Aging and Identity, 1*, 37–50.

Trapnell, P. D., & Campbell, J. D. (1999). Private self-consciousness and the five-factor model of personality: Distinguishing rumination from reflection. *Journal of Personality and Social Psychology, 76*, 284–304.

Upchurch, S. (1999). Self-transcendence and activities of daily living: The woman with the pink slippers. *Journal of Holistic Nursing, 17*(3), 251–266.

Urgesi, C., Aglioti, S., Skrap, M., & Fabbro, F. (2010). The spiritual brain: Selective cortical lesions modulate human self transcendence. *Neuron, 65*(3), 309–319.

Vaughan, F. (1991). Spiritual issues in psychotherapy. *Journal of Transpersonal Psychology, 23*, 105–119.

Wade, J. (1996). *Changes of mind: A holonomic theory of the evolution of consciousness.* Albany: State University of New York Press.

Wilber, K. (2000). *Integral psychology: Consciousness, spirit, psychology, therapy*. Boston: Shambhala.

Wong, P. T. P. (2009). Positive existential psychology. In S. L. Lopez (Ed.), *Encyclopaedia of positive psychology*. Oxford, UK: Blackwell.

Wong, P. T. P. (2011). Positive psychology 2.0: Towards a balanced interactive model of the good life. *Canadian Psychology, 52*(2), 69–81.

Wood, A.M., & Joseph S. (2010). The absence of positive psychological (eudemonic) well-being as a risk factor for depression: A ten year cohort study. *Journal of Affective Disorders, 122*, 213–217.

Wicklund, R. A. (1975). Objective self-awareness. *Advances in Experimental Social Psychology, 8*, 233–275.

Williamson, M. (1996). *A return to love: Reflections on the principles of a "course in miracles."* New York: Thorsons.

Winseman, A. L. (2002). *Religion and gender: A congregation divided, Part II*. Retrieved from http://www.gallup.com/poll/7390/Religion-Gender-Congregation-Divided-Part.aspx

Wispe, L. (1991). *The psychology of sympathy.* New York: Plenum.

Young, C. A., & Reed, P. G. (1995). Elders' perceptions of the role of group psychotherapy in fostering self transcendence. *Archives of Psychiatric Nursing, 9*(5), 338–347.

Zappala, C. R. (2007). *Well-being: the correlation between self-transcendence and psychological and subjective well-being.* Palo Alto, CA: Institute of Transpersonal Psychology.

8

The hero's journey

Our single greatest act of creation is our own life. The quest of the hero is the journey towards our individuality, uniqueness and wholeness, meeting all of what life may ask of us. The stories of the hero show us wisdom of how this has been accomplished over time.

Learning objectives – at the end of the chapter you will be able to do the following:
- Identify the stages of the hero's journey
- Relate these to lifespan development transitions
- Understand illustrations of the journey found in modern stories and films

List of topics:
- Background description of the hero's journey
- The 12 steps or stages of the journey

PP advocates we seek to know and develop ourselves to our best: subjective, psychological and social wellbeing, our strengths and a meaningful life. At the same time we know life is not all 'positive' and commonly a mix of experiences. To deal with both, finding ourselves at our best and coping with what may initially be perceived as dark or negative is a journey. This is a transition away from what we have learnt about ourselves, what our social world mirrors to us, or a resistance to experiences that may be uncomfortable or painful. This chapter draws on the idea of the 'story' as illustrative of that journey, or to use another term, the 'quest'. It argues that many of our life experiences are experienced or felt as 'stories', and big or unexpected changes may seem like a 'hero's journey' to face. The 'dark side' refers to unexpected or sudden challenging experiences, thoughts, emotions and behaviours as we face change which triggers discomfort in us. Such discomfort in the face of change or difficult events is frequently avoided as it carries an engagement with fear, pain, distress, uncertainty or confusion. However, engaging with the challenge and discomfort has great potential for growth, healing, insight and transformation. In other words, the 'dark side' contains the seed for a potential positive outcome, even when the path towards this outcome is testing. The 'hero's journey' argues that encountering and embracing these experiences is central to our growth and development.

Linley and Joseph (2007) drew on the work of Carl Rogers to propose that the concept of the 'actualising tendency', our natural unfolding over time (given the right conditions for growth) to be our best, as fundamental to our practice of PP. This chapter links that idea with that of the story to portray how the experience of finding and living the best in ourselves, or dealing with the 'dark side' of life, is a journey and quest through time.

This chapter proposes that our primary processes and experiences of psychological growth and change occur (or are encoded) in our 'big' or most popular stories. The basis of this idea is not new. It occurred via the world's most notable mythologist Joseph Campbell (1949). This idea is reflected again in the subsequent work of Dan McAdams (e.g., 1988, 1995, 2001), which illustrates how we think of and explain our lives via the characteristics of story.

After years of study Campbell proposed that the world's great myths of the hero and his or her exploits were a 'mono myth' or a single myth, and a recurring pattern appeared within them. He believed that this structure or steps represented the way in which humankind faces great challenges and in particular the challenge of personal growth and self-realisation at a point in time and particularly over a lifetime. He argued that one of the most powerful messages of myth was the call to lead our own unique and authentic lives, a concept that is echoed in PP in theories and practises such as strengths, meaning, positive emotions and hope. He published these ideas in 1949 in a book, *The Hero with a Thousand Faces*, which has been in print ever since. He lectured over decades and became well known with the wider public for his television series *The Power of Myth*. Implicit in Campbell's arguments was that we know and recognise the structure of these stories and respond to them; they are deep within us. For example, this means we are not only seeing the hero's myth in old or ancient stories; we see it in stories that resonate strongly for us now, such as *Star Wars*, *The Lord of the Rings* and *Harry Potter*; the fact that they reflect the hero's journey is a reason for their popularity. Writers write to the structure of the hero's quest, intentionally or unintentionally, and we as readers and viewers respond to it because it is also within us (Vogler, 2007).

Campbell always asserted the hero's quest applied to men and women equally. Given his years of teaching only women at Sarah Lawrence College, he would have reasons for that view, even though the majority of myths appear to have male characters. We can accept his assertion at the outset and revisit it at the end of the chapter.

Cousineau (a writer Campbell mentored) cited Jerome Bruner in arguing that it is in the act of telling a story that we as individuals can make sense of our experiences (Cousineau, 2001) and that the mythic and hero's stories reflect an evolution in our cultural and individual consciousness.

The messages carried by myth have a powerful link to PP. Drawing on the 12th-century myth, the 'Grail Legend', Campbell argued for our individual uniqueness and that it would be in our uniqueness that we brought our gift to the world (Flowers, 1988). This idea is reflected in PP concepts of strengths (Linley & Joseph, 2007) and eudaimonia (Ryff & Singer, 2008). The hero's story is the journey and quest to our uniqueness and unique expression over time, and the potential for a deeper connection and understanding of the world that surrounds us. In words that presaged Barbara Fredrickson (2009, 2013) and her research, Campbell saw a recognition of our uniqueness as an act of love. This expression, he believed, in words that also reflect ideas on eudaimonia, is also a sign of health (Osbon, 1991).

Campbell proposed a structure of what he called the 'hero's journey'. This has been modified or simplified by other writers over time, yet given the depth of Campbell's study, the stage names of the original structure will be cited here, with some additional phrases used in combination to clarify meaning for current times.

Influenced by the mythical stories and adventures we know, we could see the steps of the quest or journey as involving an external challenge or problem that may unfold in a relatively short period of time, the kind of unexpected or uncertain change we might associate with 'dark side' feelings. This could be the case. However, there is also a clear argument that this description represented an inner journey and the unfolding of our adult lives, when we begin to question the social context in which we find ourselves and seek our strengths and a path of our life that is a fuller or more complete expression of ourselves, knowingly but also unknowingly (Campbell, 2004). We can interpret the journey from both viewpoints, but within this chapter emphasis is given to the whole-life perspective.

Further, Campbell described the hero's story as drawing us towards and involving what we need and can face now. The hero's journey or quest draws out or, in Campbell's word, 'evokes' our character (Flowers, 1988), which may change over time with what we experience and learn, reflecting current history and culture. From a limited perspective, or an outer challenge alone in a short period of time, the writer infers this might not involve all of the steps of the hero's quest. When seen as a portrayal of our growth and unfolding over time, this quest is almost certainly our life story.

This idea is reflected in the work of Carl Rogers' concept of the actualising tendency: these journeys may occur outside our awareness and through a deeper part of ourselves that knows how we need to grow; given the right conditions we will grow to our potential (Rogers, 1961) and Carl Jung's concept of the 'self' (Hollis, 2005).

In his writings Campbell repeatedly used the term 'transcendent'. He saw the messages and content of the hero's story as connecting any of us to a larger understanding and relationship with the broader nature of our lives. Linking to PP, this is the path to the best in ourselves or how we encounter the challenges of our growth and life. Central to Campbell's views was that whatever we know of ourselves, this is not our final form; we must be constantly open to both letting go of self-understanding and recreating it. This, in mythical terms, is a constant 'death' and 'rebirth' of our selves (Flowers, 1988) and a fundamental part of the journey to our uniqueness. For Campbell, this implied and raised the question of our willingness to let go of a life we had planned to encounter a life that he believed was waiting for us (Campbell, 2004).

This idea and proposal sits in parallel to extensive work done by Dan McAdams (e.g., 1988, 1995, 2001, 2006) and his colleagues, arguing that we think, explore, change and even remember via stories we construct about ourselves. If we see ourselves as static or accomplished in a moment or period of time, then the prospect of change may be perceived as an unwanted challenge or threat. However, if we see ourselves as moving, unfolding or growing through eras and phases of our lives, even if these experiences may be difficult, then periods of transition can be anticipated and accepted. If we recognise or accept that periods or events in our lives may represent the polarity of experience, the negative and the painful, then a perspective such as the hero's quest on how the harder changes of life may be faced (what the authors have termed the 'dark side' experiences in the context of this book) may prove valuable to us all. This type of experience may be a reflection of how our consciousness changes and evolves with time (Campbell, 2004). This is, in turn, reflected in Vaillant's (2002) startling work on positive ageing.

Reflecting and illustrating the spirit of this book, Campbell didn't hesitate to describe life as a mixed and often challenging experience. He was blunt: this is the nature of life. However he also asserted that our choice is to participate fully in the joy and the sorrows of life (Osbon, 1991). Living life to the fullest does not involve choosing one aspect of our experience, the positive, and avoiding the negative. He argued the fullness of life is accepting all we encounter (Osbon, 1991), which includes the experiences we might consider the dark side of life. The paradox of 'creation' is it also involves a 'de-structuring', or destruction (Barron, 1988; Osbon, 1991), a change of form. In the anticipated arguments for posttraumatic growth, Campbell suggested that it was in the challenges of life that we found new strengths and potential in ourselves so that we may open more completely to who we are. He went further in his view that in these experiences of challenge, we may find the best in us, a deeper capacity for the recognition of others, compassion and particularly love. He believed that if we brought love to these moments and experiences, we would also find love (Osbon, 1991). Campbell asserted via his understanding of these myths that when we see and move beyond the polarities of our life, when we see a space or perception that integrates them, then our capacity for compassion expands, and we realise the extent of our connection with others (Osbon, 1991). The fear of the polarity in life, our resistance of the 'negative', blocks us to experience and growth.

Towards the end of his life, Campbell repeatedly suggested what Erikson, Erikson, and Kivnick (1986) asserted, that when we look back and see the path of our life over time, we have the potential to recognise its completeness so that what might feel like a mess as we live the story forward may show a coherence when we reflect on it in hindsight as our story and the only one that could have been (Osbon, 1991).

While we can view the hero's journey as experiences of a challenge coming to us from outside ourselves, we also can see it as an inner journey that comes from breaking away from society's expectations on us and proceeding with our story. This perspective is also found in Vaillant's (1977) work where Grant Study of Adult Development participants in their late 30s and early 40s made reference to an internal 'voice' emerging for the first time that was different to that of their parents or their social context. Moving towards the best and unique in us or encountering 'dark side' challenges can both result in us being questioned or pressured by our social context to behave a certain way or maintain a status quo. Levinson et al. (1978) and Vaillant's (2002) recording of this phase of life also mirrored that of Erikson (1980) and the failure of our facing this, for all three writers, was a personal stagnation, a 'drying up', a sense of life lost (Campbell, 2004).

Given the length of time, the thousands of years in which these myths have appeared, Campbell's views that these story patterns are within our mind and particularly our heart, and arguably now genetically encoded, may not be surprising. He saw them as a central part of a powerful paradox: we both desire and fear to discover the best in ourselves (Campbell, 1949). This perspective might add descriptive words to Rogers' concept of the actualising tendency and the process of our unfolding and growth (Joseph & Linley, 2006).

Campbell offered a powerful symbol for the change we see within our lives that links with optimism, hope and the unfolding of our potential. He saw these changes as the 'birth' of new aspects of our lives (Campbell, 1949), even if it did imply the letting go, or 'death' of other aspects of our selves or lives. One of the attitudes of the hero was an acceptance or submission to this perspective (Campbell, 1949). Life is an inner unfolding and journey, and the invitation and the need is to face what is happening, and caused, from within us. The facing of this brings us into a connection with our unfolding and the destiny of our own energy. It brings us in connection with ourselves, not what our social context is asking or pushing us to be.

Campbell implies in his opening description of the journey that it is a 'virtue' that we need to seek, the acceptance of the cycle of change, the death and rebirth cycle that goes on in our lives over time. Using the term 'virtue', he links to PP writing by pointing to this potential strength in our being (Campbell, 1949). A fundamental quality of the journey is mirrored in what we understand about change and many aspects of creative work, now increasingly recognised as an aspect of PP (Parks & Schueller, 2014). We have to let go or separate from what we already know, step into a place of uncertainty, explore the unknown and then give form and return with what we have found (Campbell, 1949; Cousineau, 2008).

We now turn to the steps of the hero's quest.

THE CALL TO ADVENTURE – THE CALL TO CHANGE

It is striking that Campbell would use such a title to introduce this process: 'adventure'. For many of us it might infer excitement and bravery. For others, the need to change might be an invitation we would wish to resist.

Campbell (1949), in his writing and in his lectures, suggested that this 'call' involved the outer world in some way ceasing to work for the hero, that existing ideals and values have been outgrown and change needs to occur. Our consciousness, or the world that surrounds us, is limited, restricting us, and needs to change. Viewed as the inner journey, whether small or great, it involves our actualising tendency which, if faced, also will involve a change of form or some part of our outer world dying for the purposes of change to give birth. Within the concept of the 'dark side' experience, this may contain discomfort, uncertainty, anxiety and/or fear. Gilligan and Dilts (2009) give us a powerful reminder that the call to change may occur in joy or challenge. We may wish to change in work or a relationship where we find energy and self-expression. This is a call to bring our uniqueness into a new form and in the world around us. At the same time, some aspect of our world may have been changed, lost, decayed or wounded, and this, in turn, may press or force us to respond or move into a journey of change.

Descriptions of experience which reflect these characteristics can be found in the work of Levinson (1978, 1996), where participants entered periods of transition in life. This might be the individual who now knows that choices made have to be consolidated or even changed, or the individual approaching a midlife phase may seek to revisit decisions made and unmade and readjust his or her life structure as a result. (These ideas are explored in the 'Positive Development' chapter earlier in this book.) Mirroring Campbell's ideas, these transitions may involve insights into strengths and possibilities within us that have not been previously conscious or accepted and that now will be acted upon.

Campbell (1949) described this experience as one where we know that our centre of gravity has shifted. The social world in which we work and relate has changed, and we know that we must move into the unknown. However uncertain, when our centre of gravity has changed, we are called upon to change as well.

EXAMPLES

In *Star Wars Episode IV*, we see Luke Skywalker had pleaded with his aunt and uncle to let him go from the farm and join the space academy. His uncle insisted that harvesting the crops is more important. Luke stumbles outside the home from the discussion in frustration into the sunset. The sun is setting on his world, and change is about to happen.

In the *Lord of the Rings: The Fellowship of the Ring* we see the pleasure and mischief of Frodo in Gandalf's magic and how he may be out of step with the hobbits.

The characteristics of innocence and mindfulness displayed by Frodo allow him to handle the danger of the ring and the journey.

In the Harry Potter stories, perhaps more generally, we are seeing the call to adventure as the alertness, curiosity and openness of the trio of friends – Harry, Ron and Hermione – which suggest an openness to the call and movement of life around them.

REFLECTION

Is there some part of your life calling for more attention from you – a strength or skill unused or not yet expressed?

Is there some part of your life where you are being pressed for or into change?

How do you feel about this possible change?

REFUSAL OF THE CALL

We are not forced into the call to change, nor do we necessarily believe we could cope with it if we let this happen. Individuals refuse the 'call'. In the context of this book, the refusal may, in turn, be an unwillingness or a felt inability to face or embrace the 'dark side' of our experiences. However when the energies of life appear to ask us to change, a refusal is, in part, an attempt to keep the world unchanging or as it was before, to keep existing goals and values fixed and secure Campbell (1949). Levinson et al. (1978) gave examples in his work of participants who failed to respond to a transition and needed change. In his admittedly small number of examples, these individuals appeared to encounter work difficulties and illness in the circumstances that resulted. Life was unchanged, and in the rigidity of seeking it to be unchanged, Campbell (1949) implied starkly that it became the 'wasteland'. This is a classic term from the T. S. Elliot poem the 'Four Quartets', which infers that if we do not respond to the unfolding of our lives, we are hounded from within by the 'living self' that is constrained and disoriented by this resistance. Our uncertainty or unwillingness to face the 'dark side' and change deserves compassion. Yet what this stage of the hero's quest tells us is that the call to change will not go away.

EXAMPLES

As a potentially powerful illustration of the refusal, Campbell used the graphic image of Darth Vader, from the Star Wars films, as the individual living an inauthentic life within a system imposed externally (Flowers, 1988).

REFLECTION

Have you faced change and wanted to resist it or stop it?

Why was this case?

What were you trying to stop or protect?

SUPERNATURAL AID – THE SUPPORT OF A MENTOR

Campbell proposed that when an individual responds to the call to change and the willingness to live our unique life, characteristically an 'external helper' would appear. Indeed, he implied that the call was also an indication that help would be at hand for this change.

In more modern language, perhaps the wise helper is the mentor. Learning also from Zukkerman's (1977) classic work, we must remember that we have the choice to seek out or choose a mentor and, from Worth (2010), to choose new mentors for different periods of our lives. Campbell, in his interviews with Bill Moyers, implied that the input of the wise figure may connect us as individuals with our true self. He emphasised that it was one of the roles of teachers to support students into connecting with their 'pictures', or dreams of themselves, and their unique potential. This is reflected in Levinson et al.'s (1978) description of the role of the mentor in supporting an individual in the identification of his or her personal or life dream. In PP, this may be our role as coaches or mentors in the support of others in the exploration of the positive characteristics of their lives.

EXAMPLES

In *Star Wars Episode IV*, Obi Wan Kenobi appears when Luke is in mortal danger, attacked by the sand people, which was the point when his new life direction began.

In *The Fellowship of the Ring*, Gandalf turns for Frodo from a visiting wizard into guide and protector.

In the *Two Towers* and *Return of the King*, the appearance of Aragorn with the Rohan prompts the Princess Eowyn to assert her ability as comparable to the men and eventually to act upon what she most seeks.

In the Harry Potter stories and films, Professor Dumbledore protected Harry after his birth and in school.

REFLECTION

Have you now or in the past had a mentor? What qualities did this person have? How did these qualities help or support you?

If you could choose or seek a mentor now, who would this person be? Why?

Using a concept of a mentor 'at a distance', is there an author or teacher whose ideas you might wish to make part of your life?

In what ways might you 'mentor' yourself, or self-mentor (Worth 2010)?

THE CROSSING OF THE FIRST THRESHOLD – COMMITTING TO THE JOURNEY OF CHANGE

With an acceptance of the 'call' and the appearance of a helper or mentor, the hero crosses the threshold and commits to action and the experience in the path of his or her own adventure (Gilligan & Dilts, 2009). A common image that occurs in our language is the fear of facing our demons or dragons. We can walk past the 'dragons' unconsciously because we do not know them. We can walk past them knowingly and must summon the courage to face the threshold of the adventure, the 'dark side' of our experience and the journey of change. The power and pressure of the expectations and norms of our social world are such that the normal person is often proud to accept and stay within the boundaries of his or her expectation (Campbell, 1949). These social expectations provide us with the cognitive map of what is, or is not, in our world. Going against them may leave us with feelings of fear of rejection and being alone. Yet it is only when we challenge the expectations of our world that we move beyond established boundaries, potentially provoking (in myth) a destructive response, such as 'dark side' feelings, yet also moving us into a new type of experience and the possibility of change and growth.

The act of facing what we seek in contrast to the expectations placed on us moves us directly into the realm of the 'dark side' of PP. Campbell argued that our growth, our unfolding, occurred in facing the pairs of opposites, the polarities, that form our world. Customarily we live beliefs and norms of 'right' and 'wrong', what we seek versus what we resist, what we hope for versus what we fear. This is our ego, or reason, insisting what may or may not be within our lives. Our world is defined by our perceptions of such opposites and many more. The tension involved in these opposites, particularly in the belief we 'should' be at one end, and not the other, is a powerful illustration of a 'dark side' experience. Potentially the deepest part of the hero's journey and quest is to learn to see beyond the opposites into a space that contains them both, a 'third space' in which a different type of understanding occurs. The hero's journey is into the tension of these opposites and eventually beyond them.

EXAMPLES

In the *Fellowship of the Ring*, Frodo and his friends cross the threshold by being willing to walk beyond the boundaries of the Shire, to literally step further from home than they have ever done before and face what then may happen.

In *Star Wars Episode IV*, Luke is pressed across the threshold into his new life and adventure by the Imperial Stormtroopers chasing the droids R2D2and C-3PO, killing his aunt and uncle in the process.

In his curiosity, Harry Potter and his friends notice the world around them, put pieces of information together and question their meaning in a way repeatedly leading them into adventure.

REFLECTION

Think back to a time in your life when you crossed the threshold of change, willingly or unwillingly. What were your feelings?

How did you cope with these feelings? Was it a positive way of coping?

How could you choose a positive way of coping with future change?

What part of PP might help or support you in future change?

'THE BELLY OF THE WHALE' – SITTING IN AND ACCEPTING THE UNKNOWN

While this is a graphic and potentially frightening image – having to be contained in, digested and travel in the belly of the whale – it is at the same time one of creativity and incubation. Having committed to the hero's journey, Campbell described the belly of the whale as a journey into darkness and the unconscious. The 'belly' is a place where digestion occurs, and through this energy is created. The whale, symbolically, lives within the water of the unconscious. This is a phase were the hero enters her or his unconscious to connect with what was previously outside her or his awareness (Flowers, 1988). This phase illustrated Campbell's view that our conscious and unconscious must work in collaboration. Not to do so, in his view, made the limited and defensive ego a 'dragon' which eventually had to be faced (Flowers, 1988). When we step back from believing that what we now know is all, we open to a mindfulness in the present moment, and learning and new possibility. Maybe this is an indication of how any of us might encounter or embrace a 'dark side' experience. In PP, this could present us with un-manifested strengths or emotions, such as gratitude which we may not have previously acknowledged.

The hero's journey implies that we start a process from which we emerge transformed in some way. The symbol of the belly of the whale is that we have been swallowed by and are sitting in the unknown. Campbell (1949) suggests this willingness to face change represents an acceptance that there is more to us than our previous sense of our ego may suggest. This willingness for some part of us to be changed, transcended or mythically 'annihilated' is an illustration and a highlighting of that part of us that is imperishable within us. Attempting to grasp Campbell's writing nearly 65 years later, we could argue that the 'belly of the whale' is a mix of the need for creative incubation and a willingness to accept that we are part of a process that is incomplete; we are having to wait for the shape of possibility to become clear and take form inside and outside us.

EXAMPLES

In *The Fellowship of the Ring*, one image of the belly of the whale is Frodo and his companions being willing to enter the underground world of the mines of Moria and face the dangers there.

In *Star Wars Episode IV*, a classic image of the belly of the whale is when Luke, Leia, Han and Chewbacca were being trapped in the garbage compacter as they tried to escape from the Death Star.

In many aspects of Harry Potter's adventures, he has to wait and work out what aspects of 'magic' are present and available to him to help or move him on. In *Harry Potter and the Philosopher's Stone*, music calms the danger of the three-headed dog. Sunlight saves the trio from the danger of the Devil's Snare plant. Harry has to enter the chaos of the flying keys to find the way of entering the next step of the journey.

REFLECTION

In the face of difficult change, have you been able to find a way of pausing and allowing yourself to understand what faces you?

How did you do this?

How might you do this in future?

THE ROAD OF TRIALS – FACING THE CHALLENGES OF OUR QUEST

In the road of trials we are, perhaps, seeing the stages of experience overlap and potentially what we might most readily feel are 'dark side' experiences. While the belly of the whale represents a need to be 'swallowed' by a new phase of life and to take time to understand it and its possibility, the road of trials implies there may be difficulties and tests along the way. Campbell describes the myths as showing us these 'landscapes' of the unknown maybe dreamlike and uncertain. However he also emphasised that the mythic helper or mentor also may be available to us. In PP terms, potentially the 'coincidence' of luck occurring or our ability to show gratitude for aspects of our lives and experiences may in turn change aspects of this experience.

Campbell wrote movingly, suggesting that these times of uncertainty may call on, or evoke, strengths that we did not know we had. He argued that anything a time of change and difficulty brings out in us was latent within us and waiting to be made manifest. The qualities and characteristics of our fears, tension and reactions also reflect our prior experience and our deeper selves. If we can understand our reactions to such change as not merely objective, but representing our past and history, then the road of trials is an opportunity to move beyond who we believed ourselves to be and grow and mature into aspects of ourselves we had not yet known or accepted. He believed that when we can face fear, we also find energy for life (Campbell, 1949; Flowers, 1988). Maintaining a fear takes energy. Facing and transforming it releases energy back to us for use. Perhaps Campbell is telling us that facing 'dark side' experiences may give energy and vitality to our lives. This point touches on one of the strongest arguments Campbell would make for myths over the hundreds and thousands of years in which they have been present in our culture. These templates of stories and the dynamics within them show us the change we face and the growth we can make from within; we are not alone, and these stories can reassure and guide us. Campbell argued that these tests or trials, however uncomfortable, may teach or show us aspects of life and bring about self-realisation (Campbell, 2004).

EXAMPLES

In the *Fellowship of the Ring*, having agreed to venture beyond the Shire, Frodo, Pippin and Merry travel on the road alone, carrying the ring of power to Rivendell. They face the dark horsemen chasing them and much more. Later, when the fellowship is attacked by orcs, Frodo decides to proceed alone, to live his destiny as the ring bearer.

In the face of great difficulty, Frodo tells Gandalf he wishes the ring had never came to him. Gandalf responds that we cannot change the difficulties that face us but can choose only how to live our trials.

In *Star Wars Episode V*, Luke Skywalker chooses to be taught by Master Yoda. Echoing the symbolism Campbell would use, he does this in a misty swamp-filled world reflecting the waters of our unconscious and containing what we fear.

In the Harry Potter story and film *The Prisoner of Askaban*, Harry deliberately chooses to learn how to face experiences that he most fears.

REFLECTION

Do you have a memory that reflects the road of trials?

How did you deal with those challenges or difficulties?

With what you know now of PP, would you use a different way next time? For example, have you resources available to you that you were not aware of – a mentor or a guide that may be available to you?

Could you use the structure of 'hope' advocated by Snyder (e.g., 1994, 2000)?

'THE MEETING WITH THE GODDESS' – SEEING LIFE AS A CYCLE OF CREATION

The understanding Campbell displayed, after decades of reading myths cross-culturally, was at times poetic, philosophical and psychological as well as grounded in these ageless stories. The titles of this and following sections may not seem readily understandable in more modern times. What is being offered here are interpretations of the writer.

In acknowledging the change and growth we all face within our lifespan, bodily and psychologically, Campbell (1949) saw this as the process of creation that is evident throughout the natural world. He described change as 'the river of time' and 'the fluidity of existence' (p. 115) and the ocean of our existence. In the times in which these myths emerged, creation, the cycle of existence, was the work of the 'feminine' and the 'goddess'. Examples of this personification of the creative world as goddess include the Greek goddess Demeter and the Hindu goddess Kali. What Campbell argues for in this and the subsequent stage is that the hero encounters and accepts not just rationally, but with his or her heart the process of creation, decay and death before re-creation as part of the cycle of life. If we can accept this process as underway, what Frank Barron (1988, p. 81) called 'creation and destruction . . . de-structuration' preceding the building of new structures, personal or physical, then these times of change lose some of their power to worry us. Change becomes something that is not separate from us, or being done to us, but part of a natural cycle that is our life which we can participate in and accept. Arguably this description of letting go, allowing change and accepting change is a core part of 'dark side' experiences and their processes and is reflected in the developmental eras and phases of our life.

Some of our tension in the face of uncertainty and change might fall away when we can acknowledge it as a creative process which we can participate in and influence. Campbell, again writing as if the process of change is a personification of the feminine, suggests that we see it as an attempt to draw us towards growth and to break the limitation of who we currently are. Campbell (1949) suggested that if the hero can accept change, the goddess, as she is, the process of creation in action, without 'commotion', then the capacity for kindness and some form of assurance enters, and the hero in some way may find a mastery of this experience, even though it eventually involves decay and death. Conceivably this process links to the experience of mindfulness and the perception of positive emotions within PP which in turn may help us to broaden and build, to create.

EXAMPLES

The Fellowship of the Ring meets with the Lady Galadriel and is sheltered by her at a time of danger. Frodo particularly recognises the power she holds and may wield. She gives each a gift that reflects his need and danger he may face.

In the Star Wars films, the writer infers that the 'force' is itself the energy of creation and this goddess.

Harry and his friends trust that the resources and help they need are around them and will be made clear to them. For example, in *Harry Potter and The Chamber of Secrets*, the phoenix bird belonging to Professor Dumbledore brings Harry the Sword of Griffindor at a time of peak danger to him.

'WOMAN AS THE TEMPTRESS' – LIVING LIFE AS A CYCLE OF CREATION

Campbell (1949) argues that the preceding stage and this stage are the final test of the talent of the hero because if we can embody, em-body, and live this insight, this in-sight, then it changes our capacity to relate and love, to accept change and to do so mindfully. This allows each moment to be a mirror of what we may become in our wholeness over time. Our capacity to see life in this way changes and amplifies our consciousness, allowing us to accept our abilities and participate in the process of creation and becoming.

ATONEMENT (AT-ONE-MENT) WITH THE FATHER – RECEIVING GUIDANCE AND SUPPORT

If the encounter with the 'goddess' is the ongoing creation that is life, then there is a counterbalancing, symbolic perspective that is also needed, that of the encounter with the 'father'. 'Specialised adult action' (the term used by Campbell) or goal-driven behaviour reflects the lead or role modelling that often comes from an older male, in his writing, the 'father'. The task of the 'god', the older male, is to introduce the younger person to the skills, duties, techniques and demands of a vocation and potentially society more broadly. Campbell (1949) acknowledged the tension that may occur between the younger and older generation, yet also moves into words that echo more classically the role of the mentor to guide and support a younger person into his or her choices and dreams.

Perhaps this is both the acceptance of the good we can learn from a guide, but in turn, as we integrate and grow, we can offer this to others as a mentor ourselves? As we move through the hero's journey, we may move from a position where we are being helped to one where we in turn help others; we pass on what we have learnt.

Campbell implied that this is a time when the hero must see and accept the polarities and the pain that exist as well as the positive experiences of life. Perhaps life and certain positive psychology interventions create in our 'attention', an intent or capacity only to wish to see the positive. This stage of the hero's journey and quest creates the depth of the challenge that comes with the willingness to encounter 'dark side' experiences. Campbell wrote that if we can achieve this, then potentially paradoxically we also are accepting the energies of faith and hope. These words reflect and precede those of Vaillant (2002), who described graphically the experiences of generativity that occur in midlife, when older individuals give of themselves to the younger generation.

There is a staggering depth and challenge in Campbell's words describing this stage. Reflecting a depth of spirituality within these experiences, he saw the creative processes of life as reflective of the birth and growth of our own spirit and in turn, via the myths, that this process involves a resting and trusting in the processes of what would otherwise be called 'god' (although he understood many names might be given to this). He acknowledged that our development would proceed only to a point that we personally could cope with, that the demands on the hero reflect our capacities and abilities at any point in our life, and that these will change. Remember this implication: this argues 'dark side' experiences challenge us *within* our personal capacity to digest and work with them. At the same time he was explicit that our development and growth involved the acceptance of the polarities of life and that these did not only exist outside ourselves but inside as well. Using Freudian terms, he said we must find the 'superego', the internalized demands of our society in us, and what they have done to us, along with the potential demands of the id, the ever-present yet instinctual drives that exist within us. Both of these, acknowledged by Campbell (1949), and psychology, are demands often outside our conscious awareness, and it is an act of the expansion of our own consciousness to become aware of them. Drawing on myth, images, poetry and philosophy, Campbell wrote movingly of the experience of accepting life in all its forms and the polarities outside and inside us, and one of our deepest challenges is to see the 'negative' as also a manifestation of life itself.

For Campbell, this is not an act of resignation or the acceptance that life is 'bad' but an act of 'compassion', a word and a state which means 'suffering with'. He goes further, drawing from myth, to explain that an acknowledgement and acceptance of the whole-ness of polarities involves the 'tears of life', a capacity for us to open our hearts to our own needs and the needs of others, and to give of ourselves accordingly. To resist these polarities involves living in a state of tension within 'dark side' experiences, where we struggle to stay in one polarity and resist the entry of the other. Campbell argued that life involved the acceptance and living of sorrow, along with all else life brings us. For him, to do otherwise, was to have a resistance and a blind spot to the origins of life; life itself originates the positive and the negative or 'dark side' of life. If we can do this, Campbell believed we are atoned, at one with life and the creative energy of the symbolic father.

EXAMPLES

In the *Fellowship of the Ring*, Gandalf protects the Fellowship and his friends by facing the Balrog. He falls deep into the fire, darkness and under-ground caverns fighting the evil. Maybe this is Gandalf's evil? Gandalf the Grey 'dies', is transformed in facing this evil and becomes Gandalf the White.

In Star Wars' *Return of the Jedi*, we see Luke Skywalker and Darth Vader confront each other, the opposite goals and expression of self, yet we see an at-one-ment when Vader saves Luke, and in turn Luke has healed Vader to return to his role as father.

Harry Potter has both to seek leadership from Professor Dumbledore while at the same time trusting his own path and journey to act individu-ally, not solely from direction.

REFLECTION

Can you think of an example where in having received a gift, an experi-ence or lesson from outside yourself that you in turn wished to share or give to others?

What was that experience like?

Why?

Can you see ways in which you might do this in future?

APOTHEOSIS – A CHANGED PERSONAL CONSCIOUSNESS

Using a term for this stage of the hero's journey that few of us would recognise, Camp-bell again wrote with a profound depth of understanding that challenges and points us towards what he believed myth was asking us to undertake and do. 'Apotheosis' is a point where you have an experience of the extent of who you are, your capability, found via this search and journey (Campbell, 2004).

Campbell used the example of two ancient figures in Buddhist and Eastern myths, the male Avalokiteshvara and the female Kwan Yin. Both, in stories that would be seen as religious or spiritual journeys, pause to acknowledge and absorb all they have learnt and who they are before entering 'eternity'. This is intended to illustrate the understanding that time and eternity are opposites, another form of polarity that dissolves and then are the same. The insight represents the knowledge of a mind that has transcended the pairs of opposites. By having grasped or understood who we have become in our journey through time, this in turn becomes part of our presence that we can embody, mindfully, in the moment.

Campbell believed that once we have gained the insights of the lifelong hero's journey, the acceptance of all aspects of life and ourselves, both positive and negative, the process of creation, decay and re-creation, we will recognise our commonality with all of human-kind, above our differences with them. In turn, he believed this opens up the ability in us for acceptance, compassion and above all love. Paradoxically, accepting the light and dark sides of life's experiences opens us to a deeper experience of love. In offering this, Camp-bell (1949) is describing this process. He is highlighting that the best of us and that with which we struggle are in the same space, same body and every body.

EXAMPLES

In the *Return of the King*, we see many of the main characters in mortal danger. It is a striking lesson in individualistic times that each are brought through the danger by the relationship and love of one of their friends. For example, Aragorn, Gandalf, Merry, Pippin, and many more, go in to battle when Aragorn says, in an act of love, 'for Frodo'. In Mount Doom, Frodo has fought with his dark self and opposite Gollum. Gollum has gone over the precipice into the fire following his obsession, the ring of power. Frodo clings to the cliff. We can see in the film, so beautifully cut at this point, he looks down into the abyss and knows it would be so easy to follow Gollum. It is his friend Sam who shouts, in turn with love, repeatedly, 'Don't let go'. Perhaps these powerful stories illustrate that we find ourselves in relationship and love.

In the Harry Potter films, we see a repeated quality in Harry: a recogni-tion that we eventually learn that he carries the horcrux and some of the essence of Voldamort's soul, but he chooses in turn not to act on them or display them. He chooses love. This illustrates for us that we may contain opposites, yet we can choose what we express.

REFLECTION

On your PP journey, as you experience and live what you learn, how does the world around you change?

Do you see the world differently?

Do others respond to you in a different way?

Why do you think that is?

THE ULTIMATE BOON

Whether the hero has undertaken an inner or outer journey, the ultimate end is a transformation of the consciousness of the individual. This could be small or large, reflecting Campbell's insight our change is in proportion to our capacity or readiness to change. The hero may find strengths that she or he had not previously acknowledged. Fears may have been faced and transcended or now seen as different in character. Abilities may have been developed and grown. The capacity to be part of a challenging experience will have been expanded. Resources inside and outside the hero may have been identified and drawn upon. Yet in the context of Campbell's writing, this summary is simplistic. He appears to argue that in the experience of our personality, something we may believe fixed and permanent, we find that it can be grown and expanded; it no longer will limit our view of possibility, internally or externally. Further, if we can recognise life as in the constant process of creation, change and decay, then we can accept the experiences of challenge and change more readily than if we were to resist it. In a light and hopeful view of what can happen within our consciousness, then, he suggests the challenge of change can become as light and simple as a childhood dream. Reflected in myth, the hero's journey involves finding and returning to what was in our individual hearts all along (Cousineau, 2001).

THE RETURN

For Campbell, a core part of the purpose of the hero's journey was that the changed hero returns to his or her world, and the changes in perceptions and consciousness may contribute in turn to the society of which she or he is part. This contribution, this gift to the hero's context, is a key final phase to the journey. Campbell acknowledged that the experiences of the hero may be such that he or she could choose to resist or refuse a return. However the return is a labour and one that may take effort given that others may have chosen not to change or travel. Campbell suggested that wherever there is life in the hero, the hero's social context would seek a return.

While acknowledging again that the outcome of the hero's journey will always reflect the readiness and the consciousness of the hero, Campbell's descriptions of this stage resonate with the work of Vaillant (2002) and his descriptions of an individual ego that has been grown to positive strength and which is, in turn, being given away to those younger in need of support. Biology and the river of life flow downhill.

EXAMPLES

Using a personal example, 40 years ago the writer was given the opportunity to research a topic of interest to him (career development) anywhere in the world for a three-month period. This involved taking the risk of a leave of absence from his job. In the final interview of the project with Dr Edgar Schein, at the time a world-renowned expert in career development, Schein asked, 'What are you going to do on your return to your workplace?' Out of intuition the writer answered, 'Bo back, be quiet, and live what I have learnt, not talk about it'. Dr Schein replied, 'Right answer'. Others have chosen to stay and not to change. You have changed. Let your work and life illustrate that change rather than pushing it at others'.

In the *Return of the King* film, in perhaps the most clear and poignant illustration we see, Frodo and his friends ride back into Hobbiton. The villagers, still going about their normal days, look with puzzlement and even irritation at the returning young men. The villagers have no idea what they have been through, how they have changed, to support them in turn being safe.

PRACTICE ESSAY QUESTION

Pick three PP interventions that would support you or others in undertaking a hero's journey, and explain why.

CONCLUDING THOUGHTS

Campbell believed, with the depth of work he undertook over time to create these insights, that he was describing a process, a quest and a journey which was enduring. Yet more than 60 years on from the publication of the *Hero With a Thousand Faces*, might we suggest or claim that something is changed or different from these descriptions?

From a careful review of his writing, there is little doubt that Campbell was describing a lifetime process. If this is the case, and with the dynamics he described, perhaps it is not a single hero's journey but one that recurs over time as our conscious needs and seeks to expand. This being so, perhaps the central steps of the journey are a spiral and recur over time as we change? Indeed, and the 'dark side' is an ever-present invitation within this spiral – engagement with it and acceptance of it fuels the process and allows the growth process to take place.

Is this journey a description of the experiences of men and women? Campbell asserted that it was. However we have to acknowledge the huge majority of myths have a male figure as a hero. The characters of Psyche, Persephone and Demeter are examples of a few female characters. Murdock (1990) and Frankel (2010) write movingly of how they see the woman's hero's journey. From these the author infers that while the stages may be the same, the difference is in an experience that reflects gender experiences. Yet there is a commonality between the male and female experience: that of being willing to step away from what society shapes us to do and listen for and encounter an awareness of our uniqueness and unique contributions, from within. Given the depth of Campbell's descriptions of the final stages, it is hard to believe that this is solely a male outcome but a reflection of where our life's journey takes us all.

Campbell's opening words in describing the hero's journey echo why this refers to humankind rather than men alone. We embark on a life journey that is about expanding our consciousness, living our uniqueness and self-realisation. The journey is about becoming more fully who we truly are. Yet in the act of doing so, we meet a paradox: in finding who we truly are through the creative incubation of the belly of the whale, in the road of trials, by experiencing the creativity and destruction that is part of life, and in encountering not just the good in life and ourselves but also the negative, we also find our commonality or shared humanity. If we find, as Campbell believed, an increased capacity for compassion and love towards others, we in turn start to give away, to share that self we have discovered as a means of contributing to and changing the world in which we live.

SUMMARY – THIS CHAPTER HAS ACCOMPLISHED THE FOLLOWING

- Summarised the stages of the hero's journey
- Illustrated the stages of the hero's journey by examples from famous literature and film
- Offered reflective questions to support the reader in exploring these topics
- Offered resources for following up these ideas in other literature

RESOURCES AND SUGGESTIONS

The DVD series of the *Power of Myth* programmes shows us Joseph Campbell as an engaging and influential speaker. The website for the Joseph Campbell Foundation (https://www.jcf.org/new/index.php) offers audio downloads at reasonable prices of many lectures given by Campbell.

BIBLIOGRAPHY

Albert, R.S. (Ed.). (1992). *Genius and eminence* (2nd ed.). Oxford, UK: Pergamon.

Barron, F. (1988). Putting creativity to work. In R. Sternberg (Ed.), *The nature of creativity: Contemporary psychological perspectives*. Cambridge, UK: Cambridge University Press.

Campbell, J. (1949/1988). *The hero with a thousand faces* (Paladin ed.). London: Grafton.

Campbell, J. (2004). *Pathways to bliss: Mythology and personal transformation*. Novato, CA: New World Library.

Cousineau, P. (2001). *Once and future myths: The power of ancient stories in modern times*. Berkeley, CA: Conari.

Cousineau, P. (2008). *Stoking the creative fires*. San Francisco: Conari.

Erikson, E. H. (1980). *Identity and the life cycle: Areissue*. New York: Norton.

Erikson, E.H., Erikson, J.M., & Kivnick, H.Q. (1986). *Vital involvement in old age*. London: W. W. Norton.

Flowers, B.S. (Ed) (1988). *The power of myth*. London: Anchor Doubleday.

Frankel, V. (2010). *From girl to goddess: The heroine's journey through myth and legend*. London: McFarland.

Fredrickson, B.L. (2009). *Positivity*. New York: Crown.

Fredrickson, B.L. (2013). *Love 2.0*. London: Hudson Street.

Gilligan, S., & Dilts, R. (2009). *The hero's journey: A voyage of self-discovery*. Carmarthen, Wales: Crown House.

Hollis, J. (2005). *Finding meaning in the second half of life*. New York: Penguin.

Joseph, S., & Linley, A. (2006). *Positive therapy: A meta-theory for positive psychology practice*. London: Routledge.

Levinson, D. (1996). *The seasons of a woman's life*. New York: Knopf.

Levinson, D. J., Darrow, C. N., Klein, E. B., Levinson, M. A., & McKee, B. (1978). *Seasons of a man's life*. New York: Knopf.

Linley, P., & Joseph, S. (2007). Therapy work and therapists' positive and negative well-being. *Journal of Social and Clinical Psychology, 26*, 385–403.

McAdams, D.P. (1988). *Power, intimacy and the live story: Personological inquiries into identity*. London: Guildford.

McAdams, D. P. (1995). *The stories we live by: Personal myths and the making of the self*. London: Guildford.

McAdams, D. P. (2001). The psychology of life stories. *Review of General Psychology, 5*(2), 100–122.

McAdams, D.P. (2006). A new big five: Fundamental principles for an integrative science of personality. *American Psychologist, 61*(3), 204–217.

McAdams, D.P. (2006a). *The person: A new introduction to personality psychology* (4th ed.). London: John Wiley and Sons.

McAdams, D.P. (2006b). *The redemptive self: Stories Americans live by*. Oxford, UK: Oxford University Press.

Murdock, M. (1990). *The heroine's journey*. Boston: Shamballa.

Osbon, D.K. (Ed). (1991). *A Joseph Campbell companion: Reflections on the art of living*. London: Harper Collins.

Parks, A.C., & Schueller, S.M. (Eds.). (2014). *The Wiley Blackwell handbook of positive psychology interventions*. London: Wiley Blackwell.

Rogers, C. (1961). *On becoming a person*. Boston: Houghton Mifflin

Ryff, C.D., & Singer, B.H. (2008). Know thyself and become what you are: A eudaimonic approach to psychological well-being. *Journal of Happiness Studies, 9*, 13–39.

Snyder, C. R. (1994). *The psychology of hope*. London: Free Press.

Snyder, C. R. (Ed.). (2000). *The handbook of hope: Theories, measures and applications*. London: Academic Press.

Vaillant, G. (1977). *Adaptation to life*. Cambridge, MA: Harvard University Press.

Vaillant, G. (2002). *Aging well*. Boston: Little Brown.

Vogler, C. (2007). *The writer's journey: Mythic structure for storytellers and screenwriters* (3rd ed.). London: Pan Books.

Worth, P. (2010). *Four questions of creativity: Keys to a creative life*. Bloomington, IL: Trafford.

Zuckerman, H. (1977). *The scientific elite: Nobel laureates' mutual influences*. New York: Free Press.

Index